Everyday Life
in the United States
before the Civil War

# Everyday Life in the United States before the Civil War 1830-1860

*Robert Lacour-Gayet*

*Translated by MARY ILFORD*

UNGAR • NEW YORK

*Translated from the French*
*La Vie quotidienne aux États-Unis, 1830-1860*

© *Librairie Hachette, Paris*

*Fifth Printing, 1986*

Standard Book Number 8044-1500-5
Library of Congress Catalog Card Number 70-81571

# FOREWORD

The year 1850—three hundred fifty-eight years after Christopher Columbus' ships sighted the unknown island of San Salvador, two hundred thirty years after the Pilgrims landed in Plymouth, three-quarters of a century after the signing of the Declaration of Independence in Philadelphia. . . .

The United States had only just begun its national existence. It was still far less populated than France: the 1846 census showed a population of 35.4 million in France; four years later, the statistics showed only slightly over 23 million Americans. Of this total, some 20 million were native born; the rest were immigrants. Nearly 13 million lived between the Allegheny mountains and the Atlantic, and 8.5 million in the Mississippi valley. The gulf states, bordering the Gulf of Mexico, accounted for about 700,000, distributed fairly evenly to the east and west of the river. California and the Northwest territories, the latter as yet barely inhabited, accounted for the rest. Negroes made up about 15 per cent of the population.

The growth rate had been rapid. In 1800 the thirteen

original colonies had had a population of no more than 5.3 million inhabitants. Thirty years later, that figure had risen to 12.8 million, and by 1840 it had reached 17 million. From that date, the pace of population growth was constantly accelerated through immigration. Whereas from 1800 to 1810 the population had grown by only 2 million (from 5 to 7 million), in the ten years preceding the Civil War it rose by 8,250,000.

At the same time, the main center of population kept moving westward. In 1800 it was located forty miles northwest of Washington; thirty years later, it had reached West Virginia; on the eve of the Civil War, it was approaching the eastern frontier of the Ohio.

And during this period the area of the United States expanded substantially. At the time of the signing of the Declaration of Independence, the United States comprised only 820,680 square miles; by 1830 it covered 1,787,159 square miles and in 1850, 2,981,166. After the admission of California in that year, states and territories divided the area of the country fairly evenly. In the Union itself, the slave states covered slightly more space than did the "free" states. The young republic was caught up in a veritable fever of imperialism: "the Americans," wrote James Truslow Adams, "were intoxicated by the map." This intoxication with geography led them to the Mexican wars and the annexation of Texas in 1845; it brought them to the brink of war with England over Oregon in 1846. The obscure journalist by the very commonplace name of John Sullivan, who at about this date coined the expression "Manifest Destiny," was doubtless unaware how aptly it applied to the territorial ambitions of his contemporaries.

The period covered in the present study extends roughly from the election of Andrew Jackson to the beginning of the Civil War. Since we are dealing with a country which developed so rapidly, it would appear necessary to focus our research on a fairly large number of years. Were we to confine ourselves to too specific a date, the result might well be a superficial, and above all an all too ephemeral, description of modes of life which were in constant flux.

There is another problem. Obviously, customs varied greatly from one region to another. For example, what was there in common between the life of a Boston patrician and that of a Midwestern pioneer? Not wishing to neglect these differences, we have devoted special chapters to those aspects of everyday life which were clearly distinct from others; thus the reader will find separate descriptions of the great migrations to the West, of the gold rush, and of the slave system. In other cases, we have sought to emphasize predominant features, while only incidentally mentioning those which constituted exceptions. We have not sought to give an exhaustive account of so vast a subject; we have tried only to be as accurate as possible.

We should like to thank all those who in various ways gave us their help and collaboration.

In particular, we wish to express our very deep gratitude to Professor Allan Nevins for the valuable advice on bibliography which his exceptional knowledge of the period enabled him to give us. We also received extremely useful suggestions from the New York Historical Society, whose director, Dr. R. W. G. Vail, gave us the benefit of his encyclopedic knowledge. We must also recall the inestimable value of the assistance given us by the American Library in Paris and of the personal support which we received from its head, Dr. Ian F. Fraser. Our research was also greatly facilitated by the courtesy of Dr. Edward L. Tinker, who let us make use of the University Club library, and by Mr. Mark Riley, the librarian, who guided us through his most uncommon collection with tireless competence. The New York Public Library and the Society Library also welcomed us in their turn.

We must also thank the information services of the French Embassy, to which we appealed on so many occasions, Mr. Jacques Habert, director of France-Amérique, who permitted us to consult his files on the French in the United States, Mr. Jean Piveteau, of the Institute, and Mr. Paul Marois, commercial director of the French Railways, all of whom provided us with valuable information. We would also thank the Otis Elevator Company, Western Union, and the New York Academy of Medicine, which we had occasion to consult.

Finally, we owe much to the understanding and interest shown us by our colleagues of St. John's University, especially Professor Gaetano Vincitorio, who was good enough to check our bibliography.

The actual correction of the manuscript was performed by Mr. and Mrs. Antoine Bruel, to whose devotion we wish to pay a sincere tribute.

# CONTENTS

# PART ONE

# The Framework
## of Life

# Chapter I
# TOWARD
# THE PROMISED LAND

Never, observed an American of a somewhat pessimistic turn of mind in 1852, never since the Gothic hereditary kings led their tribes from the shores of the Borysthene to invade Greece, Germany, and then the entire Roman Empire, had the world seen a wave of human migration such as was now breaking on the shores of the United States. The analogy was absurd. What would his country be today, if it had not been for the "Goths" of a century ago? Nevertheless it is true that their arrival raised serious problems.

From the Declaration of Independence to 1840, immigration was relatively insignificant. The immigrants were mostly Welsh, Scottish, and English, nearly all Protestant, and had little impact on local ways of life.

The position changed completely after political disturbances and economic difficulties led Europeans of every class and type to cross the Atlantic. Some were proscribed from their countries—for example, Garibaldi and Kossuth; dreamers like Cabet formed another group (we shall tell the extraordinary tale of the French phalansteries, or cooperatives, in Illinois and Texas); others were weary of their poverty; others, again, were influenced by religious arguments, and were inclined to liken their wanderings to the exodus of the Hebrews.

Often they would leave on the advice of a member of the family who had preceded them. But there was as yet no international postal service, and letters were expensive: it cost a day's work to send a letter from New York to Europe. They received few letters and in any case were doubtful of the veracity of the contents. It was rumored that false messages, in faked handwriting and with forged signatures, were sent by unscrupulous employers in search of workers. In most cases the emigrants would decide for themselves, without much notion of what awaited them beyond the ocean. They had had enough of their lot and were ready to try anything. In Ireland, entire parishes emigrated under the leadership of their parish priests; the eve of a departure would be an occasion for general celebration, enlivened by much liquor.

The shipping companies, which brought tobacco, cotton, and grain to Europe, did their best to lure a return freight in the form of emigrants. In the British Isles, sailings would leave Liverpool or London two or three times a month for New York or Canada. There was a monthly sailing from Hamburg. But the great embarkation port on the Continent, especially for Germans, was Le Havre, until it was supplanted by Bremen. The Germans would arrive in freight cars from Basel or Strasbourg, or travel in wagon trains through France. Some took the opportunity to visit Paris; they could be seen camping on the banks of the Seine before they sailed down the river on barges. They would arrive, finally, wave upon wave, at Le Havre, where they would engage in lengthy negotiations with sea captains or with brokers only too ready to promise the earth. Guidebooks and papers would be placed in the emigrants' hands describing the promised land in the most inviting terms. A boat would weigh anchor approximately every ten days. At the last moment, some would lose courage for this leap into the unknown. Often, their wives would dissuade them. They would remain, anguished, on the dock, and a thousand interpretations—rarely generous ones—of their defection would be offered by those who had not changed their minds.

The voyage was a lengthy one—usually forty days—and the discomfort extreme. The migrants were herded together like cattle, and slept on floors scantily covered with sawdust. In the beginning, they had to bring their own provisions and eat them cold; gradually they were permitted to use stoves, but not until 1855 did the shipping companies begin to provide food. Epidemics of cholera, smallpox, and typhoid were frequent, and many never reached the shores of Eden. For those who survived the ordeal, the magic touch of hope charmed away the memory of suffering and privation. In their moments of discouragement they could cite that most encouraging example of John Jacob Astor, who had come from Germany with $25 in his pocket and accumulated a capital of $20 million.

Germans and Irish streamed into the country in the decade preceding 1850. The former were of two contrary types: a minority, conservative by inclination, hoped to find beyond the Atlantic a purely agricultural form of life which was beginning to be precarious in Europe as a result of the Industrial Revolution; the majority were liberals fleeing the reactionary policies which followed the Frankfurt Assembly of 1848. Few of them came penniless. They settled mainly in the Ohio valley, in the region of the Great Lakes, and in New York, which for a time was the largest German-language city in the world after Berlin and Vienna. They were hard-working and industrious, and their assimilation gave rise to very few problems. They taught the

Americans horticulture and viticulture; they introduced a taste for beer and a certain form of gormandizing; they spread their love of music, the tradition of the Christmas tree, and the sentimentalism of the German Romantics. Although many of them were Catholics, they did not constitute so homogeneous a religious group as did the Irish.

The Irish were altogether different. They arrived in full force after the 1847 potato famine, which still further increased the distress of their unfortunate country. They were all poor, if not destitute, Catholics to the point of fanaticism, realists and at the same time dreamers. Their presence made itself felt; indeed, powerfully felt. The Paddies, as they were known, conglomerated in the great cities, where they exercised every kind of trade. In New York, they were employed as porters, carriers, shoeshine boys, newspaper venders; in New England, they worked in the spinning mills; in the West, they served as ships' firemen, carters, cooks. They hired themselves out wherever they could as manual laborers and diggers, and their wives as domestic servants. Their condition was little better than that of the Negroes, whom they both despised and feared. They soon succeeded in playing a political role. Tammany Hall, the original focus of Democratic party organization, was their domain even before the Civil War.

In comparison with these two national groups, the others hardly counted. The French numbered some 200,000 in the United States in 1860—few indeed compared with 1,600,000 Irish, 1,270,000 Germans, and 430,000 English. Some of the French exiles, it is true, had borne illustrious names: after the Napoleonic wars, Joseph Bonaparte spent sixteen years in New Jersey; the Duponts offered hospitality to Grouchy; Lakanal was a university president in Louisiana; Lallemand organized an agricultural association in Philadelphia, and then settled in Alabama after an unsuc-

cessful attempt at settlement in Texas; not long after, Louis
Napoleon arrived in his turn to discover America.

The major wave of French immigrants arrived in
the dozen years following 1840. Some, like their predecessors, were refugees: Victor Considérant, Elysée Reclus,
Charles Delescluze, Marc Caussidière arrived after the coup
d'état of December 2. Most of the immigrants, however,
were not driven by political considerations and simply came,
like so many others, to seek their fortune in the new El
Dorado. Some, as we shall see, pushed on to California.
Most remained in New York, some as teachers, lawyers,
doctors, architects; others—the majority—as tailors, hat
makers, hairdressers, waiters, clock makers, printers. Their
skill as chefs, in particular, was soon recognized; from now
on, the best families prided themselves on serving only
French food and French wine. So-called Parisian manners
served as a status symbol in 1840, and the 1848 revolution
set off an explosion of warm feeling for France. Dancing
masters, housemaids, tutors, and governesses all profited
alike. At the same time, the increase in the number of
French Canadians in New England made it possible for
them to establish centers for the preservation of the French
language and culture—centers which have in fact withstood
the test of time.

Add to these ethnic groups a few Swiss; a few Scan-
dinavians; a handful of Italians—especially after 1850—who
lived wretchedly in the great cities of the East as hawkers,
confectioners, tailors, organ grinders, exhibitors of trained
monkeys; small groups of Poles in Texas and Wisconsin;
Dutch settlers in Iowa and Michigan; about 25,000 Chinese
in California; the Jews in the New York Bowery—some
peddling, others already active in the garment industry—
and we shall have a fairly complete picture of the nature
of immigration in the twenty years preceding the Civil War.

Its extent is apparent from the figures. Between 1840 and 1855, 3,545,741 Europeans decided to try their luck in the New World. Men outnumbered women by three to two. According to the statistics, 48,408 new arrivals declined to state their sex.

The newcomers were not all apostles; many were former convicts. Some of them brought with them vices and diseases which horrified the local population. It has been said that the great cities of the East served as filters for these elements. What they retained was not always the best. Nevertheless, voting rights were conferred on every male immigrant as soon as he became a citizen. And the naturalization procedure was short, taking not more than five years. Since the new Americans were poorly prepared for their role as citizens and cared little about their civic duties, they fell an easy prey to the politicians. The urban corruption which Jefferson had predicted was thereby hastened. The salaried classes accused the newcomers of unfair competition, because they accepted starvation wages. And indeed, unscrupulous employers took advantage of the poverty and ignorance of these unfortunates.

But quite apart from the question of the honesty of the immigrants or their means of livelihood, the mere presence of this mass of Europeans often aroused antagonism. They were disliked for their clannishness. The Irish were recognizable by their breeches and top hats; most of them had cudgels and were only too eager to use them. The Swedes stood out by their multicolored vests, the Germans by their caps, their short jackets, and especially their meerschaum pipes. Were these Americans or not, people would often ask on observing these heterogeneous crowds. And again: why did they have to come to the United States, if they wanted to preserve their own language, dress, and prejudices? These grievances were not without foundation.

A little over a century ago there were already German, French, Italian, and Spanish language newspapers in New York. The ex-Europeans even insisted on organizing their own military units: The La Fayette guard, for instance, which formed an independent French company attached to the 12th regiment; or the 69th Irish regiment, which displayed its independence when, under the command of Colonel Corcoran, it refused to take part in the ceremonies arranged to honor the visit of the Prince of Wales in 1860.

A still trickier question was the religious one, to which we shall return later. It led to some horrifying incidents, but on the whole fairly rare ones. It would be altogether misleading to overestimate them. The American melting pot was powerful, and the assimilation of the immigrants took place at a surprising rate of speed, sometimes within less than a generation. With the exception, possibly, of the Germans, who were more particularist than the others, the new arrivals usually had only one desire: to be assimilated as fast as possible in the new homeland of their choice. This was apparent at the time of the Civil War, when they demonstrated their loyalty to the Union on the field of battle.

## Chapter II
# THE CITIES

Just over a century ago, only forty-four cities in the United States had a population of more than 8,000 inhabitants. The development of urban concentrations was nevertheless rapid, and kept gathering speed. Between 1800 and 1860, the number of rural dwellers quadrupled, but at the end of that period there were twenty-four times as many city dwellers as sixty years previously. At the beginning of the nineteenth century, the combined population of the five largest cities—Boston, New York, Philadelphia, Baltimore, and Charleston—did not exceed 125,000 persons; by 1830, that figure had risen to 530,000; in 1860, New York alone had a population of 800,000 and was already the third largest city in the world.

We cannot all live in the cities, Horace Greeley lamented, dreaming of the wide open, solitary spaces of the West.

What was New York City like in those days?

The largest city in the United States did not extend northward beyond the present sites of Washington and Union squares. The rest of Manhattan and a part of

Brooklyn were given over to farm houses, which were hard to reach owing to the condition of the roads. In 1835 a miniature railroad was inaugurated which led to the village of Yorksville (now 86th Street). The streets, which were usually narrow, with the exception of Broadway, were frequently winding, as in most of the old towns of the Atlantic coast, but were beginning to be laid out at right angles to one another. They were bordered either by wooden houses of the cottage type or by brick or stone houses three, four, or five stories high. The noise was deafening. Newspaper venders, little chimney sweeps, strawberry venders, old-clothes men, itinerant repairmen vied in shouting each other down. Gas lamps lit up the darkness, at least in the center of the city. The streets were totally unpaved.

Visitors to the city were stunned by its filth. No garbage collection existed. The city council left that job to an incredible number of pigs which moved freely about the streets. Dickens described these street cleaners in unforgettable terms. They were republican pigs, he wrote, going where they liked and mingling with the best society as equals, if not superiors, for everyone was quick to yield them passage as soon as they appeared. No one looked after them, he continued, no one fed them, no one drove them away, and no one claimed possession of them—which meant, of course, that it was no pleasure to walk about New York in rainy or snowy weather. Moreover, even then, pedestrians were complaining about the number of vehicles on the streets. A visitor—perhaps a Southerner—wrote in 1850 that when she crossed Broadway, her one hope was to reach the other side alive. Every type of vehicle passed through the streets—the clarence and the rockaway for large families, the landau and the landaulet, with its convertible top, the open coupé, the phaeton for speed-lovers, the double tandem mail coach. A variety of omnibuses were the pride of New Yorkers. They carried between twelve and twenty passengers, seated on two parallel benches, and were drawn by either two or four horses. A seat cost 2 or 3 cents. The competition between them was fierce, and the coachmen cracked their whips noisily to attract the attention of the passers-by.

The business section was concentrated in the Wall Street area; the entertainment section around Broadway. The latter, which extended over some four miles, was already famous. In the morning, and again at about 5 P.M., it was frequented by businessmen and clerks going to work or returning home; at the beginning of the afternoon it was the hub of the life of fashion. In the evening, people crowded into the Mille-Colonnes café, into Contoit's, the ice-cream specialist, but especially into Niblo's, at the corner of Prince Street. This gigantic German-style establishment, the center of "beauty, wealth, value, and fashion," as it was called, included a "spacious and magnificent" opera hall, a concert hall, reception rooms, and a dining hall and ballroom with a capacity of over 1,000 persons. Not far from this eighth wonder of the world were situated theaters and an opera house of which we shall have something to say in another chapter.

On a fine day, you could have dinner at Madison Cottage Road House (at what is now the corner of Fifth Avenue and 24th Street), or you could cross the river for a walk in the Elysian Fields, the "enchanting" woods of Hoboken on the far side of the Hudson. But the society there was a very mixed one, and ladies of doubtful virtue abounded. That breed, incidentally, flourished everywhere. In the suburbs these ladies sold hot corn, pending more lucrative business. Those of Broadway, more sophisticated, disdained such artifices; their beauty, which was often genuine, appeared to them sufficient. Nevertheless, to be doubly sure they would touch up their features with paint and bedeck themselves in equally glaring finery.

The "gentry" lived in the neighborhood of Park Place, St. John's Park, or Bowling Green. Murray, Chambers, and Warren streets remained fashionable until about 1840. After that date, "they" began to live in Washington Square. New Yorkers sought, with varying success, to adopt the tastes and manners of the best Boston society. But there was always a little something that differentiated them. Perhaps a "bigger dose of mercantilism," perhaps "more ostentatious dress, more vying with one another in luxury and expenditure." In one respect, however, they stood second to none: their women were "singularly beautiful."

Far from these residences, immigrants and Negroes were herded together in what were virtually ghettoes, living squalid lives on the banks of the Hudson and around the Five Points. Yet despite these poverty-stricken districts, New York was already turning into a fine city, although less spruce than the cities of New England. To cite one observer, the colors of the houses were not quite as vivid, the signboards not quite as bright, the gold lettering not quite as shining, the bricks not quite as red, the stone not quite as white, the shades and trellises not quite as green, the door knobs not quite as polished. Even so, Manhattan had quite an air about it. Fanny Elssler, who made a triumphal voyage to the United States in 1840, could not get over it all. Who could have imagined, she exclaimed, that such a city, in a natural framework of such beauty, of such astonishing splendor, should have existed in young America, in barbarous America! The illustrious dancer was, of course, wholly ignorant of the country. Writing to a friend before setting off on her voyage, she asked for information about America, adding that her foolish old teacher had probably never heard of the country, since she could not recollect his ever having said a word about it. She expected to find savages, and brought over with her even her own tablecloths, convinced that she would be unable to find any west of the Atlantic. It is hardly surprising, then, that New York should have caused her some amazement.

Washington—the city of magnificent intentions, as Dickens rather condescendingly described it—was quite insignificant compared with the young giant of Manhattan. In 1850 its population did not exceed 40,000 persons. Its ground plan, as we know, was designed in 1791 by a Frenchman, L'Enfant, who was both a soldier and an architect. But the very ambitiousness of the plan led to his expulsion a year later; and it was not until the early part of the twentieth century that the excellence of his ideas was finally recognized. After his departure, the city grew somewhat haphazardly. When Andrew Jackson took possession, it had an unfinished air about it. Clumps of houses could be seen dotted here and there, separated by vast deserted areas.

The White House was still practically isolated in the countryside. With the Capitol, it was the only building of any architectural merit. The State Department, situated in a garden and surrounded by trees, retained a rustic air which would have delighted Thomas Jefferson. As today, the capital was primarily an administrative and diplomatic center, and few people involved in government made their home there.

Boston and Philadelphia could boast of an older lineage. The former, lying along the banks of the Charles River, concentrated around its historic Commons, priding itself on its connection with Harvard—then known as Cambridge—which was already two centuries old, exuded an English atmosphere. English visitors breathed more

freely when they looked upon the little dark-red brick
houses with their white shutters, the churches with their
Gothic spires, the winding, well-paved, carefully maintained streets, the shady squares. The capital city of
Massachusetts was an exception in their generally un-
favorable judgment of the country. They felt at home in
Boston; hence Boston must be perfect. Philadelphia they
found more disconcerting. The Quaker city had an unin-
viting austerity about it: dark colors, rectangular avenues
(Dickens commented that, after walking about Philadelphia
for a couple of hours, he would have given anything for
a winding road), and it was completely deserted after ten
o'clock at night. Baltimore, 100 miles to the south, was
altogether more attractive. Its streets were gay with the
splash of fountains, and the steps leading up to the red
brick or marble houses positively shone with all the polish-
ing they received; their cleanliness was in fact legendary.
The city could also boast of its Catholic cathedral, the
most beautiful and the largest church in the country.

The cities of the West were only just beginning to
take shape. Chicago, for example, with its mysterious
Indian name—interpreted by romantics as "apple blossom,"
by cynics as "onion smells," by pessimists as "mad hole of
the prairie," for it was built on swamp land—was in 1840
a village of 3,000 inhabitants; when it received the future
Edward VII in 1860, it was a city with a population of
100,000 inhabitants. The manner of its expansion was
certainly unusual. In 1855 it was decided to elevate the
entire city area seven or eight feet in order to facilitate
drainage. The object—a very simple one—was to cover the
ground with fresh soil. Unfortunately, the soil was not
evenly spread, so that some roads were turned into flights
of steps which could be negotiated only on foot. Houses
were often hoisted up in one piece. George M. Pullman,
then an obscure storekeeper, who was later to invent the

carriages which bear his name, conceived of the means of bringing off these feats of ingenuity. His method was used, in particular, to move a hotel—the Tremont; there was no damage, so the report ran, and none of the guests was disturbed.

Then there was Pittsburgh, with its hectic pace; save during the space of three meals, writes an observer, the longest of which took barely ten minutes, the people there devoted their whole time to business, six days a week. Detroit and Buffalo, both boom towns, were about to launch their phenomenal expansion. Cleveland, more refined, had elegant villas surrounded by gardens and orchards. Saint Louis, with as many as 160,000 inhabitants on the eve of the Civil War, was privileged by its position at the junction of the Mississippi and the Missouri, since it could channel the riches of the Great Lakes toward the south; it was a center of trade and of culture, an outpost of Catholicism thanks to its strong minority of inhabitants of French ancestry.

Then Cincinnati, whose population grew from 24,000 to 115,000 inhabitants in thirty years. It was a city of extremes. Its enthusiasm for literature conferred upon it, among the cities of the West, the role played by Boston in New England. It was at the spearhead of progress: in 1853 it tried out a letter postal service by balloon; in the same year it inaugurated the only really efficient fire engine in the country. By contrast, its garbage removal system was even more primitive than those in other cities. What filth! enough to shame Constantinople itself, lamented a local newspaper in 1843. Although the malicious had nicknamed the city Porkopolis, the porcine street cleaners were inadequate to the task. Their "republicanism" made them wholly contemptuous of authority. One of the street urchins' favorite sports was to try to ride astride them, but the pigs would have none of it. An elderly and particularly wise pig would always lie down as soon as it observed a potential tormentor. After the terrible cholera epidemic of 1849, the superintendent of hospitals, very appropriately named Absolom Death, insisted on the expulsion of the animals. But the mountains of refuse became unendurable, and the industrious street cleaners had to be brought back.

Cincinnati boasted a magnificent, almost modern mansion, which was famous throughout the country. But its visitors were no credit to it. The splendid hall was covered with refuse; the spittoons were not used; instead, groups of men seated around the columns preferred to fill the flutings or to aim at less immediate targets. Every morning the place was washed, and the result was a brownish cataract which swept down the front steps. Morals were very strict, and a novel like *La Dame aux Camélias* had to be read in secret. On the other hand, there were constant riots, and open warfare between the anti-immigrant "know-nothings" and the Catholics. Reformers were a dime a dozen, and so were the homeless children who roamed the streets.

Turning now from these extremes, let us move south. Here we find dreamy Charleston, slumbering in its magnolia gardens, lulled by the bells of its ancient churches. Or romantic New Orleans, divided into two distinct sectors: that of tradition and that of progress. The American sector prided itself on being in the vanguard of progress. The old French and Spanish districts, with their wisteria-covered walls and their sculptured balconies, had just the opposite ambition. This was another world, in which the past was sovereign. Puritans and Pilgrims had no part in it. The Northerners were still called " 'Merican rascals," and there was great antagonism between Creoles and Americans. The Creoles did all they could to preserve their ancient ways. They claimed to have the best opera in the Union. Their Mardi Gras parade and ball were of extravagant splendor. They engaged in dueling; their hero, Bernard de

Marigny, was famous for his nineteen encounters. And their young ladies had a habit of blushing, growing pale, or fainting at the slightest provocation. Girls were not allowed to go out alone or to read the newspaper, and it was bad manners to refer to them by name in public. Married women, when they went out, protected themselves with little veils from the stares of the curious. However, they were as concerned about their appearance as they were bashful. Their pale ivory complexions, which their suitors compared to the magnolia flower, must not be marred by contact with the fresh air; for protection, they made judicious use of rice powder. For their cheeks and lips, nothing would do but toilet water concocted of rose petals. Their hair was exquisitely perfumed; this was their pride, and every night their Negro maids would brush it admiringly. They were clothed in satins, silks, and lace. Bouquets and fans enhanced their charms. They played on their weakness. But behind these appearances, they lacked neither energy nor courage, as they showed in the Civil War, when they refused either to admit defeat or to receive their victors into their houses. General Butler, who occupied New Orleans for the Northerners in 1862, was angered by their contempt; a military man with a sketchy knowledge of history, he declared that these women combined the duplicity of the Stuarts with the imbecility of the Bourbons.

The contrast was striking indeed between the "belles" of Louisiana and the pioneer women of Texas. For in Texas there was no trace of refinement. Urban life had barely begun. Dallas in 1842 had a population of twelve, and at most 400 in 1855, when the 200 disciples of Victor Considérant arrived there to attempt the experiment which we shall refer to later. Motionless as yet, but ready to spring, Dallas was the hope of an arrogant Texas which for all its optimism had no inkling of the great adventure awaiting it in the following century.

Crossing the continent, we find San Francisco. In 1847, when John C. Frémont took possession of the city, its population numbered 459 persons; by 1860, that figure had risen to 50,000. Bemused by the Gold Rush, quivering with ambition on the shores of the Pacific, it dreamed of the Golden Gate which it would one day build, facing Asia.

Fire and thieves were the twin plagues of American cities.

The wooden houses were an easy prey to the flames. Fires were not always spontaneous, either, for would-be looters could anticipate substantial rewards. Whatever the cause, fire alarms were a regular feature of everyday life. Often fires assumed catastrophic proportions. In 1835, 1840, and 1845 major fires ravaged New York. In 1845 Pittsburgh was almost entirely reduced to ashes within five hours; four years later, six fires in the space of a few months turned nascent San Francisco into a rubble heap.

There were no official fire departments. Cincinnati was the first city to establish a municipal fire department in 1853. Other cities followed more or less reluctantly, for the tradition of voluntary aid societies was very strong. It was a point of honor with citizens to belong to them. The members were recruited from every social class and received no remuneration. A bell would sound the alarm, its cadence and volume varying from one district to another. At once the town would be in an uproar; everyone rushed out into the streets, shouting, asking questions. Wedding nights were interrupted. An enthusiast reports: "On the very night we married, a fire broke out. I could see it from my window and wanted to go there at once. But in the early morning, just before breakfast, there was another fire and I rushed off to see it. You can imagine that we weren't very pleased!" In any case, it was hard to remain indifferent. Not to rush to the scene of a fire would have smacked of cowardice.

Rivalry was fierce among the volunteers; each man sought to outdo the next in the speed with which he donned his red flannel shirt, boots, leather hat marked with the emblem of the association, and broad belt.

Each company had its richly decorated fire engine, with its well-polished brasses, drawn by a score of men moving as quickly as possible, preceded by a runner blowing into a trumpet worthy of the Last Judgment, and followed by a gang of little boys bellowing their lungs out in token of cooperation. Sometimes several rival companies would turn up simultaneously, and there would be added trouble. The intensity of their zeal blinded them to their purpose. They wanted to be alone in saving the situation. What matter if the fire spread? Epic battles would take place between the valorous rivals, to the accompaniment of the cheers of the onlookers and the probably less friendly looks of the victims. The strongest carried the day. American folklore preserves the memory of one of the legendary heroes of these fights, the inimitable Mosi, whose foes found it very hard to best him, since his favorite weapons were trees, which he pulled up by the roots, or street lamps, which he used for juggling.

Eventually the fire would be put out, for the zeal and daring of these volunteer firemen knew no bounds. In the meantime, it was unfortunately not unusual for rogues to be attracted by the confusion and to abscond with a number of objects. They too, especially those of New York, were organized in gangs bearing such picturesque names as the Forty Thieves, the Shirt Tails, or the Daybreak Boys. These ancestors of the modern gangster liked to confront one another in bloody battles. The Fourth of July, 1857, was the occasion for a pitched battle between the Dead Rabbits and the Bowery Boys. Little reliance could be placed on the police in such cases, for there was, practically speaking, no police force. "Every American is his own policeman," wrote an English observer, very much shocked by the fact. Actually the police had been issued uniforms since 1850 in New York, Philadelphia, and Boston—they had previously worn plain clothes. But the change of garb had not made them any more effective. Nor had it taken place without protest. As a fervent believer in equality put it, "no man who bears the glorious name of an American citizen can wish to wear clothing which sets him apart from his fellow citizens."

*Chapter III*

# HOUSES
# AND FURNISHINGS

Even in those days it was the dream of every American to own his home. Except for the poor in the big cities, people did not live in apartments. Obviously not everyone could be a home-owner, but to live in a house that belonged to you was a mark of success which no one could ignore.

A curious point, and characteristic of the time and place, was that this instinct for a home of one's own was entirely compatible with a love of change. The practice of moving houses had been inaugurated as far back as the late eighteenth century. Dickens, with his irrepressible wit, claimed to have seen such a house coming down a hillside at a good trot, drawn by some twenty oxen. Such migrations of real estate mattered little, since all that was uprooted was objects; the spirit did not change, whatever the site. Should this be regarded as proof of the predominance of ideology over practical considerations in the forming of the United States? Moving day was May 1 or October 1. On that day, the streets of New York or any other city would be filled, from east to west, from north to south, with furniture of every kind, from the most luxurious to the most meager, with carts, carriages, wagons, with canvas, straw, rope, string, with moving men, drivers, porters, of every race and color, white, yellow, and black. Contemporary prints show cities apparently caught in the grip of panic; everyone rushing, excited, pushing and shoving as though to escape some dreadful plague. Even the rural areas felt a mounting excitement at the approach of the great day. The animals, we are told, felt it too: hens and chickens would come out of their coops and of their own accord cross their feet to be strung up for the move.

Greek architecture had been widely adopted at the beginning of the century. The fashion had originated in a vague feeling that considerable affinities existed—in the area of politics at least—between ancient Greece and youthful America. Nicholas Biddle, the poet, diplomat, banker, and above all the sworn enemy of Andrew Jackson, gravely proclaimed on his return from Athens that there existed only two truths in the world: the Bible and Greek architecture. This simplistic statement was just to the taste of his compatriots. Soon peristyles, porticos, and Doric, Ionic, and Corinthian columns could be seen everywhere. Biddle set the example by having a house built for himself on the banks of the Delaware which was supposed to reproduce a temple of Poseidon, despite its name of Andalusia. When Philadelphia inaugurated its water supply system, it was deemed necessary to erect the new buildings in the Greek style. The South was particularly enthusiastic about the Greek revival. It was a type of architecture particularly suited to the climate of the region, and was adopted almost as a matter of course. Houses with colonnades became increasingly popular, among both the very wealthy and those of more modest means. One of the most celebrated was built in Tennessee by a cousin of President Polk; it was appropriately named Rattle and Snap, the owner having acquired the site by playing dice. Most of these fashionable houses, in the North as well as in the South, were decorated by a furniture manufacturer named Duncan Phyfe, who built an unrivaled reputation, especially in the Hudson valley, between New York and Albany.

About 1840, Gothic came into style. Gables appeared, and towers, and oriel windows. Brick walls, often painted in dark colors, were embellished with stone ornaments. Wrought iron decorations appeared with flamboyant curves. At the same time, in reaction against the systematic imitation of Greece, there appeared Swiss chalets, Tuscan villas, Norman-style manor houses. Octagonal houses were also briefly in fashion, under the influence of a phrenologist who specialized in marital problems and who regarded such houses as the solution to the problem of large families. The most sought-after construction materials were limestone and marble, regarded as indicative of good taste and luxury. After 1860, they began to be replaced by brownstone, quarried in New Jersey, at least in the East.

Houses varied in appearance, of course, from one part of the country to another. Those of the South were unlike any others. They were usually built on an elevation, sometimes overlooking a stream, with great trees enfolding them in a misty luxuriance by night, and by day protecting them against the extreme heat of the sun. The most sumptuous houses were surrounded by parks; sandy walks gave access to the mansion, and here and there among the well-tended bushes could be seen marble statues, copies of antiques, or works by fashionable sculptors of animals.

A porch, supported by Greek columns, covered the whole or a part of the front of the house. In the hottest regions, it rose right up to the roof, giving greater protection from the heat but also shutting out the light. At the back of the entrance hall, on the main floor, a magnificent staircase led up to the second floor, where the bedrooms were located. The reception rooms, drawing room, and dining room were situated to the right and left of the anteroom. All were high-ceilinged, adorned with an abundance of flowers, and simply furnished. The floors were sometimes strewn with rugs, but were often bare; portraits of ancestors or celebrities hung from the walls. The library was the pride of the old houses; there you would find the Greek and Latin classics, works of law and history, English novels; the tables were covered with well-chosen reviews and newspapers: the Charleston *Mercury,* the New Orleans *Picayune,* the Richmond *Enquirer; Harper's* was tolerated, but not the *North American Review,* which was regarded as too "Yankee."

In other parts of the country the housese were less sophisticated and more functional. They were usually made of wood, including the roof, were two or three stories high, square in shape, and designed for no other purpose than to provide an agreeable dwelling place. The sash-windows were protected by shutters or half-shutters, usually green. The exceptions to this rule were the palatial mansions of the "millionaires" in New York, Washington, Boston, and the fashionable resort towns, often built in imitation of some ancient European residence. In these extremely sophisticated edifices, slate took the place of wood, and the windows opened outwards, French style. A striking example was the house built by George Whetmore in Newport around 1850, which dazzled all visitors by its proportions and luxurious appointments.

Let us look at an average house. The old Dutch traditions which still prevailed required that it be kept spotlessly clean and neat. In the small towns and the country, the open porch was a must; there the family would assemble, gently tilting back and forth in their rocking chairs, more

or less in unison. Whatever the type of house, it was never
surrounded by walls; if houses adjoined, the neighbors
would converse; if they were isolated, they would be completely unprotected from the outside world. However, there
was often a mirror in the entrance hall which allowed one
to see who was at the door.

   A visitor to a traditionalist family would use a knocker;
in most cases, he would pull a brass bell. In the foyer he
would find a hat stand with hat and coat pegs and a mirror.
An umbrella rack was part of the standard equipment, as
was a grandfather clock with a pendulum enclosed behind
glass. In the living room he would find another clock, of
brightly colored marble, standing on a more sober marble
mantel and flanked by impressive vases filled with gaudy
artificial flowers. A marble-topped table would stand in the
center of the room about which the family would gather;
it would be adorned with a lamp with an enormous lamp-
shade, samples of ladies' fancy work, and a variety of books,
particularly the Bible, in which the major events of the
family's life would be chronicled on special pages. The room
was lit by metal wall brackets; the lady of the house would
long to possess a crystal chandelier, as in the fashionable
houses. The visitor would be offered a seat in one of the two
or three armchairs which graced the room; the master and
mistress of the house would seat themselves on more austere,
straight-backed chairs. If the vistor was an intimate, he
might sit on the sofa set against the wall or between two
windows. All around him he would find bookshelves and
glass cabinets. The former must perforce contain a Shakespeare (expurgated), a Gibbon, and some other master-
pieces; in the glass cabinets there would be a collection of
bric-a-brac and little souvenirs, often including Chinese
ornaments brought back from the East by some traveler.
Family portraits, sometimes under glass, and locks of hair
would give the room a greater sense of intimacy, and an

inscription—"God Bless Our Home"—would recall the family to the practice of prayer.

The visitor gone, father, mother, and children would gather in the dining room for dinner. This was the principal room, where the family assembled three times daily. The wooden table, sometimes ornately carved, could be extended by leaves. An ornament or a basket of fruit formed the centerpiece between meals. Father and mother sat facing each other, English fashion. Only they were entitled to sit in armchairs. Father always carved the joint; mother served the dessert and coffee. The massive sideboard, with its inevitable marble top, was adorned with various pieces of silver. Knives and forks were carefully arranged in the drawers; in elegant homes the fruit knife was coming into fashion. The table linen was carefully stored in a huge cupboard with a heavy cornice which completed the furnishing of the room.

A pantry separated the dining room from the kitchen, which nearly always contained an oven and a range. The oven was often immense; in Northern houses before the Civil War, it was sometimes used to conceal Negro fugitives. The fuel used for cooking was wood and later coal. The water flowed into the sink from a cistern on the roof; the cistern was fed by an air pump which brought the water up from a well. Copper pots were being increasingly supplanted by pewter utensils. Coffee grinders were becoming more and more common, for coffee was in a fair way to becoming the national beverage.

There was no running water, of course, in the bedrooms on the upper floor. The number of bedrooms varied with the importance and means of the family. Nor, with few exceptions, were there any bathrooms before 1860. Bathtubs existed around 1832, but in Boston, as late as 1845, it was forbidden to use a tub without a doctor's prescription. "Conveniences" consisted of a wooden closet installed behind the house and therefore known as the backhouse. The term

"water closet" came into use a little later, when sanitary
installations had improved.

The parents' room, which was larger than the others,
generally contained a double bed surrounded by tall posts
decorated with acanthus and laurel leaves. The fashion of
twin beds did not become widespread until much later. It
was almost impossible to climb into bed without a stool;
a few of the more daring, however, introduced low beds,
Empire style.

The children's rooms were cluttered with mementos of
early childhood and school days. In all the rooms, beds and
windows were draped with hangings. The favorite color
combinations were blue and gold, green and gold, purple
and gold, blue and tan.

The walls of most rooms, at least before about 1850,
were hung with paper purchased from two French manufacturers, Jean Zuber of Mulhouse and Joseph Dufour of
Paris. These wallpapers sought to reproduce the effect of
tapestry and often represented scenes from history; Washington and Rochambeau at Yorktown receiving the surren-
der of Cornwallis were among the familiar heroes. The
paper did not extend all the way to the floor; it was bordered by a strip of stained wood, with the rest of the wall
painted a solid color. The ceiling was bordered by a cornice.
The living and dining room floors were covered with brightly
colored floral carpets; everywhere else the floors were waxed
or untreated, and partially covered with mats or rugs. Mirrors and hangings abounded in the two reception rooms;
indeed, according to mid-nineteenth-century tastes, these
items constituted one-half of the furnishings. Heavy silk or
satin drapes, framing the window casings and weighed down
by tasseled pelmets, effectively shut out both air and light.
In the North, at least, they served as a protection against the
cold. Double windows and doors served the same purpose.

Houses were heated mainly by open fires; each room had its fireplace, and the ashes were emptied into a chute running from the upper floor into the cellar. Wood or coal burners helped to warm the house. Central heating was first introduced in the form of hot-air pipes laid under the floors and regulated by valves. This was followed by steam heating through radiators, and then hot-water systems.

Around 1830, the oil lamp—mainly whale oil—began to replace candles. Edwin Drake's discovery of the first oil well at Titusville, Pennsylvania, in 1859 soon generalized this new form of lighting.

The main furniture styles were Gothic and Louis Philippe. Around 1840, black enamel, inlaid with mother-of-pearl and simulated lacquer, was all the rage. It was used for tables, chairs, and desks. At the same time, walnut replaced mahogany. It was used in the manufacture of the two types of furniture to be found in nearly every house: the ottoman, a very low, eastern-style divan, without a back or arm rests, surrounded by a fringe and decorated with pom-poms, and the "what not," a set of five shelves decreasing in width from base to top. Most furniture was machine-made, but there were still many craftsmen. One of them, John H. Belter, won fame through a manufacturing process known only to him. Working with laminated rosewood, he fashioned pieces with backs and arms of an almost ethereal elegance, contrasting strikingly with the opulence of the upholstery and the brilliance of the red damask coverings.

Were we to cut short our description here, we might be tempted to conclude that the similarities between the America and the France of 1850 were great. We find the same "middle-class" homes, the same furnishings of questionable taste, the same heating and lighting methods, and the same primitive hygiene. However, these analogies pale before the differences.

Take the log cabin, the only refuge the conquerors of the prairire had from nature and the Indian. The whole family worked together in building it. With the spirit of mutual aid so typical of the America of that period, neighbors, whenever there were any, lent the isolated a helping hand. Otherwise, it would take several weeks to finish the humble home. The first job was to strip branches from oaks, beeches, maples, or poplars and to pile them up on the site of the future house. There they were trimmed, smoothed, and notched. Next the ground was leveled and the first logs placed. At each corner a hatchet was used to fit the notches together properly. As the cabin took shape, the logs were fixed with nails and clamps. Gaps were filled with moss or dried mud. The roof battens were supported by rafters, and a gable crowned the structure. The door was fastened by a wooden latch, reinforced at night by a strong crossbar. The windows, which people of refinement decorated with muslin curtains, were generally covered with oiled paper or greased buckskin. A fireplace, one or more beds—innocent of springs, to be sure—built into the wall, a table for meals, a few stools, perhaps a rocking chair, a chest to store the linen, clothes pegs on the walls, an almanac hanging on a string, a map of the United States, a portrait of the President, a Bible close at hand—and the furnishings were complete.

Even more austere was a trapper's winter camp. It would ordinarily be sheltered to the north by hills or rocks in order to take full advantage of the rare rays of sun and to escape the eyes of Indians on the prowl. A woods in the vicinity would provide the timber, and water would be drawn from a stream. In front of the hut, a fire would always be burning, which the trapper would try to keep alive all night beneath the ashes. His shelter would be made of pelts piled on a semicircular framework of thin, light wooden poles carefully set in the ground. During the day he would work on his skins, first stretching them on a square frame made of slats firmly bound together, then scraping them energetically with a hard stone or a scraper of his own makeshift fabrication. Afterwards, he would grain them on a board set at counter-slope for convenience.

Behind the hut on a stick laid across two forked poles five or six feet high he would have hooked pieces of meat—sides, shoulders, and heads of deer and sheep and the hides, particularly the fleece, of the bison he had bagged. One of the major problems would be feeding his horse. Failing pasture, he would feed it cotton husks. He would keep his saddle and his pack close at hand, carefully hung up to protect them from the damp. And he would never be separated from his rifle, his powder horn, or his bullet bag; he would sleep with them by his side.

All around was cold, solitude, and danger . . . .

*Chapter IV*

# DRESS
# AND FASHIONS

The forty-two years from 1822 to 1864 were, according to an expert on fashions, the ideal period of the perfect lady. Alas, all good things come to an end. The following thirty-five years were, in the same expert's view, marked by a more complex atmosphere of sexual readjustment. We must confine ourselves here to those American women who needed no "adjustment."

Having been "romantic" until 1840, they became "sentimental" afterwards. We would not venture to trace the boundaries between these subtle shades, but shall content ourselves with considering how they were reflected in dress. Around 1820 the waistline, tired of being raised to the bosom as fashion had required early in the century, fell back to its natural position. Dresses continued to grow fuller from that time on, until they reached several yards in circumference. They were held out by one or more petticoats stiffened around the bottom with horsehair padding. The apparent freedom that the fullness of skirts gave women's legs contrasted dramatically with the strict discipline that their tight bodices imposed on the rest of their bodies. Corsets were, of course, a must. Any means of making them as effective as possible was acceptable. When a fashionable lady had no strong-armed chamber maid, she would attach her laces to the bed posts, hold her breath, and walk as far as possible before imprisoning her waist. A few doctors dared to criticize these barbaric practices and were severely reproved by a professional journal which expressed the hope that, for the honor of the medical profession, such opposition would cease. Women continued to delight in making martyrs of themselves. Although "romantic" they did not seek to hide their shape, and the plump type was not displeasing to their admirers.

Hairdressers demanded that the hair should be flat on the forehead, with corkscrew curls falling around the ears and sometimes an unruly lock or two deliberately creating an impression of involuntary negligence. The crown of the head was also flat, and a part was indispensable. It was also stylish to gather the hair into a chignon or a roll, generally decorated with feathers, flowers, ribbons, or lace, above the nape of the neck. Thus, following the counsel of the phrenologists, who then ruled supreme, the daughters of Eve disguised "the animal passions revealed by the back of the head," while on the contrary giving prominence to the "higher instincts manifested by the forehead." Perhaps scientific considerations also explained the use of bonnets carefully tied under the chin, but which coquettes liked to wear tilted back as though they were about to fall off.

Bold girls sometimes, it is true, lost another, more intimate part of their attire in public. The legs of their long batiste drawers were held together only by a string around the waist; a little inadvertence and a "leg" emerged from beneath the lady's dress.

These disturbing signs of "romanticism" disappeared around 1840 with the triumph of "sentimentalism." No

more kiss curls, no more provocative bonnets, no more slip-
ping underclothes. American women decided to be seductive
by emphasizing their dependence. The body was immobilized, tightly enclosed in nearly rigid casings, protected from
all contact. Fashion demanded a languishing air; women
must appear submissive, sweet, resigned. Their arms were
enclosed in long, full sleeves; their bodies were meticulously
fitted and bristled with whalebone; their low-cut necklines
were attenuated by lace ruffles. The cut of clothing eschewed
all boldness, and no bright colors were tolerated by proper
ladies.

The milliners also imprisoned them in bonnets which
played a role quite similar to that of horses' binders. The
idea is plain: not a glance to the right or the left—cast down
your eyes, my lady!

There were no restrictions on perfume, however. The
"sentimental" American ladies of 1840 appear to have used
it rather liberally. Bergamot, frangipani, and patchouli were
highly popular scents. It was above all essential that the
label bear a Parisian name. Guerlain's lustral water, Pivert's
soap, Pelletier's toothpaste, and Micheau's lotion were to be
found on the dressing tables of all fashionable women. Even
cosmetics not made in France were baptized with French
names. In women's conversation, all the talk was of *eau de
rose, eau de cédrat, blanc de neige, poudre de riz,* and *huile
ambrée.*

Does this reflect French influence? The French coutu-
riers were affirming their prestige at the same period. Or was
it a whim of "sentimentalism"? Whatever the reason, austerity was less fashionable in the period immediately preceding the Civil War. In the United States, as elsewhere,
crinolines were all the rage. With them, color and imagination reappeared. A slightly abrupt movement, and the
foot—carefully hidden ten years earlier—could be glimpsed.
It was shod in daytime in a high-heeled black leather shoe

and in the evening in a black or white sandal tied with ribbons around the ankle. It soon became permissible, in graceful gestures, to lift the skirts enough to reveal the white silk or cotton stockings and the lace and embroidery of the petticoats. At the same time, the gait ceased to be so rigid as corsets were made more flexible.

Women wore their hair straight or curly, more and more drawn back on the nape of the neck in masses of curls or braids, often covered with a net. Brightly colored shawls or short coats were the rule outside. Little by little, hats of various shapes replaced the bonnet.

The interpretations of fashion varied, of course, from region to region. The South was probably the center of true elegance. Even if they have been idealized by legend and misfortune, there is no doubt that the women descending from the old families of Virginia or the Carolinas knew how to give their dress an undefinable touch of elegance and refinement which further enhanced their natural charm. In Boston, too, women prided themselves on their refinement, but with less subtlety and nonchalance, for their Puritan heritage would have prohibited any caprice. Philadelphia, home of the Quakers, allowed only austerity—no feathers, no flowers, no rucking, but dark-colored hats and dresses. In New York, on the other hand, ladies were not averse to show. As Dickens summed it up in 1842, there was an abundance of multicolored parasols, and of silks and satins of all colors of the rainbow, dainty shoes, fluttering ribbons, and luxurious coats with gaudy linings. Everywhere, he said, women sought to excite attention by wearing bright colors, ermine-lined capes, luxurious furs, ostrich feathers, and bright pink or blue hats. Dickens claimed he saw more colors in ten minutes on Broadway than he would have seen elsewhere in ten years.

Needless to say, there was little of the ostentation of

New York or the refinement of the South in the regions of
the West where America was accomplishing its destiny.
The pioneers' helpmate gave no thought to dress or styles.
Her favorite attire was that which best allowed her to do
her work. For every day, she wore only a coarse woolen
dress, but given the chance to attend a party, she would
perch gaily on the horse behind her husband got up in a
light-colored calico dress, proud of her colored bonnet, and
joyfully humming the tune to which they were already
impatient to dance:

> Grab your honies, don't let 'em fall,
> Shake your hoofs and balance all,
> Faster, faster, and swing the partners,
> Until they kick the ceiling, if any.

The movies have made the Don Juan of the prairie
a popular figure: soft woolen shirt, a handkerchief (usually
red) around the neck, buckskin vest with pockets generally
stuffed with tobacco, long leather-fringed trousers, closely
fitting boots, buckskin gloves with wide gauntlets, and
above all, the essential item in the uniform, an enormous,
wide-brimmed ten gallon hat, in dark grey or tan felt, with
a thong on each side to hold it beneath the chin. In truth,
this type of figure was still fairly rare in the mid-nineteenth
century, and only became common with the development
of the ranches and cowboys around 1860 or 1870.

Before the Civil War, the traditional pioneer no more
sought elegance than did his wife. Sometimes allowing his
hair to hang down nearly to his shoulders, but clean-
shaven (his only refinement), he was wont to wear only
a shirt, heavy wool trousers, and moccasins. While hunting
or traveling, he supplemented this indoor attire with a
buckskin jacket and leather chaps, not to mention, of
course, his gun, powder flask, knife, hatchet, and axe. Anyone west of the Alleghenies who had become so middle-class

as to dress in the manner of New England or Virginia would have become a laughing stock. Two types of men were, however, more conventional—the ministers, dressed all in black, who crisscrossed the region on some old nag, and the politicians, who hoped that their alpaca frock coats and silk cravats would confer upon them the respectability to which their ethics did not permit them to aspire.

The apotheosis of the "perfect lady" was accompanied in the East by a renewal of masculine elegance. "Romantic" women's husbands did not eschew bright colors: a blue frock coat with copper buttons, a beige waistcoat, and a white cravat were essential items in their wardrobes. Even more striking was their underwear, consisting of long red flannel pants and a singlet of the same color concealed beneath the shirt.

When, in a "sentimental" style, women's dress tended to subdued tones, the men followed suit. Their choice fell to black, grey, and dark colors in general. The clothes remained the same, with a high stovepipe hat; a long frock coat, at first full and later fitted; trousers with straps beneath the instep; a puffy cravat skillfully knotted to create an impression of deliberate negligence. Any gentleman worth his salt bought the cloth for his suits himself, the tailor's job being confined to the stitching. Around 1860, imperials and sideburns began to appear (Abraham Lincoln was the first bearded President). Beards and mustaches had been strictly ruled out before. Shaving brushes and lather bowls played a prominent part in men's lives. It was fashionable to have one's initials stamped on them in gold and to vary their color according to the owner's profession.

We should not conclude from these remarks that the Beau Brummel type was commonplace in the United States. Some examples might be found in a few large cities. There was doubtless a hereditary snobbery in the South which even extended to men's clothing; elegant planters, for example, affected the habit, after the English fashion, of never wearing suits which might look new, and made sure that their clothing had a subtle air of carelessness. Those, however, were only exceptions, and it would be more accurate to suppose that American men of a century ago were the despair of their tailors. Diplomats long aspired to remain an exception. They clung to court uniform: a blue coat, lined with white silk, white knee breeches and black silk stockings, cape, and three-cornered hat. "Old Hickory" (the nickname given to Andrew Jackson in memory of the defense of New Orleans in 1812 and his extermination of the Florida Indians six years later) suggested that they should adopt a more "democratic" costume, but they paid no heed. Finally, in 1853, the Secretary of State formally ordered them to dress like American citizens. Sick at heart, they had to obey. James Buchanan, then ambassador at the Court of St. James, when forced to content himself with a coat and a white cravat, buckled a sword to his side so that he would not, as he said, be taken for a butler. But the gesture of protest had no tomorrows, and "democracy" soon won out, even in the Foreign Service.

# Chapter V
# FOOD
# AND BEVERAGES

It is said of Americans today that they eat little but often; it does not seem erroneous to say that their ancestors of a century ago ate much and often.

Hence they attached enormous importance to matters of supply. In small towns, direct contact was established between farmers and townspeople. The large cities organized markets. The Fulton Market in New York was admired by visitors for the variety of produce on sale there —for one could buy meat, fowl, vegetables, fruit. A few butchers' shops and bakeries also facilitated supply. Then there were the pedlars selling muffins and crackers, berries, milk, spring water for the fearful, and ice cream for the refined. Ice cream made its appearance in Jackson's time. The ice cream habit spread like wildfire as soon as the railways began to use refrigerated cars in 1842. The first soda counters appeared in 1855.

In such a strongly meat-eating country, the problem of meat was vital. It received no systematic solution for a long time. Cattle and pigs were transported by road from

the Ohio valley to the Atlantic coast. Each community had
its slaughterhouse, usually located in the center of the
town, which emitted a stench. Cincinnati gradually mo-
nopolized this trade. The animals were slaughtered there
and the meat salted and smoked, then packed and sent by
rail to the rest of the country. It was only after the Civil
War that Chicago predominated in the field.

Three or four meals a day were customary, at least in
the cities. Breakfast was taken at 7 o'clock, when the members of the family, completely dressed, met around the dining table; dinner, generally eaten at noon, was delayed
until 2 o'clock on Sunday; the men were always present,
except in large cities, where the distance of the business
areas from residential areas was beginning to prevent them
from coming home at noon; supper was at 5 or 6 o'clock
and lastly, in some cases, a snack was taken at about 11 P.M.

Two types of cooking vied for popularity among gour-
mets. In New England, people boasted of knowing how to
make clam chowder, baked beans, squash, apple pie, pumpkin pie, and every imaginable pudding from plum pudding, and bread pudding to Indian pudding, better than
anywhere else. Shellfish and ordinary fish, especially lobsters
and cod, also sparked the culinary imagination.

To so much talent, the South replied by its uncontested mastery in cooking meat, particularly pork and ham,
and its equally great ability in the preparation of turnips
and, even more, yams and sweet potatoes. Once a year the
two camps agreed on the standard Thanksgiving Day menu:
the most imposing stuffed turkey possible with cranberry
sauce, turnips, pumpkin, boiled or fried potatoes (then
known as German fried potatoes), and puddings or pies.

No European visitor failed to be astonished at the size
and, it must be added, the strangeness of the daily fare. By
way of example, a standard breakfast menu included oat-

meal or cornmeal mash, soft-boiled eggs, a meat dish (beef-steak, lamb or veal chops, or sausages) accompanied by potatoes, cheese, bread or crackers with butter, and sometimes buckwheat pancakes with Vermont maple syrup; the usual beverage was coffee or tea. It is understandable that five hours of digestion until the next meal were not amiss. Dinner or supper was no less copious: soup; red or white meat served with potatoes, corn, green peas, cabbage, or beets; chicken and other fowl garnished with jellies and jams; pudding and pies. The salad habit appeared only later. The only raw vegetables were usually lettuce or dandelion greens seasoned with sugar and vinegar. Such nourishment, which would make modern dietitians throw up their hands in horror, was pleasing to women as well as men. Godfrey T. Vigne, Esq., who visited the United States in 1833, deplored the fact, and observed that American women should know that overeating was unfeminine. Since ladies, sitting in the presence of gentlemen, did not conceal the fact that they were really hungry, obviously something was wrong with the national manners. The honorable visitor was full of warnings concerning the future of a country in which such unfortunate customs prevailed. He predicted that it would collapse of its own weight, probably in less than fifty years.

While waiting or the inevitable *mene, mene, tekel, upharsin* to appear on their walls, the langorous creatures of 1840 or 1850 were, it must be admitted, hearty eaters. They did not confine themselves to adoring the sweets, ice creams, and cakes in which the pitiless Mrs. Trollope claimed they indulged so extravagantly. (Mrs. Trollope, the wife of an English lawyer, who went bankrupt trying to operate a novelty shop in Cincinnati, published a book which quickly became famous, *Domestic Manners of the Americans,* after her return to England in 1832.) One of the favorite dishes of American women was oysters, which remained constantly in vogue from 1810 to 1870; they were eaten all year round and on all occasions in the form of oyster stew, oyster sauce, fried oysters, oysters *au gratin*, oyster tart; in bars, they were dipped in whisky before being served; sometimes they were mixed with eggs. These bold combinations were not the only ones in which American cooking delighted. Pork—the eternal pork, as one visitor said—was never served without stewed apples; steak with peaches was most popular; and salt fish set off with onions frightened only absurdly delicate palates. Vegetables and meats were served fresh, for the canning industry did not develop until around 1880.

Coffee, served black or laced with cream, was already the customary beverage at meals. It was only after the discovery of the condensation process by Gail Borden in 1853 that milk consumption became widespread. In the country, water was drunk as a matter of course. In the cities, on the contrary, fear of cholera often prohibited its use. When, in 1842, construction was begun on the aqueduct that was to bring Croton water to New York, the "drys" were pleased, affirming that no one would any longer have an easy excuse for pouring cognac or rum into the water. That was a particularly reprehensible weakness in their eyes, since there was always root beer, the widely consumed ancestor of ginger ale, to fall back on.

Outside of Europeanized circles, where Madeira, Bordeaux, Rhine, or Mosel wines and champagne were favored, wine was virtually unknown. Lincoln gave proof of this upon his arrival at the White House. A well-schooled headwaiter asked him whether he preferred white or red wine. Lincoln answered that he hadn't the faintest idea and inquired which the waiter himself preferred.

Around 1825 a first wave of prohibitionism broke upon the country. The American Society for the Promotion of Temperance soon counted more than 4 million members.

To make war on demon rum, it used all areas of propaganda—Sunday schools, medical societies, brochures, public lectures and, above all, revivals. It managed to give
alcoholic beverages a stigma of hypocrisy. In the Senate
bar, purchases of champagne were concealed under the
heading of office supplies. When the largest of the clipper
ships, the *Great Republic*, was launched in 1853, it was
baptized with a bottle of water. The drys thought at first
that they had won a victory. A book with the melodramatic
title of *Ten Nights in a Bar-room*, which described the
tragic consequences of alcoholism, was almost as successful
in 1854 as *Uncle Tom's Cabin* had been two years earlier.
At about the same time, Maine, Oregon, Minnesota, Iowa,
Illinois, Ohio, Pennsylvania, New York, Vermont, and
Massachusetts adopted total prohibition. But those were
more symbolic gestures than actual achievements. Most of
the laws remained a dead letter or were quickly repealed.
The Civil War put an end to the first noble experiment.
An initiative based on a different principle was more durable. The Washington Temperance Society did not pro-
pose that alcoholic beverages should be prohibited, but
that former alcoholics should be assigned the task of curing
their brethren still in sin. The campaign of this ancestor
of Alcoholics Anonymous, an organization which of course
plays an important role in present-day America, achieved
appreciable results. John D. Gough, a repentant drunkard,
won as much fame through it as William Lloyd Garrison
won through his anti-slavery campaign. Nothing, it seemed
could damp his ardor; as long as he had a voice, he said,
he would speak, and if he could only whisper, he would
make signs—and it was said that he knew how.

Was so much zeal justified? Scenes of drunkenness
were frequent, it is true, and there was no dearth of bars,
but in the small conventional towns, at least, they created
a lugubrious atmosphere that somewhat disheartened cus-

tomers. They drank in silence, dejectedly, made downcast, it would seem, by their remorse at satisfying, despite themselves, a shameful vice. An exceptional atmosphere such as that created by the discovery of gold was required to free them of their complexes. In the Far West and in California, drinkers were apt to be very glib; they would not drink before a brawl. Creatures of diabolical seductiveness (as is well known) stirred noisy reactions from them, and the vamps themselves did not hesitate to join in the men's libations. But elsewhere, what would have been said in 1850 of a woman who "drank"? Perfect ladies barely touched their lips to a glass of sherry and, not to offend their modesty, gentlemen, when they felt temptation too strong, took refuge in their clubs or in bars like the one at the Metropolitan Hotel in New York, where Jerry Thomas, "the king of bartenders," operated, or the famous Gem Saloon on Broadway, which boasted the longest mirror in the country. There gin slings, mint juleps, sangarees, sherry cobblers, timber doodles, hot buttered rums, blue blazers, and other refined and comforting drinks awaited the men.

As a rule, meals were dispatched with a speed which astounded foreigners; the slang of the period put it very picturesquely as "Gobble, gulp, and go." One visitor exclaimed at the voraciousness, haste, and hustle. Everyone stuffed himself at an incredible speed. Another visitor remarked that in barely twenty minutes, he had witnessed two series of meals in his hotel. A third added that in New York the waiters, impatient at his slowness, had virtually withdrawn the tablecloth from under his plate; it was little wonder, he observed, that dyspepsia should be a common complaint under such conditions.

The term "dining room" was perfectly appropriate for the room set aside for the purpose; although dining was done in it, pleasure of conversation was out of the question. Dickens sadly commented on the staggering boredom occasioned at funereal banquets, where to joke would have seemed a crime. Judging by the silence, he went on, one might have thought that the diners were gathered to lament the passing of some dear friend rather than with the idea of joyfully ensuring their survival.

It was obviously a far cry from the little suppers of Versailles.

# Chapter VI

# MEANS OF COMMUNICATION AND TRANSPORT

In a country in full development like the teeming, feverish America of a century ago, means of communication were essential to progress. Indeed, national cohesion was largely dependent on their development. George Washington had understood their unifying role and had said that every single one of the roads provided by nature between the Atlantic states and the western territories should be opened and their use encouraged to the utmost, for there was no surer means of cementing the Federal Union.

Roads, canals, and railroads were built in turn. Even balloons were for a time in vogue. They provided Edgar Allan Poe with the occasion for a famous practical joke: in 1844, a special edition of the *New York Sun* published as front page news a tale he had written about a supposed crossing of the continent by air. But this form of transport turned out to be not at all practical. The same was not true of the others, and the greatest diversity had soon been achieved—stagecoaches, wagons, boats, and trains were all being used simultaneously. In the course of a single trip, even a short one, a series of different forms of transport frequently had to be employed. To go from Washington to Richmond—a distance of 100 miles—Dickens took a boat, a coach, and a train. Another traveler who went from New Jersey to Cincinnati—a journey of 450 miles—at about the same period took a train from South Amboy to Philadelphia, where he changed to another train for Columbia; there he boarded a horse-drawn canal barge as far as Pittsburgh; finally, an Ohio steamer carried him to his destination. Another typical example of these itineraries with continual changes was New York to Mobile by boat, Mobile to Augusta by stage, Augusta to Charleston by boat, stage again from Charleston to Norfolk, boat from Norfolk to Baltimore, stage from Baltimore to Philadelphia, riverboat from Philadelphia to Trenton, stage from Trenton to New Brunswick, and finally a ferry across the Hudson back to New York.

Thus, journeys did not lack variety. The unforeseen, and discomfort, as we shall see, were also far from being ruled out. As to recuperating in the evening from the fatigue of the day's travel, that could not be counted on. The road inns were worse than primitive. A traveler would arrive at 11 o'clock at night, to leave again at 5 in the morning. All the travelers were crowded into the few available rooms, several to a bed. Not to mention the vermin. The food was inedible. On the prairie, there were not even any organized relays. From time to time, a wagon tavern was to be found on the most frequented routes. Hotels in the small towns were with few exceptions, extremely primitive. Those in the South—where courteous private hospitality compensated for their inadequacy—were especially notorious in that respect. According to bitter descriptions, they provided no bell, no bed curtains, no wash basin, no water jug, no coat rack, no mirror, no towels, and no table cloths. In fact, only the large cities had more than rudi-

mentary facilities. And that was not saying much. Dickens
claimed that Baltimore was the only city where he had
been able to obtain water for washing. He had been better
pleased with his hotel in Washington, but what service!
To call a servant, you had to strike a metal triangle in the
hall a certain number of times, from one to seven, depending on the part of the building to which the servant was
supposed to come. As all the servants were constantly being
called and none ever came, the din never ceased the whole
day long.

Several years later, the situation had considerably improved. Tremont House in Boston offered travelers 140
rooms which could be locked with a key, each having a
wash basin, a water jug, a bar of soap, a nail brush, and
a tooth brush. Eight toilets, eight bathrooms, and gas lighting in all the lounges bore witness to the magnificence of
the place. Barnett House in Cincinnati, Mansion's House
in Philadelphia, the City Hotel in Baltimore, Godsby's, the
Italian Queen, and Fuller's in Washington, Shepherd's in
Utica, the Saint Charles in New Orleans, and especially
Astor House in New York, around 1840, and a little later
the Metropolitan and St. Nicholas', were renowned for
their luxury. In St. Nicholas', according to a visitor, all the
mantelpieces and tables were of marble, all the carpets of
pile, the chairs were covered in silk or damask satin, and
the curtains matched. Room and board cost about $2.50 in
the North and $3.00 in the South. Room service was un-
known, and meals were taken at a fixed hour at the call
of a gong at long common tables. As it was fashionable for
a newly married couple of a wealthy family to spend their
wedding night in one of these very luxurious hotels, each
hotel had its bridal suite, especially reserved for that purpose. In Cincinnati it was once given to Ralph Waldo
Emerson out of courtesy. For a moment he ceased to be tran-

scendental and commented that it was quite beautiful, but wondered how one could think in such surroundings.

During the thirty years following Independence, the roads had been virtually the only means of communication apart from the navigable rivers. Most roads were no more than somewhat widened paths twisting and winding across the countryside with poorly defined outlines. Little by little a network of roads took shape, and even after the construction of the canals and railroads, the roads remained the scene of intense activity.

The first roads, known as corduroy roads, were built of large logs placed parallel to the track, across which were laid other, smaller logs the width of the road. The whole was covered with earth and sand, intended to serve as a cushion. Unfortunately, little remained of this thin protective layer after the first rain. The plank roads, much in vogue from 1845 to 1857, were less primitive. Their tarred boards stood up better in bad weather, and they sloped slightly to the outside to facilitate water drainage. The planks, which were held in place neither by nails nor by clamps, were supposed to adhere to the ground by their own weight. In general, they covered only half the road, which carried heavy wagons bringing agricultural produce to the city. The unloaded wagons returned to the country on plain beaten earth.

With the turnpike, macadam roads, or at least properly drained ones, made their appearance. Most were built by private firms to which the state granted concessions. Approximately every ten miles a toll was collected, from which those living in the immediate vicinity, those on their way to church, voters on election day, soldiers, and jurors were exempt. One of the most famous was the National Cumberland Road, which started from Baltimore and

linked the Atlantic coast to the Mississippi. Most of the
rivers were crossed by covered bridges, always made of
wood.

Many kinds of vehicles traveled on these roads. Some,
called liners, had schedules fixed in advance. Others were
rented for specific trips and were known by the colorful
name of tramps. Goods were transported in enormous Conestoga wagons, which gradually disappeared as the canals and
railroads were developed. Their maximum capacity was ten
tons, and their floors sloped slightly toward the center for
the sake of load stability on inclines. They were pulled by
six horses harnessed in pairs. The driver rode the left-hand
horse of the last pair. The team and wagon together measured up to 60 feet in length. The goods were protected by
a heavy canvas top held in place by iron bars of roughly
semicircular shape. Their height from the top to the ground
exceeded 11 feet. Some wagons were amphibious; with
wheels high and strong enough, it was usually possible to
ford streams up to two feet in depth. The Conestoga wagons
must have been quite impressive with their blue and red
bodies and their white cloth tops. The lighter and faster
"prairie schooners," less imposing but better suited to the
terrain of the West, also transported goods across the Alleghenies.

As far as appearance went, nothing could be too beautiful for the prospective travelers. Brightly colored and decorated diligences bore the owner's name—Concord Coaches
or Deadwood Stages—on their sides. Their four-horse teams
were glossy and harnessed as though for a drive in the park.
The coachman wore great buckskin gloves which reached
halfway up his arms. The comfort inside was not, however,
commensurate with the outer show. The passengers were
crowded onto three parallel rows of benches, each seating
three, only the last of which, reserved for women, had a
back rest. Leather curtains afforded them some protection

from bad weather. Two passengers sat next to the driver, and the baggage was piled into a rear bin or onto the roof. A crack of the whip, and the coach leapt forward. The complete absence of suspension, springs being unknown, made this type of transport singularly uncomfortable. An exasperated Frenchman wrote that it was a new kind of steeplechase and genuine torture. Another victim observed that he had felt he was being made to fly through the air. An Englishwoman observed in astonishment that if there was the slightest truth in phrenology, enormous changes in character must have been caused by a trip across the Alleghenies. Dickens went one step further; during their trip, he wrote, the coach had not for a minute been in the position in which one was accustomed to find ordinary coaches; the passengers would be touching the roof one minute, and flung to the floor the next.

But speed was the supreme law. The eastern stages did an average speed of about ten miles an hour. That, however, was nothing beside the records achieved between the Missippi and the Pacific. The distance was usually covered in twenty-four days. What a strain, to judge by one witness' account—perhaps he was a bit of a softy! He described it as twenty-four killing days, twenty-four killing nights, passengers who, from drinking whiskey and going without sleep, went half mad and had to be tied to their seats, abominable meals swallowed in ten minutes at halts, a climate conducive to malaria, no light allowed at night for fear of illusory Indians; in short, the suffering endured on that unhappy road knew no bounds. What would that pessimist have said had he been driven by the illustrious Ben Holliday, the "overland Napoleon"? For that king of the stagecoaches, distances were really nonexistent. In a specially equipped wagon, he once covered the 2,000 miles between Folsom, California, and Atchison, Kansas, in twelve days and two hours. His exploits were legendary. An American child, it is said, when he learned that the Hebrews had taken forty years to cross the desert under Moses' leadership, exclaimed that if Ben Holliday had been there, the journey would have taken less than thirty-six hours.

The canals afforded the most restful means of transport. They played an important role in American life for some forty years before the Civil War. Some relatively short ones were designed only to transport products from the hinterland to ports such as Boston and Charleston; these were built by private undertakings. Others were the result of more ambitious programs; in the minds of their promoters, they were to constitute a vital link between East and West. The states and cities assumed their financing and operation. The material difficulties were sometimes considerable. Pennsylvania, which was attempting to attract the products of Ohio to Philadelphia, was particularly interested in this type of communications, but the canals it decided to build had to cross the barrier of the Alleghenies. The lock system was not sophisticated enough to provide a complete solution to the problem. The canal stopped when it reached too sharp a slope; the boat was placed on an incline and, with the aid of a machine, transported to the top of the obstacle and then lowered into the opposite valley, where another waterway awaited it. These trans-shipments were carried out along a distance of more than 150 miles and across mountain chains sometimes reaching nearly 2,600 feet.

New York's supremacy was assured by the opening of the Erie Canal, which linked Albany and Buffalo, thereby establishing direct contact between the Great Lakes and the Atlantic by way of the Hudson Valley. From that time on, $10 and eight days sufficed to transport a ton of freight from Buffalo to New York, whereas $100 and twenty days had previously been required. It was a gigantic task, one which Jefferson, despite his optimism, had called folly, to construct a canal 363 miles long, 40 feet wide, and 4 feet deep across an area of almost unbroken wilderness. It was completed on October 26, 1825. At the inauguration, a ceremony reminiscent of the traditional marriage of Venice and the sea took place at the tip of Manhattan. Water from the fourteen largest rivers on the five continents was mixed with that of Lake Erie and thrown into the ocean in a symbolic gesture of the international role to which New York aspired.

The cities of the West did not intend to play second fiddle to the great metropolis; in the following years a dense network of canals also linked the Great Lakes to the Mississippi valley. It greatly contributed to the prodigious development of cities like Chicago, Detroit, and Cleveland.

Only goods transport was originally provided for, but it soon became customary to use the canals for passenger service as well. The passengers could not be in a hurry, for the average speed hardly exceeded 3 or 3½ miles an hour. At that rate, for example, to travel from Philadelphia to Pittsburgh (400 miles), Cincinnati (900 miles), or St. Louis (1,750 miles), one had to allow 6½ days, 9½ days, or 13 days, respectively. The fare, it is true, was nominal—$6, $9, or $13—but the comfort was on the same scale. In the daytime, the passengers were obliged to go below deck or to lie flat on their stomachs whenever the boat passed under a bridge, and heaven knows there were many. At night, forty or fifty had to gather in a room as small as it was dirty, where they were accommodated on three tiers of bunks, 5½ feet long and 2 feet wide, separated by a space of 2 feet. For washing, they had two towels, one wooden wash basin, one bucket of more or less clean water drawn from the canal, two pieces of soap, one comb, and one brush.

River navigation, so characteristic of the mid-nineteenth century, was more poetic, or in any event more picturesque. All types of boats were used. Some, flat-keeled,

20 to 30 feet long and 3 to 5 feet wide, were propelled by pole or oar. To run against the current, sails were used. Others were mere rafts made of dozens of logs chained together and propelled by oars. At the destination, they were broken up and the wood sold. The arks which floated with the current were more durable; they were 75 to 100 feet long and 15 to 25 feet wide, had a draught of 3 to 5 feet, and were steered by means of a tiller 40 feet long. The flat boats, a kind of wooden box which hardly emerged above the surface of the water, were the most unusual of all. One observer remarked that, seen from afar, they had precisely the appearance of coffins afloat on the water. One was quite surprised from time to time to see a child's or a woman's head emerge from one of the openings in the roof. Or, as this observer did not venture to add, a gun—for they served as forts when necessary. Families crowded in with pigs, chickens, furniture, and tools. Finally, there were innumerable canoes, skiffs, and dugouts, speedier although less reliable, in which the impatient made haste. Trying to keep up with them, some barges with sails, specially equipped for speed, managed to do four or five miles an hour sailing downstream and two miles sailing upstream.

All this paled beside the paddle-wheel, then propeller, boats—the pride of the major rivers, and especially of the majestic, romantic, incomparable Mississippi. It is estimated that, around 1845, 10 million tons of freight, or double the United States' foreign trade, were transported on the waters of the giant river or its fifty-four affluents, some of which, such as the Arkansas, the Ohio, and above all the Missouri, dared rival it in power and splendor.

Mark Twain has left unforgettable descriptions of the hard, adventurous life of the Mississippi River pilots. He led that existence for four years, and according to his writings, it was not a precisely restful job. To succeed, he noted, a man had to learn more than anyone should be allowed to

know, and he had to relearn each day in a different way
what he had learned the day before. The passengers were
not exactly of the placid tourist type—they were businessmen for whom time was money and who ceaselessly complained that the boat was going too slowly, or adventurers
leaving first one town, then another, when they had run out
of luck, or Southern belles around whom there hung an
aura of desire and jealousy. There were many professional
gamblers. Strangely enough, they wore what was virtually
a uniform——black sombrero, black frock coat, full cravat,
ruffled white shirt, colored vest, high-heeled black boots, a
massive diamond shirt button, and an enormous gold chain
and watch. This standard apparel did not prevent them
from finding victims—far from it. These they fleeced with
dexterity. Nonetheless, scruples sometimes held them back.
As one explained, after having taken from a traveling
preacher all his money, his gold-rimmed glasses, and his sermons, he had felt badly and had decided to return the sermons and the glasses. This impulse of Christian charity was,
we are sure, appreciated by the beneficiary, but most of the
time the atmosphere was not so harmonious. Incidents were
frequent, and the crew had its hands full to put an end to
the brawls between winners and losers. The showboats had
so bad a reputation in that connection, that they were finally
prohibited before the Civil War and reappeared only in
1878.

There were many accidents, especially when, as was
constantly happening, two rival captains indulged in races.
Explosions and fires were the usual consequences. Even at
a slower speed, a disaster could occur at any moment. It was
therefore recommended that passengers should keep their
life preservers at hand. The rear cabins were much sought
after, for it was usually the front of the boat that exploded.

In the East, too, the rivers were commonly used as communication links. The Hudson, in particular, from New

York to Albany, was plied by boats of all sizes and types. Their departure around 5 P.M. took place amidst the greatest uproar. The captains shouted orders through megaphones, bells rang, passengers gesticulated, and, on the quays their friends waved flags. Some boats were quite primitive. At night, men and women slept in a common room, separated only by a curtain. Other boats afforded more comfortable facilities. Some were even reputed to be of singular magnificence. For example, there was the famous *Drew* with its double-deck bridge, its white and gold decor, soft carpets, sparkling gas chandeliers, great stairway, and orchestra, whose tones communicated an atmosphere of culture, harmony, and rhythm. And then there were the amorous affairs, for the night boats were said to be literally invaded by prostitutes. "The night boat to Albany" has remained a proverbial expression.

The first rails seem to have been used in Massachusetts in 1825. They were made of wood, 1 foot high, 6 inches wide, and covered with a layer of iron 3 inches wide and $\frac{1}{4}$ inch thick. They were placed about 5 feet apart. Initially, traction was provided by sails, as with boats, or by mules and horses. When steam engines (fired first with wood, then with coal) appeared, pessimists in the United States as elsewhere foresaw the worst catastrophes. A newspaper in 1830 wailed that all citizens would start flying like comets and asked what would remain afterwards of the country's gravity. At least for the moment, these fears were a little exaggerated, for the very year when they were expressed, a locomotive was unable to outstrip a horse in a race whose outcome temporarly comforted the adversaries of change.

These, however, represented only an infinitesimal minority. The Baltimore and Ohio Railroad started operating in 1827. Twenty years later, the railways were a part of everyday life in the East and were increasingly common between the Alleghenies and the Mississippi. According to a witticism which illustrates this development well, when a locomotive collided with a cow in 1830, it had to be sent to a repair shop; but by 1850, the company had to pay for the cow. The total railway network before the Civil War is estimated at approximately 31,000 miles. The establishment of the New York Central by Commodore Vanderbilt in 1853, coming after the founding of the Pennsylvania Railroad in 1847, accelerated the movement. At about the same time, a study of four transcontinental railway routes was undertaken. However, the Atlantic and the Pacific were to be permanently linked only in 1869, with the completion of the Union Pacific.

After alarming the timorous, the railway soon fascinated the imaginative. Walt Whitman, the great prophet of progress, sang of what he called its savage beauty, its raucous beauty. Thoreau, the solitary lover of nature (but who did not shrink before paradox), found in it a justification of humanity. In a poetic vein, he exclaimed that when he heard the roaring of the iron horse echo like thunder across the hills, and when he saw it make the ground tremble as it passed, breathing fire and smoke through its nostrils, it seemed to him that the earth was at last inhabited by a race worthy of it.

In the heroic age when the iron horse was still taking its first steps, the passengers were perhaps not absolutely convinced of the exalted dignity to which the new invention had raised them. Judging by their tales, train trips were no pleasure outings. Thirty, forty, or fifty persons were crowded into wooden wagons connected by chains. Stuffed seats and springs appeared only around 1850. The windows were sealed, and ventilation was provided only by two doors at each end of the cars. In summer, when they were left open, soot, sparks and dust poured in. In winter, when they were closed, the occupants nearly suffocated. Departures and arrivals were not gentle, and it was difficult to relax even on the way. This is how Dickens described it: a great deal of jolting, a great deal of noise, a great many walls and few windows, the puffing of the locomotive, the noise of the bell, an oven that made the atmosphere unbreathable—and everyone trying to talk to you. One never knew when the train would leave or when it would arrive. Stops of ten minutes at most were allowed for meals. There was in any case no guarantee that a passenger would arrive at his destination, for accidents were frequent. Burned bridges, which were primitively built of wood, were the main cause, and not all the engineers were as lucky as Phineas Fogg. The cinder-spitting locomotives set fire both to the travelers' clothes and to bridges and the countryside.

Then, on the prairie, there were the celebrated herds of bison, and there were the train robbers. Lastly, a breakdown could occur at any moment. Fortunately, good humor was the rule. A foreigner found himself in a train thus immobilized a few hundred yards from a station; the passengers, he observed, were not in the least disconcerted but simply set their shoulders to the cars and pushed until a horse was found to replace both them and the locomotive. Travelers were in any case accustomed to patience, for they had constantly to change cars on account of the different gauges (seven times between Buffalo and Albany, for example), or in order to cross rivers by ferry. Night journeys were particularly hazardous, and at first a pilot machine would always precede the train to bear the brunt of any obstacle. Lighting, for many years, was provided only by an enormous candle protected by a glass lantern. Around 1840 its feeble gleam was reinforced by a reflector.

By the middle of the century, the average speed had increased from its original ten miles an hour to thirty. Iron tracks had everywhere replaced wooden ones, and many bridges were constructed of steel. At about the same time, a double track and a uniform gauge became generalized.

Night journeys became somewhat less burdensome, for some coaches—forerunners of the Pullmans, which did not come into operation until after the Civil War—were arranged as three-tiered sleeping cars. Facilities were at a minimum, consisting only of planks covered by mattresses. This innovation did not meet with unanimous approval. Moralizers pointed to the promiscuity of these dormitories, deploring that young ladies should be thus familiarized with the hardly engaging spectacle of men still half asleep and unwashed; that trial, they felt, should be spared them at least until marriage made it unavoidable. The cautious, too, were not always wrong in hesitating to travel in these coaches, for the upper tier occasionally collapsed on the lower berths. In any event, it was long the fashion among businessmen to spurn even the problematical comforts of the new coaches which, they were wont to say, were signs of a disturbing lapse in American austerity. Tougher individuals, therefore, continued to travel in ordinary coaches.

The interior arrangement of the train cars soon became similar to what it is today, with parallel rows of two or three seats separated by a center aisle. The conductors wore top hats but no uniform, and moved from end to end of the train. To avoid being constantly disturbed, male passengers adopted the habit of sticking their tickets in their hat bands. For a while, there were special smoking cars for men and special cars for women, but the integration of the sexes speedily took place. The same could not be said of the races. From the outset, the South demanded the segregation of whites and Negroes; the slaves traveled with the baggage.

As long as the United States was confined to the eastern part of the continent, the postal problem was not acute. Distances were relatively short and the communication links fairly easy to use. Even in the East, however, service was still fairly primitive in the mid-nineteenth century. It is estimated that, in 1837, there was approximately one post office for every 1,500 inhabitants. Stamps appeared in 1847. The postage for an ordinary letter was between 5 cents and 10 cents, depending on the distance, but a 2 cent supplement was imposed for any collection or delivery elsewhere than at the post office counter. This extra charge was not abolished until 1863, in cities of over 20,000 inhabitants, and continued until 1897 for rural communities. Money orders were not introduced until 1864. Before that time, money was transferred by sending actual coins or bills in envelopes.

Westward expansion brought seemingly insoluble problems. How were letters to be transported over such long distances and, above all, how was their safety to be guaranteed? Private enterprise undertook to solve those problems, at least at first. The first "express company," founded by William F. Harnden, a former conductor on the Boston and Worcester Railroad, started operations in 1839. A series of competitors soon emerged. By about 1860, American Express had already absorbed many smaller enterprises. Side by side with it, and also powerful, Adam Express, National Express, United States Express, and above all Wells Fargo, which is so closely bound up with the folklore of the Far West, were in full activity. These organizations had a hand in everything: the transportation of letters, packages, and even passengers. On the eve of the Civil War, six lines linked the Mississippi and collected $100 in gold for each passenger and 10 cents for each half-ounce letter for the maximum distance.

The trip from St. Louis to San Francisco usually took twenty-three days. When the famous Pony Express started operation, the time was reduced to ten days. The idea had been advanced in 1854 by a senator from California, William A. Gwin, who was unable to convince the Congress that it was practical. Once again it was a private undertaking, Russell, Majors, and Waddell, which assumed the responsibility. Now it was no longer a matter of launching wagons or coaches into the vast expanses of the prairie and transporting passengers or packages. A single horseman, relayed at regular intervals, was to transport letters and documents in record time from one end of the country to the other at the maximum speed of a series of horses. The price for letters, to be written on very fine paper, was $5. America swelled with pride when, in March 1860, Abraham Lincoln's inaugural address was carried from the Mississippi to California by relays of horsemen in seven days and seven hours.

One month later, on April 3, a regular service started to operate. From the point of departure in Saint Joseph, Missouri, to the terminal in Sacramento, Salt Lake City was the only city on the route. The messengers usually galloped on in complete solitude. On some routes, they managed to travel 25 miles an hour. They were not permitted to bear arms. Each one covered 100 to 140 miles, changing horses every 20 or 25 miles. At relay points, they caught their breath for barely a few seconds. No obstacle and no excuse could stop them. They earned between $120 and $125 a month. The total distance they covered is estimated at 650,000 miles, and the mail was lost only once. Buffalo Bill, Jack Slade, Robert Haslam (known as "Pony Bob"), "Wild Bill" Hickok, and innumerable others took part in this probably unparalleled adventure. Mark Twain immortalized these centaurs of the prairie, saying that at whatever time—night or day—they might set out, whether in winter or summer, in rain, snow, or hail, whether the roads were icy, straight, or twisting along the brink of precipices, whether they crossed pacified or Indian-infested regions, they must always be prepared to leap into the saddle and leave as though borne on the wind.

This epic gradually came to an end with the entry into service of a transcontinental cable 3,595 miles long, from New York to San Francisco, on October 24, 1861, and the opening of the Union Pacific eight years later. Even in the Wild West, the machine began to replace man.

The beginnings of telegraphy, however, had been difficult. In 1832, Samuel Morse, then thirty-nine years old and living not very opulently on his painting, returned to New York on the *Sully*. On board, a Dr. Jackson told him about discoveries by European scientists which proved that electricity could be instantaneously transmitted over any length of wire. Morse reflected that if electricity traveled in that way, there was no reason why information could not also be instantaneously transmitted by electricity. That sensible reflection was at the origin of his discoveries. For ten years, he encountered public indifference and eked out a living as an artist. Finally, in 1843, Congress authorized the laying of a cable from Washington to Baltimore (40 miles). One year later, it was completed. On May 24, 1844, Morse sent the first telegraph message from the Baltimore railway station to the Supreme Court in Washington. It was just four words, typical of the man and his country: "What hath God wrought." Thereafter, the impetus was irresistible. Western Union was founded in 1856. Two years later, Cyrus Field, after being called a madman and failing four times, triumphantly inaugurated a transatlantic cable from Newfoundland to Ireland. The new line operated for only three weeks, it is true, and regular service could not be established until after the Civil War. But even before the outbreak of the conflict, messages were being transmitted to the West and then carried to California by Pony Express. It was inevitable that the line should be extended and the Atlantic linked to the Pacific. Nonetheless, Abraham Lincoln was skeptical to the end and called the project absurd and virtually impossible. That proves nothing except, perhaps, the truism that, even for great men, silence is often golden.

# PART TWO

# The Routine
# of Life

# *PRIVATE LIFE*

*Chapter VII*
# WOMEN, LOVE, AND MARRIAGE

Contrasts abound between the United States of today and of a hundred years ago, but few are so striking as that between the status of women and the character of family life in the mid-nineteenth and twentieth centuries. Today, freedom, not to say licence, and individualism, not to say disintegration, are the rule. A century ago, the husband's supremacy and family unity were two uncontested principles.

From childhood, girls were subject to strict discipline. As stringent as it was in the cities, it was of even more extreme rigor in the country. The diary of a little girl, begun at the age of ten in 1852, is most revealing in that regard; it is but one of many such documents. After their mother's death, the writer and her sister had been sent to live with their grandparents in a village named Cumandaiga, about 300 miles north of New York. The family appears to have been middle-class Presbyterian.

Reading the diary, one feels an atmosphere in which all amusement was banished on grounds of principle and in which sin and pleasure were virtually synonymous. Religion played a preponderant part in the children's upbringing. The diarist—she was now eleven—wrote that every morning, before going to school, she read three chapters of the Bible, then three more in the afternoon and five on Sundays; in that way, she explained, she could get through the whole Bible in a year. They went to church morning and evening, attended Sunday school, learned seven verses each week and, in the evening, recited their catechism and sang hymns to their grandmother.

Every event was interpreted in the light of Scripture. In 1858, when the first transatlantic telegram was sent, their grandmother told them that this was the fulfillment of the prophecy in the nineteenth psalm: "The heavens declare the glory of God, the firmament showeth his handiwork."

Merriment was discountenanced, at least on Sundays. Their grandmother told them one Sunday that the morning's sermon must not have done them much good since that afternoon she had to tell them several times to stop laughing (they were twelve years old at the time). Card playing, of course, was forbidden; their grandfather told them that it could easily become a habit, and that nothing was more scandalous and repugnant. And when Barnum's circus visited their town, there was no hope of their going; their grandmother explained that it was certainly not God's intention for women to show themselves half-clothed, riding horseback, and jumping through hoops. Even Christmas did little to relieve the atmosphere, for their grandparents gave small thought to gifts.

Education was more or less neglected. In any case, as we shall see, it was confined to a minimum. Girls of good family had governesses and attended elegant boarding schools, where more care was taken to imbue them with good manners than to increase their knowledge. A little reading, but always in the form of selected excerpts, a great deal of sewing, a few dancing lessons, and they were ready for marriage. Poor families prepared their daughters differently, by assigning them the most difficult household chores. Rich and poor married young. In the South, fifteen, or even fourteen or thirteen, was the marriageable age. It was not unusual to encounter grandmothers under thirty years old. In other regions, a girl who had not found a husband by the time she was twenty caused surprise. In general, the choice of a fiancé was up to those concerned, and the family stepped in only in hopeless cases. DeTocqueville greatly admired this custom, for he rightly saw in it the harbinger of women's emancipation. Even with downcast eyes, American girls of a hundred years ago seem to have been quite capable of discovering the man of their dreams for themselves.

On the prairie, opportunities were rare; it was usually during the harvest and at corn-husking parties that potential suitors could be met. If the suitor declared himself, he was invited to the girl's house. But distances were vast and dwellings small. The future fiancé had to be lodged somewhere, and that was the origin of the picturesque custom of "bundling," in which the suitor and his beloved slept fully clothed in the same bed, separated by a firmly fixed plank. One is tempted to see in this custom a vestige of courtly love, in which a knight, lying on the same bed as his lady love, placed his sword between them as an impassable symbol of his disinterestedness. But we fear that this somewhat romantic interpretation would hardly be applicable to the customs of the Wild West. Furthermore, bundling was not confined to night time, but was practiced in a different form in the daytime. The young man and the girl were settled alone in a buggy and set off for a drive, carefully bundled up in covers. It was very rare that they did not return formally engaged.

The buggy ride, so conducive to intimacy, was a uni-

versal practice, with or without covers. Young hopefuls
found any number of opportunities, on such a ride, to make
their declaration. Valentine's Day provided the shy with
a discreet opportunity of making their feelings known.
Dancing, lastly, was the supreme resource. Here, the Southern belles were unrivaled. In an article entitled "Husband-
hunting," published in 1857 in the *University of North
Carolina Review*, their technique was admirably summed
up. The lady, according to the article, would make the man
waltz a turn or two. A light touch of her soft hand, a glance
of her sparkling eyes, a languishingly glamorous smile, the
soft pressure of a round white arm abandoned trustfully on
the man's shoulder as they whirled to the music, and his fate
was sealed. "Gold diggers," already a flourishing breed, were
especially feared by bachelors. Shot-gun weddings, even at
this period, were apparently not unknown. In 1860 a magazine wrote that it had become positively dangerous for a
wealthy man so much as to be polite to an unmarried
woman. That was even more the case, it might be added,
with titled European males, who were much sought after.

In "good" families, in reaction against the customs of
the "vulgar," money was supposed to play no part in decisions of the heart. Traditionally, the young man came himself to ask his future father-in-law for the hand of his beloved. But material questions were disregarded. In America,
where love was more important than wealth, the conversation was supposed to touch only on vague moral notions
such as deservingness and responsibility. Once the suitor was
accepted, he did not refuse a dowry if there was one, but he
did not count on it and felt himself solely responsible for
the future of his family. His fiancée's contribution would be
confined to a trousseau which, following an old custom, she
would have been preparing for a long time and keeping in
her hope chest. In the West, however, where practical prob-

lems always dominated, the bride usually brought with her a bed, a table, chairs, a chest of drawers, and sometimes a cow. The groom provided the house, a horse, farming implements, and seed.

In the city, at least, engagement meant tête-à-têtes only in the family living room, veiled looks, and stolen kisses. For lovers in the South, the great problem was getting rid of the merciless mammies who refused to leave their mistresses alone. Bolder couples succeeded by making these excellent creatures swallow a soporific, but woe betide them if "papa" discovered the deceit!

Once the honeymoon was over and married life began, the woman found herself entirely dependent, nearly a slave. "The wife is dead in law," and "Husband and wife are one, and that one is the husband," were common principles. Beginning in 1840, more states granted married women the title to their inheritances, any gifts they might receive, and their salaries. But the increase in legal flexibility changed nothing in the actual situation. The husband alone held the purse strings. His authority was uncontested. In the "lower" classes, it sometimes took the most concrete forms. Until mid-century, the husband was allowed in most states to beat his wife, provided that he did so with a "reasonable" instrument, no matter what, from a riding whip to a stick no thicker than the thumb, as a judge in austere Massachusetts ruled. A Methodist preacher exhorted his flock to follow the examples of the worthy citizen who chastised his wife regularly every two or three weeks. That, he said, was the only way to keep her submissive to his will and prevent her from complaining all the time. Although religion did not always go so far, it did not take the matter lightly. According to another minister, the home is the husband's and father's castle; in it, he is the ruler of a small empire, crowned by heaven and holding a scepter that the father of all mankind placed in his hands, recognizing no superior, fearing no rival, dreading no usurper.

A popular song idyllically described the atmosphere of the perfect family:

> The father gives his kind command,
> The mother joins, approves,
> And children, all attention, stand.
> Then each, obedient, moves.

Women, it seems, accepted their inferior status with good grace. The shrewdest ones, it goes without saying, managed to get around obstacles. There is probably much truth in the comments of a French chambermaid working for a wealthy family around 1845, who said that the husband, a businessman, earned money which his wife, a lady of fashion, spent; the husband, she maintained, was really nothing, his wife everything. This reversal of positions was, nonetheless, an exception.

For more than a few women, their passive role held its charm. When necessary, they exaggerated it as a stratagem in winning a man's heart. Above all, they were traditionally accustomed to it. They had been prepared for it by their families, at school, at church. They knew by heart the words Milton put into Eve's mouth, and applied them to themselves when they thought of their husbands:

> My Author and Disposer, what thou bidst
> Unargued I obey; so God ordains.
> God is thy law, thou mine; to know no more
> Is woman's happiest knowledge and her praise.

Women's dependent state did not seem to suit them physically. They lacked spirit. A mid-century observer sadly remarked that fashionable women appeared to have lost the vivacity and elegance which had been the rule in earlier generations. Pallor was compulsory. To acquire it, experts recommended drinking very strong vinegar and eating large amounts of chalk. Above all, women were fragile and of delicate health. Their bone structure and constitution seemed less solid than those of European women, one observer remarked. They lost consciousness at every opportunity, since one of the signs of good breeding was knowing how to faint. Foreign visitors were unanimous in stating that American women tended to fade quite young. Until the age of twenty, their waists were sylphlike as nowhere else in the world; their features were exquisitely modeled; they moved with grace and lightness; their bearing was at once easy and dignified. But decline was just around the corner. By the age of thirty, they could only look back on their conquests and wait until they could vicariously relive their triumphs in their daughters. In 1833 the *Ladies' Magazine* of Boston was concerned about this situation and asked a question which, we suppose, must have remained unanswered. It remarked that Europeans were often struck by the premature ageing of beautiful women in the United States and asked American men whether they thought their wives were victims of the climate and their delicate constitutions or if they were unhappy because their husbands did not give them enough money.

How did women spend their time? In rich families, they were virtually idle. A lady visitor in 1841 observed an evident tendency to "orientalism." In all fashionable circles, women lived in as idle and useless a manner as the members of a harem. It was commonly said that a woman should be kept like a jewel in its case, and should have nothing else to do but listen to insipid compliments. Another witness, a suffragette, went even farther by saying that she had never in any country been so impressed by the total inactivity of upper-class women, except, perhaps, for the wives of Turks and Arabs. A large proportion of American women led a

cloistered existence, doing nothing; the rest were also re-
cluses, but were overworked. It must be admitted that exertion was not these langorous creatures' strong point. When,
giving way to the general fad around 1840, they took to
skating, their teachers recommended that they hold on to
their partner's coat tails, for if he was capable and they were
steady enough on their skates, they should be able to enjoy
themselves without becoming fatigued.

In any event, as we shall see, sports and outdoor recreation had an infinitesimal place in American life. Women
living in the city rarely left their homes. Before the Irish
immigration temporarly solved the problem, the servant
shortage had reached critical proportions. (The solution was
not always satisfactory, however. The hot temper of the
Irish is legendary, as are their political activities. An English consul in New York in the nineteenth century finally
discovered that his kitchen had been transformed into a
meeting room for the local Irish revolutionary committee.)
In the egalitarian atmosphere of the young country, from
the outset some stigma was attached to domestic service.
George Washington is said to have had to advertise for three
and a half months before finding a coachman and a cook.
The prejudice had constantly increased with time. It was
almost treason to the Republic to call a free citizen a servant. Hundreds of girls, miserably dressed, worked in factories for half what they would have earned as servants, but
felt that their equality would be jeopardized if they became
domestics.

The obligation to have liveried valets created an enormous problem for ambassadors. The only solution was im-
porting foreign employees.

These servant difficulties compelled many young married couples to live in boarding houses, where life was unbelievably monotonous and empty. For once, Mrs. Trollope
was not exaggerating when she wrote that she could hardly

imagine a more effective way of guaranteeing the insignifi-
cance of a woman than to marry her at the age of seventeen
and settle her in a family boarding house. Mrs. Trollope
said that she could not conceive of a duller and more boring
married life.

Was a day in the life of a woman who did not live in
a hotel much more varied? We are not thinking of those
who bore the full responsibility of their households. Their
life was in no way different from that of their sisters the
world over or in any other period. But let us take Mrs.
Smith, a middle-class American woman sufficiently well off
to have domestic help. Her schedule would be approximately the following: Breakfast, as we have said, very early,
fully dressed; at about 8:30, or 9 at the latest, her husband
has left and the children, if they are old enough, go to
school. Otherwise, a maid takes care of them. Furthermore,
it is already fashionable to allow them maximum independence. Fortunately for her, Mrs. Smith has recently had
a baby. She dresses it herself and never tires of admiring the
baby's long embroidered dresses. She is indignant to think
that in Europe small babies are swaddled—unheard of in
this free country!

From the nursery, she makes a round of the kitchen,
but the menus are quickly chosen, and conserves and jams
are not made in every season. In a word, her task as mother
and mistress of the house is completed. Three hours of
morning to get through, and no telephone, no radio, no
television. Women of the twentieth century may pity their
ancestors! Sometimes there will be a religious service or a
charity meeting organized by the pastor, that will make the
hours pass more quickly. It was only from the clergy, according to one observer, that American women received the sort
of attention so dear to the heart of every woman.

At noon there is the family lunch, then separation
again. Sometimes Mrs. Smith will go shopping, but she does

not even have the entertainment of fitting, for dressmakers are nonexistent. Her dresses, for which she herself buys the cloth, are made by seamstresses who come to her home. Milliners do have hat shops, but one can hardly visit them every day.

There remain the novelty shops. Mrs. Smith thinks herself very lucky to live in New York, for it seems that there are very few cities which have such shops. A stroll around Arnold Constable, Lord and Taylor, and especially A. T. Stewart, the fashionable shop, awakens in her a host of desires. She seeks to push them aside, for she does not think she could satisfy them—her husband would call her extravagant. So she goes home.

She entertains herself by sewing or embroidering, but she is set in her ways, and it will be years before sewing machines are adopted. Other favorite pastimes are modeling with wax, embossing leather, charcoal sketching, glass or china painting, and collecting shells. A little singing, clavichord, and piano awaken romantic notes in her. If she has intellectual aspirations, she will read the popular authors—Longfellow, Oliver Wendell Holmes, and James Russell Lowell. If she prides herself on philosophy (but we don't recommend it), she will have Emerson's latest work or that of one of the self-styled members of the Transcendental Club on her bedside table. Novels and short stories are more likely to claim her attention. She will pretend (if she is bold) to be fascinated by Edgar Allan Poe, but will hardly dare mention Walt Whitman. Thoreau, Hawthorne, and Melville will carry her into the realms of dream and imagination, where she occasionally seeks to forget the uniformity of her life.

Such reading is very tiring, and in any case, with whom could she discuss it? Mr. Smith has scarcely heard of these authors. If she dared to steer conversation to literary subjects, she would receive only a condescending smile and a pat on the cheek. So she might as well return the books to the shelf. In doing so, however, she must not commit a *faux pas*, for the perfect mistress of the house must take care that books written by men and by women are properly separated. Unless the authors are married, their proximity is not to be tolerated.

To be sure, it was safest to page through magazines, although the *Ladies' Repository* was a bit too "intellectual." More popular were the *Ladies' National Magazine*, which published serials with a religious slant, and especially *Godey's Ladies Book*. This periodical had tremendous success thanks to its pictures of dresses and its articles on home life, and its stupidity, according to one commentator, was assumed to be to women's taste.

But a few friends may drop in. Mrs. Smith pours the tea herself for her guests. Her silver is her pride. This is the pleasantest hour of the day, when one really feels secure. And then the cookies and the home-made sponge cake are especially good today. There is no want of topics of conversation—everyone has read *The Young Lady's Friend*, by Mrs. John Farrar. She prescribes five such friends: a child, a picture, an animal, a piece of furniture, and a bouquet. Money, of course, is never to be mentioned, and politics even less. Literature and religion are to be treated with caution, for they could cause debate.

The ladies decide to go out together the next day. A lecture has been announced at the literary association to which they are discreetly proud to belong. The lecturer is so amusing! "Were you there the other day when he spoke on women's psychology? Do you know how he concluded? He asked: 'What is the main quality of women? Curiosity. Who was last at the foot of the cross? Women. Who arrived first at the holy sepulcher? Women.' That is better than

daring to choose physiology as a topic. Do you remember
the sensation that Paulina Wright caused when she wanted
to use a live model? Part of the audience walked out; I have
friends who fainted. Frankly, I think I would have done the
same in their place." And so they chat on, then rustle on
their separate ways.

At five or half-past, Mr. Smith is back. From his spouse
he expects affection, respect, and faithfulness, the three cardinal virtues of the perfect wife. He knows he will find them
in her and is little inclined to seek elsewhere. In any event,
the obstacles are too great and the fear of scandal too powerful. Divorces are very rare and are frowned on. If Mr. Smith
should have moments of weakness, it will be while he is
traveling, far from home—as far as possible. Houses of easy
virtue are to be found in most cities and after one whisky
too many the flesh is weak. But Mr. Smith does not even
consider a lasting attachment. He prefers his home to adventure. Outside of office hours, he is almost always there. If he
belongs to an elegant circle, he will increasingly tend to
engage in club life. Most of the famous clubs date from this
period: in Philadelphia, the Philadelphians; in Baltimore,
the Maryland; in New York, the Union (for socialites) and
the Century (for artists and men of letters); in Boston, the
Somerset; and even in San Francisco, the Pacific Union.

Six o'clock. Dinner will soon be announced. Mr. Smith
likes a whisky or two, his privilege as head of the family.
The parents go into the dining room, where the children
are already waiting. If there are boys, one stands behind his
mother's chair to help her into her seat. If not, the husband
himself discharges this gallant task. Dinner, as we have said,
is the most important meal. Mr. Smith presides over it as
the master, and his wife and children listen to him with
deference. The evening is not long, and by about nine
o'clock the house is silent.

Physical pleasure, for a woman, is out of the question. Everyone knows that a proper lady is innocent of physical desire. She may love, but calmly. And only her husband, and always without passion.

Dinners in town are rare. Mrs. Smith finds in them the opportunity to exhibit her dresses and jewelry, which do honor to her husband's wealth, but that is just about the only pleasure she derives from these occasions.

At such dinners the sexes are sometimes strictly separated, with the gentlemen at one end of the table and the ladies at the other. Parties are hardly more conducive to conversation, and even less to flirting. The gentlemen make gallant displays of their deference. At the magic words, "Here are the ladies!" everyone must rise to his feet. As to the ladies, concerned for their reputation, they try to remain as stiff as possible and mute as statues.

Respect for the weaker sex was universal. In fact, it was the natural counterpart of feminine submissiveness. It flattered men's vanity to take such weak creatures under their protection. All descriptions of American customs, including the most critical, remark on the consideration lavished on women, especially on journeys. It is said that they tended a little to take advantage of this and, playing the part of the spoiled child, excelled in obtaining the best seat in the coach or wagon. Protocol was particularly strict with respect to meals. One European remarked that there was not a boat, even in the wildest areas of the West, where a man would have dared to sit down before all the women had taken the places of honor. He had seen a hundred hungry men with a steaming dish before them wait patiently until a girl had finished arranging her curls and had come to take her place at the head of the table. And another observer maintained that America had two idols—Mammon and the weaker sex;

the two lived in a state of constant warfare—what one built up, the other tore down, what one accumulated, the other cast to the four winds.

Around 1840, a small group of heroic women began to display their dissatisfaction with these mediocre material satisfactions. This was the period when the first rumblings of the feminist movement were being heard. Previously there had been hardly a murmur. In 1792, Mary Wollstonecraft Godwin, a fanatical Englishwoman, published a violent pamphlet against social conventions entitled *Vindication of the Rights of Women,* which stirred some quickly quelled flurries. Thirty years later, Frances Wright, a Scotswoman, who at the age of twenty-nine had accompanied Madame de La Fayette on her journey to the United States, won notoriety by her lecture tours, during which she discussed religion, education, women's emancipation, and Malthusianism. At the time, she had no success except perhaps with the Quakers, who were always open to new ideas. Nonetheless, some of her theories slowly germinated.

The feminist agitation began to claim the public eye about 1848. Three years earlier, Margaret Fuller, in her *Woman in the Nineteenth Century,* had dared to maintain that there was no such thing as an entirely masculine man or an entirely feminine woman. That was a revolutionary and an "un-American" thesis. Bolder women nevertheless did not hesitate to espouse it. Elizabeth Cady Stanton, a girl of good family, had demanded that no mention should be made of the word "obedience" in her wedding ceremony. Another, Lucrezia Mott, had the rather vague but most significant title of Quaker Minister. In 1848 the disciples of the new age met at Seneca Falls, New York, and adopted a manifesto patterned after the Declaration of Independence. Joining acts with words, the most fanatical decided to begin by reforming dress. They appeared in a strange apparel, soon to become legendary—bloomers, so called after their designer. In order, as they explained, to put themselves on an equal footing with men, these ladies wore gypsy-style straw hats, short jackets, crinoline dresses to the knees, and bloomers to the ankles; their shoes were covered with gaiters. They caused a considerable sensation: they were booed in the streets and called a variety of names; they were accused of sedition, of wanting to play a part in politics, of trying to show their legs, and so on. But by 1854 or thereabouts, little remained of the bloomer experiment, and at a convention on women's rights held in that year in Philadelphia, a male member of the audience interrupted the proceedings to suggest that women must first prove that they possessed any rights at all, since both church and state agreed in denying it.

Thus not all American women of the period resembled Mrs. Smith and her friends. The women in the North who associated themselves with reform movements, those in the South who managed their own plantations, and those in the West who stood behind the pioneers and sometimes even led them forward, were of quite a different caliber, as we shall see. Here, we have confined ourselves mainly to describing a type of woman which, in the light of twentieth-century America, one can hardly believe existed in America only a century ago.

*Chapter VIII*

# MANNERS
# AND ETIQUETTE

It is estimated that more than one hundred handbooks on "common and honest civility" were published in the United States between 1830 and 1860. That figure does not take account of reprints and new editions. Some were tremendously successful and were brought out in popular editions, mostly costing 25 cents. One of them, *The Dime Book of Practical Etiquette,* was commonly found in the humblest homes.

The titles are revealing. They include *The Young Man's Own Book; A Manual of Politeness for both Sexes; The Laws of Etiquette; The Art of Conversation; Manners Maketh Man; The Young Lady's Friend; Woman in her Various Relations: Containing Practical Rules for American Females; The Bazaar Book of Decorum; How to Behave: A Pocket Manual of Republican Etiquette.* The authors of these works were mostly American. In 1843, however, a book entitled *Etiquette or a Guide to the Usages of Society* caused a sensation; the cover bore the name of Count Alfred D'Orsay. There was a rush on the counsels of so qualified a

dandy; the truth was less dazzling, for this master of protocol was merely a certain Charles William Day who had had
the lucrative idea of this fraud.

What were the reasons for such a vogue?

At the beginning of the century, the former colonies
still had what in the Old World was generally referred to
as "good society." In Maine, the Dearborns; in Boston, the
Winthrops and the Cabots; in Philadelphia, the Bayards
and the Van Rensselaers; in New York, the Schermerhorns,
the Livingstons, the De Peysters, and other descendants of
old Dutch families; the Carrolls in Maryland; the Carters,
the Randolphs, and the Lees in Virginia, had long since
taken root in American soil. They claimed, not without reason, to play the same role as a European aristocracy. In two
respects, however, they differed from their counterparts
across the Atlantic: they disliked excessive luxury and they
were not afraid to work.

The Industrial Revolution was a serious threat to them.
It brought with it the "new rich," whose fortune was no
longer based on land, but on trade. In New York the
Roosevelts, the Delanos, the Astors, the Cuttings, the Stew-
arts, the Goelets, the Brevoorts, the Lorillards, the Iselins,
and the Vanderbilts were bankers, ship owners, industrial-
ists, speculators. Aristocracy, 1850 style, counted among its
ranks the Longworths in Cincinnati; the Duponts in Wil-
mington; and the Biddles, the Drexels, the Whartons, and
the Dahlgrens in Philadelphia. Their ranks were soon
swollen by California's contribution. The Crockers and
Huntingtons in railways, the Spreckels in sugar, and the
Ogden Mills in banking and mining, quickly came to be
called "millionaires," a term which had just entered the
language. For all these businessmen, money was a god.
Emerson looked with anxiety on the rise of this financial
oligarchy; he feared, he said, that it would upset the human
equilibrium and establish a new universal monarchy, more

tyrannical than Babylon or Rome. While waiting for such gloomy prospects to materialize, the upstarts of industrialization introduced an element of crudity and brutality into society which the champions of refinement and moderation deplored. At about the same period, the strongholds from which the latter defended themselves against the mounting vulgarity were even more formidably assailed by the wave of immigration to America, which swept no Beau Brummels or purists onto its shores. These adventurers cared little for convention or courtesy. Unconstraint and crudeness came to be the rule. In the cities, it might still be hoped that the example of others would civilize the "barbarians," but if let free in the prairies, was it not to be feared that they would be more intent on conquering nature than on becoming polished?

It was therefore not superfluous to recall a few elementary rules of life in common. It is significant that, of the some one hundred handbooks published in that period, two-thirds appeared between 1840 and 1860, in other words, just at the height of the European influx.

Almost all travelers' descriptions agree on the coarseness which reigned in public places. It is true that most come from the pens of English visitors, only too pleased to ridicule a country that was so absurd as to prefer its freedom to allegiance to Britain. De Tocqueville, an exception, remarked that manners were often more sincere in America than in France. A Polish visitor also spoke of well-intentioned cordiality in social relations.

Sincerity and cordiality were sometimes disconcerting. These democratic virtues took on an unreserved spontaneity, especially in the art of tobacco chewing. Mrs. Trollope blamed that vile universal habit for a remarkable peculiarity of the American physiognomy, which almost always, she maintained, exhibited thin, pinched lips. We should not be too contemptuous of this indeed universal practice, for it provided Dickens with several of his finest pages. His descriptions of expert spitters should not be missed. It was a mystery to him, he wrote, describing a train journey, how men could so entertain themselves as to create an uninterrupted deluge of spit on the floor. On another occasion, he described a genuine hurricane, a tempest, of spitting which did not cease the whole night long on the boat on which he was traveling. Was he exaggerating? Let us listen to another witness, Alexander Mackay, who was very friendly to the United States. Mackay wrote that the floor of his railway car was so covered with tobacco juice that he had had to seek refuge on the platform. He had also seen a man take his plug from his mouth to make pictures on the window.

These habits were not the only ones which were untoward, judging by the bibles of propriety. Some of their basic recommendations were never to sleep in one's clothing during the day, never to keep one's hat on in the presence of a lady, never to tell one's hostess that one has found insects in the bed, not to tilt one's chair, not to stretch one's feet out on the andirons, not to whirl a chair around on one leg, not to beat time with hands and feet, not to touch one's partner in conversation, not to hold him by the buttons or the lapel, not to grab women by the waist or, in general, to touch them, and not to make fun of those who bathed and washed regularly, and so on.

That, it was true, was advice for the vulgar, but the experts aimed higher. They had decided to waste no time. One of them commented that he had heard it seriously maintained that three generations were necessary to make a gentleman, and that was too long. A more nuanced code of good manners was quickly worked out.

Relationships between men and women played an important part in that code. They were governed by the most stringent rules. Judging by some of the rules, conversation could not have been at all facilitated: it was recommended, for instance, that a lady should never ask a gentleman about his health; what was more, a gentleman must never ask a lady any question whatsoever. Special care was necessary regarding gifts. A bouquet or a book was the only kind of gift that a well-bred man might offer a proper lady. A lady's reputation would be gravely compromised if she accepted the arm of any gentleman but her husband, her father, or a member of her family. In general, the slightest contact was to be avoided. One traveler recounts that he saw a young woman seated at a table between a man and a woman, virtually sitting in the woman's chair in order to avoid touching the man's elbow.

What problems dancing created! In circles which did not pride themselves on refinement, the sexes were simply kept apart as much as possible. The result was strange. According to a (perhaps unfriendly) witness, the women's movements resembled those of turkeys spreading their tails, of birds of prey alighting, or of ducks waddling. As for their male partners, they seemed to be regularly wiping their feet on a doormat. Lovers of elegance and good manners resorted to less primitive techniques. Couples held each other by one hand, and the woman placed her free hand on her waist. The man graciously waved his hand over his head or over his partner's, or rested it on a part of his body. In some circles in the South, waltzing was tolerated only if nothing but the elbows touched. The woman's waist was forbidden territory, and the man was allowed to lead her only by the tip of her elbow.

The rules for young ladies were of course still stricter. Even with the elbow-to-elbow method, it was recommended that they should leave the waltzing to married women. Above all, they must never cease to be on their guard. Unless it was absolutely necessary, a young lady must never permit anyone to help her on with her coat, shawl, over-shoes, or anything else; she should never sit down next to a young man with the excuse of reading the same book; even in order to see a fascinating show better, she must never let her face get too close to her neighbor's. Above all, she must not allow certain forbidden words to be uttered in her presence. The chest was called the neck; the stomach, the chest. A stomach ache was unthinkable—one felt a pain in the chest. Legs were not supposed to exist. The English novelist Frederick Marryat learned this first hand during his trip to the United States in 1839. A girl he had taken to see Niagara Falls slipped and grazed her leg. Full of concern, he asked her whether her leg hurt. She blushed and showed every sign of being offended. By insisting, he managed to get an explanation: he should have used the word "limb" rather than "leg." Marryat later discovered that it was in fact the fashion to use that term even in the case of table or piano legs! Nor was this the last of his surprises, for upon entering the reception room in a girls' boarding school, he saw that the "limbs" of the piano were chastely covered with frilled little pants. Is this just a traveler's tall tale? Perhaps. The story, however, is less unbelievable than it may appear if we recall that at the same period, Edward Everett, a Unitarian minister (later to be United States Minister in Great Britain, president of Harvard, Secretary of State, and Senator), had a veil placed over the copy of the Belvedere Apollo in his home.

A curious detail in this atmosphere of prudishness is the fact that the custom of chaperoning girls did not really catch on until about 1850; before that time, they usually went out alone. This almost paradoxical independence is explained by the respect with which, as we have seen, women were universally surrounded.

The handbooks of good manners devoted at least as important a place to table manners as to relationships between ladies and gentlemen.

There was, it seems, good reason to do so. Mrs. Trollope did not mince words in describing a meal at which she had been present during her travels. Everything, she wrote, had been distasteful to her: the total absence of the usual rules of courtesy, the haste with which the company fell upon the food and devoured it, their strange and crude remarks, their filthy spitting, from which it was absolutely impossible to shield the ladies' dresses, the revolting use of knives in such a way that the entire blade seemed to enter the mouth, and the no less filthy habit of cleaning the teeth after eating with a pocket knife. In one respect, at least, the pitiless English-woman was not exaggerating. The use of forks did not become widespread until mid-century. Before that time, the knife reigned supreme, and was even used to eat green peas or ice cream. Its gradual disappearance worried the nationalists, who regarded it as a disturbing sign of the Europeanization of "God's country."

Without engaging in lofty considerations, the etiquette experts made countless rules of behavior for mealtime, of which the following are samples: Don't blow your nose with your fingers; don't raise your soup bowl to your mouth to drink; don't gargle noisily with the mouth-rinsing water. Here are some rules for a "perfect" dinner. Remove your gloves before eating; spread your napkin (a woman should pin it to her dress); chew noiselessly; wipe your plate with bread; avoid looking at those who are eating a little too fast; if the lady next to you has taken an unmanageably large mouthful, break off all conversation with her and look the other way. . . . Whatever the circumstances, the important thing was to keep calm. The writer of a book of etiquette illustrated this point as follows: A particularly accomplished gentleman had had the misfortune, when carving a slightly tough duck, to have it slide onto his neighbor's lap. What did he do? With admirable gravity and perfect unconcern, he looked her in the eye and simply asked her to be so kind as to return the duck to him. If a guest upset a dish—a common occurrence, apparently—he must at all costs remain unmoved, make no excuses and, in a word, ignore the accident. Why? Because if he appeared concerned, he would appear to imply that his host was not wealthy enough to stand the loss.

Actually, Americans were so often accused by foreigners of talking incessantly of money that this subtle advice is easily understandable. To take no interest, at least ostensibly, in material questions was one of the commonest forms of snobbery. Of course, no one would have refused to appear in one of the lists of wealthy citizens—the peerage, as it were, of the United States. The best known was Beach's, the forerunner of the present-day *Social Register*. In 1844 it listed 850 names, showing for each one the amount and origin of the fortune. The Astors headed the list with $20 million, followed by the Goelets and Stewarts with $2 million, Commodore Vanderbilt with $1.5 million, and the Lorillards with $1 million. A minimum of $100,000 was required to appear in this list. "Society" deplored the custom, but conformed to it.

It was long considered very bad form to have one's name in the newspapers. When the local Cincinnati paper, *The Commercial*, described the marriage of Nicholas Longworth, that arbiter of elegant society, on December 24, 1857, it humbly apologized for such "intrusion" into private life; the event, the editor explained, was of such historical significance that the readers would surely pardon their paper for mentioning it. Actually, the good people of Ohio were

a bit behind the times. Twenty years earlier, James Gordon
Bennett inaugurated a special page in the *New York Herald*
in which, to the fury of the old guard, he chronicled social
events. And on February 27, 1840, Bennett scored another
"first" in the history of American journalism: with the com-
plicity of the family, he managed to introduce a reporter
into a reception intended only for a select few. Some months
later, the visits of Prince de Joinville and Viscount Morpeth
filled whole columns of the *Herald*. On August 31, 1841, a
big costume ball in Newport was featured on the front page.

As could easily have been foreseen, the opposition of
fashionable circles to publicity gradually weakened. By mid-
century, prominent persons had even began to grant their
patronage to medicines and cosmetics.

Ah, when snobbery holds sway! Around 1840, it was
stylish to drop French words in conversation. *"Le ton"* (for
society), *"comme il faut," "élite," "robe de bal," "le meilleur
gout," "recherche," "outré," "éclat," "vieille noblesse," "coup
d'oeil," "soupé"* (sic), *"corsage," "rouleaux," "volants," "coif-
fure en classique," "tout ensemble,"* and so on became common. French was indispensable for elegant menus. An example is the banquet given for the Prince de Joinville at Astor
House in 1841, at which the menu included a *"pain de
volaille à la reine historiée sur un socle"* (sic), *"turbans de
filet de volaille à la babilonne"* (sic), *"filets de faisans farcis
à la d'Artois sauce Périgueux," "pâté chaud d'ortolans
désossés, à la Montebello," "aspic de filet de bass* (sic) *aux
truffes," "turkey à la périgore"* (sic), *"calf's head en tortue à
la moderne"* (sic), and so on.

In a country where so many knew nothing about their
ancestors, interest in genealogies was exceptionally strong.
The list of groups specializing in this type of research would
be too long to cite. One, established in 1861, by a certain
Charles H. Browning, was especially popular. It published
a list of "Americans of royal descent"; those whose lineage

could boast of descending from the legitimate posterity of
kings were entitled to appear in it. Even in those days,
Americans were infatuated with titles. They liked to call
themselves judge, colonel, general; and a court—especially
the Court of St. James—made them thrill with curiosity and
admiration. Mrs. Robert Tyler, daughter-in-law of the tenth
President, wrote to a friend in Alabama in 1842 that the
latter would surely burst with envy when she learned that
a real English lord, in flesh and blood, had been among the
guests at the White House the week before. And what a
Lord! Lord Morpeth, Earl of Carlisle, in whose noble veins
flowed the blood of all the Howards.

It is a strange but typical feature of the "you never can
tell" attitude deep down in every American that the rev-
erence shown to the royalty and nobility of the Old World
did not rule out a certain familiarity. "Why them and not
me?" In 1838, when the mother of a young attaché at the
London embassy was told that her son had had the honor
of dancing at a court ball with Queen Victoria, then nineteen years old, she commented, reflectingly, that she hoped
the encounter would not lead to a marriage for her Richard.

## Chapter IX

# HYGIENE
# AND SPORTS

Hygiene experts today would recoil in horror if they had occasion to see sanitary conditions similar to those which prevailed in the United States a hundred years ago. We have already mentioned the method of removing garbage in most of the cities. The street-cleaner swine at least acted as good citizens. The same was not true of the roaming packs of dogs, much less of the rats, which were particularly virulent in ports. In 1860, one devoured a new-born baby at Bellevue Hospital in New York. These rodents found plenty of choice pasture ground. The stench of garbage and offal rose from streams, back yards, and alleys. It is estimated that in mid-century, 5 per cent of the populations of Boston and New York, perhaps the most modern cities, lived in dark, ill-ventilated, vermin-infested basements. Washing was out of the question. In any case, city authorities concerned themselves very little with installing water-supply systems. In 1850, there were 83 such systems, and 148 in 1862.

In the wild solitudes of the West, the prairie winds swept away the miasmas, it is true, but innumerable swamps

and stagnant ponds spread malaria, the terror of the pioneers. It was a fearful disease, yet benign in comparison with
the epidemics which regularly struck the cities. Yellow fever
was chronic in the South. In 1832, one-sixth of the population of New Orleans fell victim to it in twelve days. The
treatment was always the same: the patient was put to bed
under a mountain of blankets, and doors and windows were
hermetically closed regardless of the temperature. There
followed a purge and a bleeding, both equally ruthless. Few
survived such radical treatment. One observer tells that
when it was discovered that no one remained alive in a
certain hospital—the doctors, nurses and patients having all
died in one night—the building was burned down together
with the bodies in the hope of stopping the spread of the
disease. In 1833, one inhabitant in five succumbed. Epidemics
recurred in 1842, 1848, and 1849, and achieved even more
catastrophic proportions in 1853. Smallpox was prevalent in
the East; it struck cruelly in Philadelphia and New York in
1860 and 1861. But worst of all, by far, was cholera. It struck
New York, for instance, in 1832; its effects were vividly
described in the August 20 issue of the *New York Evening
Post*. Industry, we read, was at a standstill. A hundred thousand people had left; the sky had become clear because the
usual factory smoke had been dispelled; the colors of the
houses stood out with extraordinary brightness, and hardly
a sound was heard in the streets. When, in the summer of
1849, the scourge spread from the Atlantic coast to the rest
of the country, it assumed such proportions that on August
3, President Taylor, who was not the emotional type, called
for a national day of fasting, humility, and prayer. Further
epidemics took place in 1851 and 1859.

Medical knowledge, according to contemporaries, was
still very rudimentary. Surgery took a great step forward
when, on the basis of Dr. Morton's work, anethesia began

to be practiced in the middle of the century. But drugs made no comparable headway. Oliver Wendell Holmes told the Massachusetts Medical Society in 1860 that if all the medicines in use were thrown into the sea, mankind would be better off—but that it would be a calamity for the fish. The author of *The Autocrat of the Breakfast Table* enjoyed such witticisms, and he may have been exaggerating. Nevertheless, there must have been plenty of quacks, for the examinations for admission to the medical corps were a mere formality. According to another cynic, the medical profession was no more than a bunch of "allopaths of all kinds; of homeopaths in large and small doses; of hydropaths, sometimes moderate, sometimes extreme; of chronothermalists, Thompsonians, mesmerists, Hindu magicians, seers; of spiritists who claimed to possess mysterious healing powers, and everything under the sun."

Country doctors had at least the advantage of common sense over their city colleagues. Traveling on horseback over hill and dale through rain, hail, and snow, they brought their patients devotion, if not always effective aid. Their bag contained a minimum of supplies: mortar and pestle, a scale, a few homemade splints, a stethoscope, forceps, and a few instruments for delivering babies. They relied chiefly on their fingers, eyes, ears, and noses. They are among the legendary figures in the great epic of the West, but they had formidable rivals in the professional healers, who were not averse to a little stage setting. To cite a contemporary, they liked to wear flashy suits, silk hats, and a collection of big, sparkling diamonds, one more spurious than the next, and to twirl their carefully waxed black mustaches. The flow of words issuing from their lips could be compared only to a senator's Fourth of July speech, and the description of the misfortunes awaiting those audacious enough to spurn their aid was more horrible than anything Jonathan Edwards could predict in his sermons. There was, however, one

sphere into which they did not venture, and that was den-
tistry, which was practiced by traveling tooth extractors,
who were jealous of their specialty.

Old wives' remedies and superstition played an important part in the lives of the prairie settlers. The measles?
A sheep's dung broth, more poetically referred to as "manny
tea," would cure them. Pleurisy? A tea of mint and wild
orchid leaves, together with applications of stinging nettles
or sulfur mixed with egg, would bring relief. Indigestion?
Apply compresses of rhubarb bitters or Cayenne pepper
mixed with alcohol to the stomach without delay, and drink
a lot of fluids, especially water and good whisky if available.
For dysentery, that was inadequate: you needed a strong
brew of bloodroot or mullein in milk fresh from the cow.
For colds and sore throats, wrap a thick piece of meat seasoned with pepper around the neck, and put a plaster of
goose fat, onion, and mustard on the chest; then suck barley
sugar. Croup and asthma were cured by alum, turnips in
molasses, or onion and garlic juice; the mumps by garlic
rubbed on the patient's spine; rheumatism by a twofold
system: externally with rattlesnake, goose, or bear fat and
internally with a mixture of calomel, tarter emetic, Cayenne
pepper, and camphor, and also with a tincture of mint or
hellebore leaves mixed with "French" cognac. If that was
hard to find, then it could be replaced by an additional
herb—there were about 200 or 300 with curative value.

And then, there was always superstition. In case of ear-
ache, put the kinkiest Negro hair obtainable or a little oil
from a weasel's ears in your own. But watch out! The animal
must be of the same sex as you. If you touch your aching
teeth with a bit of wood from a tree struck by lightning,
a coffin nail, a needle which has been used for making a
shroud, a claw from a nightingale's middle toe, or a wood-
cock's tongue, the pain will disappear as by magic. A spider

worn on a necklace will protect against malaria. For hemor-
rhoids, carry chestnuts or sweet potatoes in your pockets.
Fried rattlesnake is a good protection against tuberculosis.
Reptiles are very useful; in case of epilepsy, you should eat
a reptile's heart. If none is available, the patient must sleep
on the roof of a new stable or walk under the branches of
a walnut tree three times. If you have been lucky enough
to get hold of a wolf's right eye, keep it in your sleeve and
you will quickly recover from any wounds or lesions.

These peculiar practices were current only among a minority, but the rules of hygiene were everywhere minimal.
Was that the explanation for the sickly appearance of part
of the population? Everywhere, one observer said, one saw
deformed limbs, hunchbacks, and joints too weak for dis-
proportionately large bodies. And good Mrs. Trollope, going
a step further, and only too pleased to find one more defect
in her American cousins, said that the women did not know
how to walk and were never at their best when they moved;
moreover, she added, one rarely saw full and well-formed
bosoms. The men were no better. Mrs. Trollope wrote that
she had never seen an American man walk or hold himself
well; most of them had sunken cheeks and slumping shoulders. For once, the pitiless critic was not exaggerating. In
1856 *Harper's* said of fashionable young men that they were
pale, pasty-faced, had match-stick legs, and were stunted,
good only to model the creations of the fashionable tailors.
Incredibly enough, Americans in those days did not engage in sports; and that was perhaps another cause of their
physical deficiencies. In 1855, an English visitor wrote that
playing ninepins in a gaslit room or driving horses at a brisk
trot in a light buggy over a very bad and dusty road seemed
to be the alpha and omega of sport in the United States.
And once again, *Harper's* confirms these statements: Americans seemed to have a distinct aversion to sports and out-

door exercise. Big city dwellers did not for a moment consider engaging in physical exercise. Most of them, once they reached adulthood, never imagined that they might need to exercise their muscles. The idea of sports emerged with the development of the cities and the easing of living conditions. Previously, it had been a somewhat academic question; it is hard to imagine a prairie settler or a gold prospector, exhausted by incessant physical labor, embarking on sports in his leisure time. Moreover, young America was fiercely individualistic and had not yet acquired the team spirit required for collective athletics.

In a word, baseball and football were virtually unknown before about 1850. A little track, boxing (which was at first regarded as "un-American"), gymnastics (under the influence of the German immigration), "catch-as-catch-can" wrestling, and weight and dumbbell lifting (Lincoln excelled at both) about accounted for all the sporting activity of the average American.

"Society" prided itself on more refinement. Riding and hunting were a part of the life of gentlefolk, especially in the South. In winter, skating was very popular. An unsuccessful attempt was made to use it to emancipate women's fashions. In summer the gentlefolk did not deny themselves the pleasures of sea bathing, but every precaution was taken. In Newport, a citadel of orthodoxy, women wore ruffled white pantaloons reaching to the ankle and long dresses with long sleeves. This strange garb did not prevent them from dancing quadrilles in the water with their gallant partners, also appropriately garbed.

Croquet, of course, had its fans, but it lacked prestige. Cricket lent a British air to those who played it which snobbery did not disdain. It was the dream of certain local sportsmen to rival the English. In yachting, they found growing satisfaction. It was a great day when, in 1851, the yacht *America*, owned by John Cox Stevens, for the first

time won the Cowes regatta and brought back to the United
States the cup which may still be seen at the New York
Yacht Club. Its glory was, however, soon eclipsed by the
splendor of the *North Star*, owned by Cornelius Vanderbilt.
This was indeed a princely boat, in which marble and
precious woods combined with pink, green, and gold furnishings; on the ceiling of the lounge were portraits of
Washington, Franklin, Webster, and Clay. Such luxury did
not interfere with principles, for prayers were said at the
beginning of each meal and at nine in the evening. Its owner
used the yacht to sail to England. He saw Victoria and
Albert, but felt that their appearance was anything but
aristocratic. The "Commodore" returned more convinced
than ever of the beauties of democracy.

## Chapter X
# RECREATION
# AND ENTERTAINMENT

It was already good form in nineteenth-century Europe to smile at American customs, nor did English or French visitors deny themselves this pleasure, in describing the society life of the time.

It must be acknowledged that that life was somewhat artificial, at least in the North. By reaction against the general unconstraint, New England "society" affected a stiffness which created a singularly strained atmosphere in its gatherings. In New York, things were more spirited. The balls given in the years following 1840 have remained celebrated. There was the bachelors' ball arranged by 150 fashionable dandies; Mrs. Brevoort's ball, whose splendor dazzled and astonished; Mrs. Mott's ball for the Prince de Joinville, which took place in seven rooms magnificently furnished, we are told, in the best of taste. At three in the morning, the narrator continues, the Prince and his brilliant retinue sat down to supper with the mistress of the house and her family. Mrs. Mott's bodice was ornamented with diamonds; Miss Mott wore a pink *crèpe de chine* dress embellished

with "scrolls" and a lace flounce. Then there was the New
York City ball in honor of Dickens, at which tableaux
vivants of scenes from his works were presented before him.

Following Dominick Lynch—the only Irishman, it was
said, who ever brought money to America—in the role of
arbiter of elegance, was Philip Hone, founder of the Union
Club, then Isaac Brown, warden of that most aristocratic
church, Grace Church, and a little later, Ward McAllister,
who put Newport on the map. A Frenchman, Régis de
Trobriand, at once a man of the world and a man of letters,
a colorful personality rich in dollars (by his marriage to the
daughted of a local banker), also had his hour of triumph
among the lions of New York society.

There were two conditions for a party's success, namely,
a great deal of light and a copious buffet. Thousands of
candles, whose glow was reflected in gigantic mirrors, provided the lighting. The guests were served oyster stew, turkey, and stewed fruits. Champagne at $10 a bottle was a
must at a really elegant party. Elsewhere, the beverages were
wine, coffee, and tea.

Until 1840, quadrilles were danced almost exclusively.
With the German immigration, the "impure waltz with its
wanton swing" became popular. The old guard, however,
accepted it only hesitatingly. The schottische and the polka
enjoyed extraordinary popularity at mid-century, and a
Pole, "Mr. Korponay," made a fortune teaching Boston
society the new steps. We all know what enthusiasm the
revolutionary movements of 1848 aroused in the United
States. Adopting the most outlandish dances gave society an
opportunity to show its sympathy with the European insurgents. But too much familiarity between men and women
would still have seemed in bad taste. In the strictest circles,
the sexes were usually separated at dinner time. This segregation was not to the advantage of the weaker sex. One
dinner is described, at which the men were magnificently

treated in an enormous room in which the buffet had been set up. As to the poor ladies, they were handed plates as they gloomily strolled together in the ballroom; soon servants arrived with trays of candles, cakes, and puddings. The charming ladies then sat on chairs lined up against the walls, and using their knees as tables, sulkily began to eat.

The South, with its older civilization, could afford more informality. The women were not treated with less respect. Quite the contrary, but the art of courting them was infinitely more subtle than in the rest of the country. Life on the plantations has been greatly romanticized, and *Gone With the Wind* is partly responsible. Life there was neither as easy nor as refined as it has often been described. Nevertheless, are we distorting the truth when we picture young couples dancing on the verandah of some old mansion with moonlight sifting through the magnolias? Or one of those light-hearted picnics where young girls and women with lily-like complexions, pearly teeth, and starry eyes rode in light buggies surrounded by gallant cavaliers who would have thrown down in the mud not only their coats, but also their hearts, to prevent their companions' delicate feet from being even slightly dirtied? Southern gentlemen had no objection to playing the part of knights of legend. Some even entertained themselves one day by reconstructing a medieval tournament in armor of the period, wearing the colors of the ladies of their thoughts.

Visits were frequent from plantation to plantation. Sometimes they were extended for several weeks, in keeping with the traditions of faultless hospitality. The coaches used for transport before the railroads came into operation were modeled on more ancient carriages—massive, spacious, decorated with gold and gilt and with the family coat-of-arms on the door. The coachman, majestic and impassive, made a particularly splendid impression on passers-by. These coaches were used for traveling in summer to the mountains of North Carolina and in winter to the races in New Orleans and Charleston. The St. Cecilia Ball, which closed the Charleston season each February, was perhaps the most aristocratic gathering of the region. There the elegant and sensual atmosphere of the South hung even heavier than anywhere else.

It is not hard to see why many plantation owners should have had no wish to frequent the fashionable vacation spots, for they were exceedingly dull. Newport in Rhode Island, White Sulphur Springs in the hills of Virginia, and especially Saratoga Springs, near the lake region of upper New York State, vied for the favors of vactioners. We find traces there of the delicate snobbery which has always permeated American society despite its egalitarianism. At Saratoga the "old" families attempted with relative success to retain exclusive right to that most select of hotels, Congress House, but to the despair of the regulars, some "new rich" and "politicians" managed to slip in, too. The United States Hotel, a large establishment accommodating 2,000 guests, was less exclusive. Pastors, judges, lawyers, and writers preferred Union Hall.

A Victorian atmosphere pervaded all of them. A young man named Murat who had occasion to visit Saratoga has left a less than enthusiastic description of his stay. The first part of the morning, he wrote, was spent in going to drink the spring water—or pretending to do so—then returning to breakfast all together. Then the day began. Fathers and mothers resigned themselves to boredom; young girls made music; young men courted them (a special place, the Courting Yard, was reserved for the purpose); sometimes an excursion was organized; in the evening there was dancing. The schedule was strict: breakfast at 7:30 A.M., dinner at 2 P.M., tea at 7 P.M. In between, the women gossiped and loafed about while the men talked politics, smoked, and consoled themselves with many drinks, billiards, card games, and chess, and a few excursions to Flat Rock Springs sweetened their idleness for a while.

With the advent of steamers, journeys to Europe became fashionable. They attracted, however, only a very small minority, better prepared than the masses to understand Old World traditions.

Those were the entertainments of important people. Ordinary people had to settle for other joys—and a minimum of them, at that. Relaxation—all the rage today—was not at all in fashion a hundred years ago. It was looked upon as a sign of weakness and indeed of sin. Many considered ceaseless work to be the only justification for man's presence on earth.

The theater was long looked upon with an especially jaundiced eye. The Puritans saw in it the temptations of the devil. They succeeded in surrounding theaters with such a reputation for immorality that respectable women did not dare go to them. As for the men, they tended to be exhausted by their work and little inclined to go out in the evening. Around 1840, prejudices and habits began to break down. Enormous theaters, soon filled to capacity, were built in New York: the Park, with 2,500 seats, the Bowery, seating 3,500, and the Broadway, seating 4,000. Prices were low—50 cents for the best seats and 12½ cents for the top gallery. Comfort was proportionate. Benches served as seats, thinly padded and with narrow backs in the orchestra, but wooden and backless elsewhere. It was not unusual to see rats scuttle up through the floor. The theaters were icy in winter, the lighting was inadequate, and fires were frequent; ministers saw these fires as signs of God's judgment. So many prostitutes frequented the top gallery that it was ironically suggested that they should have their own special entrance.

November 22, 1847 was a great day in Manhattan—the

inauguration, at Astor Place, of an opera house built by
private subscription by the local aristocracy. It was a very
different thing from the modest Italian opera house built
in 1839. The spectators were attired in all their finery. The
*Herald* commented that the elite had achieved its aim: even
the rabble washed their faces, shaved, came with freshly cut
and oiled hair, and bought even the most expensive seats.
The yokels, it went on, assumed the manners of gentlefolk
under the influence of soft music and the presence of pretty
women.

We fear that the description may be idealized. Elsewhere, in any case, manners appear to have been rather
more free and easy. We read—again in the *New York Herald*
—that three spectators sitting behind a man who had placed
his hat on the floor, used it as a spittoon, outdoing each
other in skill in hitting the mark. Should we believe Mrs.
Trollope when she writes that she saw a woman calmly
performing her maternal duties in a loge, and men arriving
in boxes without evening dress, some with their shirt sleeves
rolled up to their shoulders and incessantly spitting? The
mingled odors of onions and whisky pervading the hall, she
continues, made one feel that the price was really high for
the pleasure of hearing a good actor. The conduct and manners of the men, writes Mrs. Trollope, were absolutely indescribable. They would prop their feet up higher than
their heads, turning their backs to the stage, or stretch
out on the benches. The noise, too, was uninterrupted and
as disagreeable as could be. Instead of clapping, the audience shouted and stamped their feet. Each time they were
prompted by patriotic fervor to sing "Yankee Doodle," one
might have thought that their reputation as good citizens
depended on the noise they managed to make.

It must not be forgotten that the author of these kind
remarks came to America at a time when the theater was
barely beginning. By mid-century, there was greater de-

corum. The life of traveling actors nonetheless continued to be somewhat irregular. There was never any guarantee of an audience. Sometimes the prices of seats had to be reduced at the last moment to avoid playing before a handful of spectators. But the big problem was the walk-on parts. In *Pizarro*, a play by Richard Sheridan, the presence on the stage of two "virgins of the sun" was indispensable. How were they to be found in Pittsburgh, where a touring theatrical company was visiting? As a last resort, the producer recruited an old Irishwoman and the wardrobe mistress. They were dressed in cotton robes and gauze veils, and everything was going beautifully when an ill-timed exclamation arose from the audience: "Look what virgins!" That set off an indescribable uproar, and the manager reportedly had to come on stage in person to chide the audience for its attitude. He probably considered himself lucky, when he remembered another incident. In another city, twenty-four pure-blooded Indians had been hired, each being promised a half dollar and a glass of whisky. Unfortunately, they were paid in advance. That put them in the highest of spirits, and nothing could keep them from launching into a war dance and tearing down the scenery.

The audience was not averse to a colorful touch. Serious plays were not at all popular. Shakespeare, played with dramatic exaggeration, was of course a must, but his works were never performed alone. Dances, jugglers, acrobats, farce, and even trained animals made him, one might say, palatable to the audience. The presence of horses on stage was also a strong drawing card. The presentation of *Richard III* was a particular favorite for that reason. Audiences were even more appreciative of comedies with broad jokes, operettas, melodramas, and above all tableaux vivants. Such tableaux were originally of an educational or religious nature, featuring scenes from mythology and the Bible, and tights were obligatory. They gradually degenerated into

more scantily costumed allegories—the forerunners of the
burlesques which the police pursued with varying degrees
of zeal.

Until about the second quarter of the century, English
actors undisputedly dominated the stage. Later, local talent
began to compete with them. There was Charlotte Cushman,
for example, or Anna Mowatt, E. L. Davenport, William
Warren, James Hackett, Junius B. Booth (father of Edwin
Booth, the great actor who made his debut in 1862, and of
John Wilkes Booth, Abraham Lincoln's assassin), and above
all Edwin Forrest, who won undying fame for his person-
ifications of King Lear, Coriolanus, Richard III, and other
Shakespearean heroes. His rivalry with William Macready,
former manager of Covent Garden and Drury Lane in London, gave rise to tragic incidents during the latter's American tour in 1849. Aroused by posters which had been plastered all over the walls asking whether New York should be
governed by Americans or by Englishmen, mobs stormed
the Astor Place Opera House, where the actor was playing,
and to the cry of "Long Live Washington," attempted to
set fire to the building. Troops had to be called out, and the
toll was twenty-two dead and thirty-six wounded.

The journeys of foreign actors were not always so event-
ful, but their success was varied. The French found proof
of this during the presentation of French ballets. The audience was scandalized; women screamed, and most of them
fled the theater. The men found the whole performance
hilarious and absurd. The actors of the Comédie Française
were more fortunate. Robert Kemp played in one of the
first theaters opened in California after the gold rush. In
1855 a tour by Rachel was tremendously successful in New
York, Boston, and Philadelphia. Unfortunately, it was interrupted by the celebrated actress' illness, and she appeared
in public for the last time in Charleston.

Despite the warmth of this reception, it appears quite cold in comparison to that given to Fanny Elssler in 1840. Two of her solo dances, the Cracovian and the Tarantella, carried her to the peak of triumph. In New York the whole house rose and acclaimed her like a conqueror returning from his victories; in Baltimore, young people unharnessed the horses and pulled her carriage; in Washington the Senate rose when she entered, and the members of the House insisted that she sit at the Speaker's place; in Richmond she was greeted by the ringing of the bells and the firing of cannons; in Boston she was asked to dance up the steps of the famous Bunker Hill Monument; in New Orleans the cushions from her carriage were sold for a small fortune and she inspired a number of duels. Adelina Patti also was so honored when she visited the city of Creole chivalry in 1853 and 1860. And then there was the "Swedish Nightingale," the unique, inimitable Jenny Lind. People paid up to $225 a seat to hear her sing during her two-year tour from 1850 to 1852. She gave 150 concerts at $1,000 apiece, all expenses paid, and her impresario still made a profit of several hundred thousand dollars. But the impresario was Barnum!

The life of this "Napoleon of public caterers," as James Gordon Bennett dubbed him, was astonishing. Born in 1810, he began his career in the fashion of the time as a peddler, selling candy, barley sugar, and gingerbread. At twenty-five he had his first inspiration: he bought an old Negress, Joyce Heth, who claimed to have been George Washington's nursemaid, generously attributed to her the age of 161, and began to exhibit her. A year later, he joined Aaron Turner's traveling circus. This type of attraction was in its infancy, but he soon perceived its possibilities. In 1837 he organized his own company, went West, bought a steamer, and triumphantly sailed down the Mississippi to

New Orleans. The year 1840 found him at the head of a troupe of singers with whom he traveled through the prairies. In 1842 he opened a museum of curiosities in New York. Here he exhibited, in particular, Charles Sherwood Stratton, the famous bearded dwarf known as General Tom Thumb, who was a little more than 2 feet tall and weighed about 15 pounds; a billboard assured the spectators that, following the "General's" 1844 tour of England and the Continent, a million of the prettiest lips in Europe had kissed him. We have mentioned the success Barnum won a little later by taking Jenny Lind across the United States. The rest of his life further strengthened his popularity. In 1856 he made another journey to England, where he gave lectures on an especially appropriate subject, the art of making money. In 1871 the "Greatest Show on Earth" opened in Brooklyn, and ten years later merged with the Bailey Circus to form the Barnum and Bailey Circus—a name destined to become legendary. He acquired Jumbo, the gigantic elephant which was the joy of children and parents alike. Barnum died in 1891 at the age of eighty-one; he had definitely not wasted his life.

What was the secret of his success? First of all, of course, his sense of publicity and his initiative. He did not fear calculated risks. One day he announced with much fanfare that a sensational buffalo race would take place on a piece of land just a stone's throw from the Hoboken ferry linking New York and New Jersey. Wonder of wonders, entrance was to be free! Twenty-four thousand spectators came rushing to the spot, only to find that the buffalo were completely dispirited, and made a rather pitiable showing. The receipts, however, were considerable, for Barnum had hired all the ferry boats for a set fee and pocketed all the profits. It would be a great mistake, however, to imagine that his success was due to such mean tricks. In a sense, he was a genius. Like all great men, he understood and seized all the opportunities that his period afforded him. His contemporaries were thirsting for miracles and asked nothing better than to be amazed. Their credulity was unlimited; anything out of the ordinary, anything that seemed bizarre, strange, or surprising fascinated them. So he presented them with more such sights than anyone else, with incomparable magnificence and originality. In this undertaking, he ran the risk of Puritan opposition, so he transformed his circus into a propagator of the faith. Only educational and morally uplifting subjects were allowed. Shakespeare was carefully expurgated. An old lady once asked him at what time the service began, and he answered with the utmost seriousness that the worshippers were taking their places. Scenes from the Bible were painted on the baggage wagons. The troupe usually went to church on Sunday, and Barnum was unequaled in discussing theology and quoting Scripture.

The circus was a splendid sight indeed when the red and gold wagons rolled past at the slow cadence set by the elephant chosen to lead the parade. By 1851 Barnum was no longer satisfied with one ring. He needed two, and soon three, in which acrobats, dancers, magicians, singers, musicians, equestrians, wild animal tamers, and masters of trained animals all performed at once. And what excitement on entering the American Museum in New York, which had become a real national institution! It was said to house 600,000 curiosities—giants, dwarfs, bearded women, hairless men, snakes of abnormal size, fortune tellers, a reproduction of Niagara Falls, wax figures illustrating the ravages of intemperance and alcoholism, dioramas, panoramas, cyloramas, and who could say what more!

Various attempts were made to imitate Barnum. The Zoological Institute boasted forty-seven cars, 120 matching grey horses, fourteen musicians, and sixty artists. Chauncey

Weeks, Lewis Jones, Spaulding and Rogers dreamed up
attraction after attraction, but to no avail. Barnum was
inimitable.

Other forms of entertainment appeared very pale beside the circus, but they had their patrons nonetheless.
People with intellectual tastes thronged to the lectures
which were so extraordinarily in vogue at the time. Among
the most popular lecturers was Emerson, who spoke with
stormy and calculated eloquence. He would sometimes learn
his material by heart and recite it, but would appear to be
seeking inspiration in the clouds. Wherever he spoke, a
crowd drawn from all classes of society flocked to hear him.
Not all his competitors had the same success, but they rarely
spoke before empty halls. In 1841, the New York newspapers observed that the theaters were deserted, but there
were never enough lectures. The tours arranged by the
Lowell Institute (in 1836 John Lowell, owner of the well-
known textile mills that bore his name, bequeathed $250,000
to finance lectures on the various branches of human knowledge) and the Lyceums were particularly popular. Everything was discussed, but certain topics were especially in
vogue. Two of these, in particular, drew public attention:
spiritism and phrenology. Andrew Jackson Davis, the seer
of Poughkeepsie, held his audience spellbound as he communicated the messages vouchsafed him from the next world.
These were so numerous that he decided to dictate them
to a secretary; they were said to fill thirty volumes. Other
speakers, less favored by the celestial powers, but just as eloquent, held their audiences entranced by describing visions
had by two young farm girls, Maggie and Katie. They
vouched for the genuineness of the visions, and the topic
was all the rage until they were forced to admit that it had
all been a hoax. In more serious vein, George Combe, a
student of Franz Josef Gall, spoke on skull formation and

its psychological significance. Gastronomy was less successful as a topic. Pierre Blot, a Frenchman, tried to convert America to French cooking, but his explanations had a chilly reception.

For all their popularity, these lectures were attended by relatively small audiences. The same was not true of concerts featuring the newly discovered songs of the South, which the audiences loved and flocked to. "My Old Kentucky Home" and above all "Dixie," later to become the national anthem of the Confederation, always brought innumerable curtain calls for the singers. These were seldom authentic Negroes, but more often whites, appropriately called "Ethiopians" or "burnt-cork comedians." They traveled from town to town, generally accompanied by other itinerant performers: sleight-of-hand artists, puppeteers, magicians whose wands and dexterity could soothe strained nerves.

Although gambling was strictly forbidden, it nonetheless went on in secret in certain ill-famed haunts whose existence was the despair of virtuous citizens. Cockfights in the South and West and horseracing almost everywhere provided gamblers with plenty of opportunities to indulge their passion. Some of the principal race courses—after those in New York state, and especially at Centerville, Long Island —were those of Washington, Cincinnati, Louisville, Nashville, and New Orleans. Boston did not succumb to the temptation until 1862. Trotting races were almost as common as sprints. A record of 1 mile in 2 minutes, 19¾ seconds created a sensation among racing enthusiasts.

These were not the only spectators. The races were among the rare opportunities for the urban masses to get out into the fresh air. They, too, excitedly followed the exploits of celebrated horses like "Lady Suffolk," which won nearly 500 races in fifteen years, or "Peytona" and "Fashion," whose rivalry for a prize of $20,000 is said to have brought operations on Wall Street to a complete standstill on May 13, 1845. More important still, city dwellers thus had a chance to see a little greenery—a pleasure they rarely enjoyed. Very few cities had public parks. Central Park in New York did not open until 1857. Days of rest were usually spent at home or loitering in the streets. A visit to an amusement park or fireworks on a holiday occasionally broke the monotony. Fortunately, the very frequent patriotic parades warmed the hearts of "true" Americans. Puritanism, however, would certainly not have let these parades be used as excuses for suggestive exhibits. What would the moralizers have said of the modern drum majorettes, with their red lips and bare legs and whirling batons!

# PROFESSIONAL LIFE

*Chapter XI*

# AGRICULTURE, INDUSTRY, AND COMMERCE

On the eve of the Civil War, America was still essentially an agricultural country. The rural population accounted for nearly 75 per cent of the total. Except in the South, where the survival of slavery had made possible the creation of huge estates, medium-sized holdings were the rule. These were sometimes grouped together in the East, but beyond the Alleghenies they were always isolated and at a considerable distance from each other. The owners cultivated the land with the help of their families; the richer ones took on a few agricultural laborers whom they paid a miserable wage. From time to time, they would go into the nearest township, which might be many miles away, to make their purchases. On such days they would exchange the deep blue overalls which they used as work clothes for heavy cloth suits and beaver-skin hats. The little towns, consisting generally of three to four thousand inhabitants, were all alike. The roads were unpaved; at the center, sometimes, the courthouse, always in the Greek architecture style, the residences of the mayor and the sheriff, the school, two or three churches, a few offices of lawyers and businessmen, and then the stores. The list of storekeepers was the same everywhere: tanners, shoemakers, blacksmiths, carpenters, masons, tailors, dressmakers, furniture dealers, and especially millers.

The production of cereals rose substantially between 1830 and 1860; that of wheat, in particular, rose from 84 to 173 million bushels. This increase was not simply the result of extending the area under cultivation. A series of inventions revolutionized conditions of work. Around 1837 the manufacture of steel ploughshares began to facilitate the breaking up of the rough closely packed soil of the prairies. Previously, anything from three to seven pair of oxen had been needed to till certain fields.

In 1833 and 1834, Obed Hussey and Cyrus H. McCormick patented their invention of harvesters: this was a discovery of incalculable importance, but it was a long time before its effects made themselves felt; it is estimated that, around 1860, no more than twenty thousand machines were in use. On the other hand, mechanical threshers were commonly employed in the 1850's. The construction of pneumatic grain silos met the need of storage facilities for this massive build-up of production. A sharp rise in prices and the thrust of the railroads into the West contributed significantly to the expansion of agriculture.

As in other sectors, science began to oust tradition. Gone were the good old days when farmers relied entirely on the *Farmers' Almanac*, that authority on virtually everything and especially meteorology, since it predicted the weather for all three hundred sixty-five days of the year! The experts were careful to give less precise but more practical, advice. *The Elements of Scientific Agriculture,* published in 1850 by John P. Norton, became the bedside book of progress. It became customary, moreover, for farmers to send their sons and daughters to attend courses at specialized colleges: Farmers' College in Ohio, Michigan Agricultural College, and Pennsylvania State College, founded in 1846, 1857, and 1859, respectively.

Compared with the expansion which subsequently took place, the changes in industry were relatively slow. Nevertheless, the 1860 census showed that one-third of the population was already directly or indirectly employed in industrial enterprises. Fifty years earlier, the United States had not yet progressed beyond the stage of production by craftsmen in family units. Factories made their first appearance after the war of 1812, but the use of coal as a source of power did not become widespread until after 1840. Before that date, new workshops were usually located beside rivers and waterfalls in order to utilize their energy resources. It was an idyllic era, at least here and there.

The model factories of Massachusetts, especially those of Waltham and Lowell, became famous the world over. Visitors from Europe simply had to visit them. They employed mostly women, who were paid less than men: 5,000 young women between the ages of seventeen and twenty-four in a work force of 6,000. Michel Chevalier likened these factories to convents, because life there was so well ordered and so exclusively dedicated to work. Whether pretty or plain—the prettier ones worked in the front rows, apparently, and the less attractive ones at the back of the shed—the women workers were well turned out, smiling, and disciplined. They lived in family rooming houses under the motherly supervision of chaperones who tolerated no nonsense.

The introduction of new techniques gradually upset this kindly paternalism. All industries were affected by them to some extent. The factories which made cotton goods—1,200 in 1840—were the first to change over and quickly eliminated foreign competition. Those making woolen goods achieved their independence more slowly; they specialized in fancy materials such as the imitation cashmeres which were highly fashionable around 1848, but the English held on to their monopoly of worsteds until after 1860. Together with textiles, the iron and steel industry formed the core of industrial activity at the time. The main source of iron ore and coal was Pennsylvania, but their extraction was not highly developed. In 1860 the production of cast iron in Great Britain was five times greater than the United States, and that of coal six times greater. As late as 1870, America was an importer of steel. Local factories held the upper hand only in the markets for cooking ranges, piping, and nails. In the last-named field, large-scale production was rapidly developed; it was responsible for the widespread introduction of prefabricated housing from the 1830's. The watch industry systematized its techniques at about the same period, and in 1835, we are told, the joys of working on a conveyor belt were discovered in a Cincinnati slaughter-house. The manufacture of locomotives, too, developed so fast that, prior to 1850, the United States was already selling them to Russia, Austria, Germany, and even England. These examples are exceptional, however. The modernization of industrial methods went forward very slowly before the Civil War, and many branches of production continued to operate along the traditional lines of craftsmanship. This was particularly true of the manufacture of boots and shoes, which took place almost entirely in very small workshops where everything was done by hand.

Labor problems did not really crop up until after 1840, along with the influx of immigrants.

Craftsmen had formed themselves into unions some twenty years earlier, and two schools of thought were at work within them. One favored political action: under its influence a workers' party was organized in New York which proved strong enough to gather one-third of the votes in the

1828 elections. However, dissensions soon crippled its drive; it was accused, in particular, of copying foreign examples. Within a few years, it had disappeared without a trace. Demands concerning conditions of work then came to the forefront. In a dozen towns of the North, federations were created which embraced the associations formed by workers of each occupational group. Strikes became current practice and, generally speaking, wages improved. The ten-hour working day was even adopted for certain categories of municipal workers.

After the depression of 1837, which continued for five years, and which was of unprecedented severity, these first achievements melted away. The middle of the century was a hard period for the working class. The labor surplus rendered it powerless; from time to time, indeed, strikes did break out, but they were conducted without hope, since their instigators knew that there was no chance of a successful outcome. A minimum of twelve hours' work at famine wages, paid partially in kind, became the regular practice. The workers' aristocracy of shoemakers, hatmakers, and printers managed to earn $4 to $6 a week. Unskilled hands could not hope to receive more than 65 cents a day and were never sure of being employed. A further slowdown of business in 1847 and the "panic" of 1857 still further aggravated the plight of the workers. It would take thirty years for the trade union movement to reach any real magnitude.

Discoveries increased—an indication of the spirit of individual enterprise. No research centers existed to encourage them, nor foundations to finance them. They were, in every case, the achievement of researchers and curious men, moved by an extraordinary passion for innovation and progress. Twenty-eight thousand inventions were patented between 1850 and 1860. The list is as varied as it is long. In 1836 Samuel Colt perfected the revolver which bears his name; this was followed in quick succession by rifles of higher and higher performance, devised by Oliver Winchester. In 1844 Charles Goodyear invented the vulcanization of rubber. About the same date, William Crompton devised improved looms: the rotary press and the daguerrotype became an increasingly integral part of everyday life; and, above all, the sewing machines of Elias Howe, patented in 1846, and that of Isaac Singer some years later, revolutionized the manufacture of women's clothing. At the same time, Elisha Otis developed the safety mechanism which was to make his elevators famous, and the use of excavators revolutionized existing construction methods.

The "gadget" civilization was already taking shape. The two international exhibitions at Crystal Palace in London, in 1851 and 1853, were a triumph for American ingenuity. American art was represented by only a single, rather poor statue, but in the technical field the exhibits dazzled by their anticipation of future lines of development. American chauvinism drew much satisfaction from this. A cartoon shows Uncle Sam busy explaining all these miraculous inventions as John Bull groans; "Oh dear, oh dear, whatever will they think of next? We must be terribly backward."

Up to the time of the Civil War, commerce was mainly in the hands of peddlers. Some sold everything: pins, needles, fasteners, eyelets, scissors, razors, combs, buttons, spoons, knives, forks, cotton fabrics, lace, books, perfume. Others were specialized; weavers and cobblers were much in demand. Sellers of tinplate, clocks, antiques, furniture, and washing coppers prided themselves on being the aristocrats of the trade. Looking down on them, in the conviction that they moved in more refined circles, came the decorators, portrait painters, and silhouettists, working the same routes. A Frenchman, Auguste Edouart, became famous in the last-named form of activity: he is said to have cut out 50,000 silhouettes, and his treatise on the subject was the standard reference book.

These commercial travelers could be seen arriving, some on foot, some on horseback, with their merchandise carried in long tin boxes on their backs or on their mounts. Each purchase was the occasion for endless bargaining. After the migrations to the West, the greater distance led the peddlers, like the pioneers, to use covered wagons which were capable of transporting heavier loads. These traveling salesmen knew all the tricks. They did not generally pride themselves on high standards of honesty, and they retailed a good many fantastic stories. A historian of this group describes them as setting out each year in their thousands, ready to lie, trick, load the dice, swindle. In the beginning, they were all of native stock. The "Yankee peddler" long remained a stock figure in local folklore. Around the middle of the century, German Jews recently arrived in the country began to offer them serious competition.

But at the very same time, peddling as a trade was beginning to be displaced by the emergence of the general store, the forerunner of the department store and of the "five and ten." The general store carried a little of everything. It was nearly always situated at the center of the village and was the focal point of village life. People gathered there to wait for the stagecoach, to gossip, and to collect their mail. In the large towns, of course, retail trade was more diversified. Shops of all sorts looked for custom. They had already taken to advertising in the daily papers, but few of them had window displays; the price of glass was, in fact, prohibitive, because it was virtually not manufactured in the United States and had to be imported from England, Belgium, France, or Germany.

The merchant marine developed considerably between 1840 and 1860.

Whaling also reached its peak at about that time. The oil so obtained was used for lighting, until oilwells were discovered. Whalebone was used to make a variety of objects: walking sticks, clothes pegs, bodkins, corset stays, umbrella ribs. New Bedford was the capital of the whaling industry. From this New England port and the rival ports of Nantucket, New London, Sag Harbor, and Mystic, many hundreds of boats set forth every year for the Pacific, crewed by men ready for any eventuality, whose primitive and picturesque lives have been immortalized by Melville.

On the Atlantic seaboard, the whalers were not the only ships to make for the open sea. Well before 1840, Salem and Boston were centers of vigorous trade with the West Indies and South America; some ships extended their voyages as far as California, and even Hawaii, whence they brought back furs and sandalwood. A series of developments revolutionized maritime trade in the years which followed. The opening up of China in 1842 gave it outlets of an incalculable potential. Six years later, the discovery of gold brought about a gigantic migration from East to West which, at the beginning at least, mainly followed the sea route.

New means of action were needed to take advantage of this situation so full of promise. And so, for a dazzling period, the clippers reigned supreme on the oceans. They quickly became legendary. There was unanimous admiration for these ships with their tapered prows and slender build, with their three gigantic masts pointing skyward—some were nearly 200 feet high—and vast sails of varied dimensions cracking in the wind. What was sensational, however, even more than their lines, was their speed. To this their romantic names bear witness: *Sea Witch, Surprise, Flying Cloud, Nightingale, Westward Ho!, Ocean Glory, Sovereign of the Sea.* Previously the passage from New York to San Francisco had taken 159 days on the average. In 1851 the *Flying Cloud* reduced this to 89 days. Record-breaking exploits followed thick and fast: 97 days from Hong Kong to London; 194 days for the round-the-world; the *Sovereign of the Sea*, product of the famous Donald McKay shipyards of Boston, covered 411 nautical miles in 24 hours; the *Lightning* soon beat this, by doing 436 miles in the same time, a record which no sailing ship has ever equaled; the *Baynes*, finally, made Boston–Liverpool in 12½ days and Liverpool–Melbourne in 63 days, a speed which only steamships could surpass.

The American merchant marine enjoyed a very brief period of supremacy. The repeal of the Navigation Act by Great Britain in 1849 allowed American ships to compete successfully with their rivals, even in their home ports. Again, the discovery of gold in Australia gave the clippers a new lease of life. English shipowners even had to place orders with New England shipyards—an unheard of thing. However, the Yankees never held the leadership in the passenger lines. And even in other lines, their supremacy was short-lived. The *Sirius*, the first steamship to cross the ocean, flew an English flag as she entered the port of New York on April 23, 1838, after a crossing of 16½ days. Two years later, regular services were functioning between Europe and America, but the lion's share was with the Royal Mail Steam Packet Co., founded by Sir Samuel Cunard. For a time, thanks to official subsidies, an American company, the Collins Line, managed to offer it some competition, but a series of untoward accidents discouraged would-be travelers. To make matters worse, American ship builders were so intoxicated by the success of their clippers and at the same time so handicapped by the delays in the modernization of the steel industry, that they persisted in building their steamers with wooden paddle wheels. At best, these could serve for the Great Lakes and coastal navigation, but they were incapable of tackling the ocean. The employment of steel screw-propellers by its British rivals dealt the American merchant marine its final blow. Around 1860, the United States merchant fleet totalled 90,000 tons, as against nearly 500,000 under the Union Jack.

## Chapter XII

# "GO WEST, YOUNG MAN, GO WEST"

The West—a magic word! "If Hell was in the West, the Americans would cross heaven to get there," so the saying ran. The mysterious lands of the setting sun had always fascinated immigrants. In the middle of the eighteenth century they had already reached the eastern slopes of the Appalachians; fifty years later, this first obstacle had been surmounted: Kentucky and Tennessee were the first territories to be added to the thirteen colonies. The movement continued, irresistibly: Ohio in 1803, Indiana in 1816, Illinois in 1818, Michigan in 1837 were incorporated in turn into the Union. In the South the expansion was no less rapid; by 1840 the Mississippi had been traversed throughout its course, from St. Louis to New Orleans. Beyond Louisiana, Texas, if not Mexico, seemed to be marked out as a future stage in Manifest Destiny. Farther north, along the Arkansas and the Missouri, there stretched an immense, almost unknown area wide open to all ambition, favorable to every hope.

The prairie acted like a magnet. Hundreds of thousands

of men and women, motivated by every desire, streamed to
gather its riches, to probe its secrets. In most cases, the lure
of a better life had set them on their way. They were ready
for any exertion, prepared to face any danger. They were
a mixed crowd: rascals and honest folk were represented in
equal proportion. They had one characteristic in common
—optimism. They were not expecting to succeed easily, but
they were sure that, in the final reckoning, they would reap
the benefit of their daring. Many of them went out of inclination rather than necessity. They were not all poor,
these pioneers who abandoned a safe existence to risk adventure. Often they left a life of ease, comfortable homes;
they faced separation from wife and children, not knowing
when they would see them again. Their motives were not
practical, like those of their fellow travelers; the risks attracted them, the unpredictable beguiled them, nature in
the raw called to them, so violently that they were unable
to resist.

Thoreau's reflections have often been quoted; they
strikingly express what so many Americans felt. Every sunset, he wrote, filled him with a longing to go westward, to
a West as far away and as beautiful as that in which the sun
was disappearing. Atlantis, he mused, the Hesperides, those
gardens of earthly paradise, must have been the West of
ancient times, shrouded in mystery and poetry. When he
went for a stroll, he continued, he always found himself
impelled to choose a westerly or southwesterly route; facing
in that direction, he felt a sense of freedom.

The mystique of unlimited, virgin lands worked on
others besides the hermit of Walden. A senator proposed
in 1848 that a giant statue of Christopher Columbus should
be carved out of the granite of the Rockies. The discoverer
of America was to be portrayed in a romantic pose, with
hand outstretched toward the Pacific; the meaning of his
gesture would clearly be: "Yonder you will find the East,

yonder you will find the Indies!" The intellectuals vied with
each other in singing the saga of the settlers. How splendid
it was, Carlyle exclaimed, to think of those Yankees, lean
and slender, tough as steel, carried away by an ungovern-
able hidden passion, on their way to the West, determined
to tame the jungle and make it bring forth meat and bread
for Adam's posterity! No myth of Athena or Hercules, he
added, could equal such a reality. Walt Whitman went
farther: a canyon in the Rocky Mountains, he wrote, or the
plains of Kansas and Colorado, extending boundlessly, like
oceans, arouse in the human breast emotions whose gran-
deur and compexity surpass those which can be evoked by
all the marble temples, all the sculptures of Phidias, all
painting, poetry, memories, even music. It was a revealing
observation: for there were, indeed, plenty of barbarians
among the tamers of the prairie.

Around 1840 the migrations took on gigantic proportions. As we know, some millions of immigrants arrived
from Europe at the same time. Not all of them settled on
the Atlantic seaboard. A large number of them helped to
swell the ranks of the columns already on the march to the
West. The discovery of gold gave this movement, as we shall
see, the force of a tidal wave. It took but ten years for the
Rockies to be reached and left behind.

The Mississippi and Missouri basins acted as points of
departure. From the beginning of the century, a series of
expeditions had explored the courses of these giants. At the
time of the Louisiana Purchase, two famous explorers, Meri-
wether Lewis and William Clark, had set out from Saint
Louis in May 1804, and followed the Missouri right to its
source; pushing further afield, they even descended the
Columbia valley and reached the Pacific. Their example
haunted the imagination of their contemporaries. Above
all, they brought back from their expedition a mine of pre-

cious information for their successors about the inhabitants
of these wild regions, their flora and fauna. The successors
were numerous. In 1819, John James Audubon, navigating
the Ohio and the Mississippi, made that famous voyage from
which he returned with the bird paintings for which he
will always be remembered. Thirteen years later, a paddle
steamer, the *Yellowstone*, following the Missouri over a
distance of more than 900 miles, managed for the first time
to reach the mouth of the Yellowstone, near the present-day
borders of North Dakota and Montana: aboard, there was
another artist, George Catlin, whose portraits of Indians
must have helped many a pioneer to picture the appearance
and habits of his future adversaries. The same itinerary was
again followed in 1833 by two explorers, this time a German, Maximilian von Wied, and a Swiss, Charles Bodmer,
who likewise amassed drawings, documents, and information. Little by little, forts were constructed along the length
of the Missouri; they were to serve as shelter and staging
posts for the caravans which risked the vastness of the plains.

The first of them, a handful of men and a few wagons,
reached the foot of the Rockies in 1830. Six years later,
Bonneville, whose exploits inspired Washington Irving, succeeded in crossing from the Platte valley to that of the Snake
by the pass which was soon to gain fame under the name
of South Pass.

It was the Northwest, at least in the beginning, that
attracted the majority of the pioneers. The missionaries had
arrived there before them: French-Canadian priests in the
far North, in the region of Coeur-d'Alène, Methodists and
Presbyterians further south in the valleys of the Snake and
the Columbia. From all of them, letters arrived full of enthusiasm about the riches of the region. In 1842 the *Wander-
lust* gripped the inhabitants of Iowa and Missouri. The
Oregon Trail—the French played an important part in its

exploration—soon became famous. It originated either at Independence or at St. Joseph, both located in the valley of the Missouri, respectively downstream and upstream of the present site of Kansas City. Crossing the plains of Kansas, the Oregon Trail reached the Platte at Fort Kearney and followed its course upstream, sometimes on the right bank, sometimes on the left, as far as Fort Laramie. Chimney Rock, with its landscape of jagged rocks of all sizes, shaped like chimneys and visible eighty miles away in clear weather, and Scotts Bluff, a favorite place for very active rattlesnakes, were spots which never failed to arouse astonishment and fear in the columns as they passed through. Before arriving at the oasis of the fort, they had to pick their way through a gorge so narrow that—so the story goes—wild goats jumped over their heads from one side of the ravine to the other. Then, heading toward South Pass, the columns left the course of the Platte after some 120 miles and came to Independence Rock, a block of granite over 600 yards long and 120 feet high, rising like an island in the plain. The names of thousands of pioneers were carved on it. Later arrivals often learned by this means what had become of their predecessors.

One obstacle after another rose up in their path. One in particular was famous above all, with the well-chosen name of Devil's Barrier. The highest point of the crossing —the Continental Divide—on the watershed between the Atlantic and the Pacific, was finally reached: this was perhaps the toughest part of the journey. Crossing the Rockies between the ranges of the Gros Ventre and the Tetons, the travelers reached the course of the Snake. There, at Fort Hall and Fort Boise, real first-aid posts, they got their second wind. At last the Columbia valley lay before them! They had now only to descend to Fort Walla and Fort Vancouver, some halting at the richest hunting and fishing grounds, while others pressed on to the deserted coast of the mighty ocean. They had covered about 2,000 miles from the Missouri.

At that time, California was practically unknown: a detailed map of it had hardly even been drawn up. Some travelers' tales, one or two books (Richard Henry Dana's *Two Years Before the Mast,* for example) had from time to time drawn the public's attention to it, but it did not exert the same fascination as Oregon. It was reputed to be a romantic country where, beneath a blue, voluptuous sky, the Hidalgos of popular imagination "slept, smoked, and hummed the lazy songs of Castille." Did the settlers of the Middle West fear to be corrupted by this decadent atmosphere? Whatever the case, before the discovery of gold spread like a roll of thunder, few had taken themselves in this direction. John C. Frémont, however, penetrated as far as Sierra Nevada in 1844, on the far side of the Rockies, and a year later he reached California. It was just before the outbreak of the Mexican war. When this began, in May 1846, Frémont's presence encouraged the few American settlers in California to attempt its conquest. In a comic-opera atmosphere, the Mexicans quickly lost the nominal control which they exercised. California officially became American territory on February 25, 1848, ten days after some mysterious golden nuggets had been seen for the first time in the Sacramento Valley.

Over the previous ten years or so, columns had been setting off from Independence toward the South. Santa Fe, with its ochre-and-red houses and seductive senoras, whose mantillas and fans dazzled the rustic Americans, had an aura of legend about it. People went there, however, not so much for the pleasure of tourism or for amorous adventures, but rather in search of the furs and silver in which the area abounded. The Santa Fe Trail across Oklahoma, Texas, and New Mexico became as famous as the Oregon Trail. Here, however, expansion came up against a political obstacle. These territories were not, like the others, vague open spaces without frontiers or government. They belonged officially to Mexico. Force, once again, brought a solution. A brief campaign, noisy rather than glorious, settled the Mexican army. Texas and New Mexico, as well as Southern California, were annexed to the United States by the Treaty of Guadalupe Hidalgo.

Suppose that we had been watching a typical caravan as it wound its way across the plains from Independence. We would have seen women, children, provisions, equipment stuffed into wagons with roofs of thick canvas, held in place by semicircular iron hoops. Each of these heavy vans was named. Among the commonest names were *Rough & Ready, Gold Seeker, On My Way, Now or Never*. When relieved of their loads, the floors could be raised up high for fording rivers. In normal movement, they sagged beneath the burden they were required to support. It was to be assumed, in effect, that, over hundreds and hundreds of miles, no resources would be locally available, other than the products of hunting and fishing. A list of food and equipment required for the journey was carefully drawn up before leaving. "For every head," we read in a report dating from 1849, "we carried 125 lbs. of flour, 50 lbs. of salted ham, 50 lbs. of smoked bacon, 30 lbs. of sugar, 6 lbs. of ground coffee, 1 lb. of tea, ½ lb. of cream of tartar, 2 lbs. of baking powder, 3 lbs. of salt, a bushel of dried fruit, a sixth of a bushel of beans, 25 lbs. of rice, 16 lbs. of sea biscuits, pepper, ginger, and citric and tartaric acid in various proportions." The amounts varied, naturally, with each expedition. Some rules, nevertheless, were fairly constant, and the figures we have just quoted seem to represent the average. To this already considerable weight there had, of course, to be added one or two axes per individual, a saw, a plane for roughing down wood, two or three carpenter's chisels, a pick, a spade and a shovel, not to mention as large a stock of cartridges as possible—all quantities multiplied, of course, by the number of males in the party.

It is hardly surprising, therefore, that the matter of locomotive power for the wagons was one of extreme importance. Opinions differed. Oxen, horses, mules—each had their advocates. Oxen had the advantage of being robust and hardy, but pulled very slowly and in sandy or marshy stretches were liable to get bogged. Horses ensured a speedier pace; however, they were suitable for limited loads only and were too fragile to be relied on in all circumstances. Mules, many people claimed, possessed qualities which the others could not match: they were tireless, light on food, obstinate; you might think, to see them, that they, too, were fascinated by the call of the West. Unfortunately, they were noisy and their braying even preceded the sunrise. Their disposition, moreover, was not pleasant; several men were needed to hitch them at departure, and in this daily operation there were frequent injuries.

The scene when the caravan set off, generally in the first shafts of sunlight at dawn, did not lack color and life. All was noise and confusion. Such excitement! Such an uproar! Everyone calling their animals, wagon drivers swearing, cattle lowing, bells clanging, the noise of chains, yokes, harnesses filling the air, whips cracking. At long last, all was ready. The column was often more than a mile long. The coaches were assembled into groups of four or five, and each section took the lead in turn so that the inevitable discomfort of the dust would be shared out fairly. The men followed, often on foot. Many, however, rode on horseback around the wagons or went on ahead as scouts; and some acted as rear guard. Some had the special job of herding before them the cattle and the spare horses, of which there was always a great number. They all wore the same rig:

a red shirt with attached collar, a rough woolen coat to the knees, with huge pockets, tight trousers tucked into high boots, leather belt, large felt hat and, in particular, a loaded pistol, a hunting knife, and a dagger.

Over favorable ground, they would sometimes make more than twenty miles a day, but that was an exceptional rate of progress; they usually thought themselves lucky when they managed 120 miles in a week. There was generally a one-hour halt around midday. The leader of the expedition, who had been selected before the departure, would take advantage of the halt to hold a council of war with the most experienced of his companions; where necessary, he acted as a judge, but in that case he surrounded himself with a jury drawn by lot. The daily stage ended around sunset. The animals were unharnessed and unsaddled and put out to graze; a portable forge enabled horseshoes to be replaced when necessary. The tents were unfolded; the men went off in search of wood and paper, while the womenfolk set about the cooking. If there was no salt or pepper, they did not have to worry: they had only to take some mule meat, season it with rifle powder, and burn it slightly—their husbands were more than satisfied with the dish. While the dinner was being prepared, the men arranged the wagons next to each other in a closed circle, to form a rampart round the camp. Sentinels were picked: they stood guard in turn, alert to the slightest noise. Sometimes they were a little too much on edge and mistook the soughing of the wind through the grass for the approach of an Indian; their premature rifle shot would awaken the whole camp and would be the subject of endless jests the following morning.

The evening was the only gentle hour of the day. Some meditated and read the Bible. Around the fire there was chatter, jokes, laughter; some wrote letters which they hoped to entrust to the next relay post; idylls took shape; if some-

body had a violin, the young men and girls broke into a
dance; sometimes the piercing notes of the flute would
awaken a sense of nostalgia in the travelers; above all, people sang. Always the same songs, and they never wearied
of repeating their happy or sad rhythms. Those of Stephen
Foster Collins, "the troubador of America," were particularly
popular. *"Louisiana Belle," "My Old Kentucky Home,"
"Old Folks at Home," "Come Where My Love Lies Dreaming,"* and so many others, soaked in a sentimentality which
easily drew tears but alternating with childish jokes—these
were the songs which softened the tough conquerors of the
Wild West. *"O Susanna,"* was their especial favorite. *"Mich-
igania,"* full of punch, revived if need be those whose courage was flagging:

> Come all ye Yankee farmers who wish to change your lot,
> Who've spunk enough to travel beyond your native spot
> And leave behind the village where Ma and Pa stay.
> Come, follow me and settle in Michigania,
> Yea, yea, yea in Michigania!

Sadder, but with a happy ending after all, was the story
of "sweet Betsy" and her loving "Ike." They had crossed the
mountains with a pair of oxen, a fat yellow dog, a fine big
cock, and a pig with spotted skin. But, alas, all these animals
died:

> Poor Ike was discouraged, and Betsy got mad
>
> .  .  .  .  .  .  .  .  .  .  .  .
>
> They stopped at Salt Lake to inquire the way,
> When Brigham declared that sweet Betsy should stay.
> But Betsy got frightened and ran away like a deer.

It was decidedly too much for "sweet Betsy":

> And down in the sand she lay rolling about,
> When Ike, half distracted, looked on with surprise
> Saying Betsy, get up, you'll get sand in your eyes.

A sweet appeal, which did not go unheeded! Betsy took courage once more.

> ... And they fondly embraced.
> And they traveled along with his arm round her waist.

Even Betsy and Susanna did not keep the caravan awake for very long. By ten o'clock at the latest everybody was asleep. Against the fatigue and dangers of the night watch and the morrow, a few hours of sleep were not excessive.

The name "prairie," given to the great plains extending from the Mississippi to the Rockies (about 900 miles), was perfectly justified at that time. Grass was almost the sole form of vegetation in this vast territory; it was thick and dense in the East, with scattered bushes at the approach to the mountains. Beside the rivers grew willow trees, silk-cotton trees, and wild plum trees. A monotonous landscape, in which a few hillocks and rocks, barely distinguishable from one another, served imperfectly as landmarks. Nothing could have been easier than to lose one's way. Before the routes were clearly marked, how many columns failed to reach their destination! Those who came after them sometimes found grisly signs of their fate: human bones, animal carcasses, abandoned wagons. Sometimes there were survivors to tell the tragic tale. In 1847, forty-eight wretched people arrived, more dead than alive, in California. They related how they had set out, eighty-seven strong, from Springfield, Illinois; they had lost their way during the winter, and the snow had effectually prevented them from moving on. Thirty-nine of their companions had perished; they themselves had kept alive only by resorting to cannibalism.

In most cases, a complete silence enveloped those who disappeared. Had they succumbed to the climate, to thirst, to Indians? A short, stifling summer, interspersed with violent storms and cyclones, is usually succeeded in this region of America by an interminable winter during which, day after day, an icy wind blows from the Northwest, heralding snowstorms. Spring and autumn are just brief interludes. The columns generally set out toward the end of May. If their leaders were experienced, they included a reserve of drinking water in their stores. Many failed to take this precaution and relied on springs and rivers; at the height of the dog days, their hopes were often disappointed, and it was quickly discovered that, at many points on the itinerary, the alkaline deposits made the water practically undrinkable. That left the whisky, but under a blazing sun that could cause madness for all but those with hard heads. Besides, it did nothing to solve the problem of the cattle. But there were, it is true, the old wives' cures. If your cows had swallowed alkali, give them a sandwich of nicotine, made from a handful of tobacco between two slices of bacon. Finding shelter for the night was no mean problem as winter approached. The cold then became just as mortal a danger as thirst. Wolves and coyotes padded round the camp; sinister though they looked, their howling nevertheless did not inspire in the travelers the same terror as did in summertime the clouds of grasshoppers, against which rifles and knives were equally useless.

But the greatest obstacle, all agreed, was the Indian, who could claim rather more ancient rights to the land than could the newcomers. Their ancestors had emigrated from Siberia to America some 15,000 or 20,000 years earlier. They had spread over the whole of what was to be United States territory. One wonders why they did not create a civilization comparable to that of the Maya, Aztecs, or Incas of Central and South America. They never developed any political unity. They were divided into innumerable tribes, torn by internal dissensions, and possessed no common language other than that of signs. They were thus never in a position of sufficient strength to be able to resist the white invasion. Their way of life, north of the Rio Grande, remained quite primitive. East of the Alleghenies many settled in hunting and fishing territory which they regarded as their own, and they did not move away unless the game and fish resources failed. By contrast, those of the Great Plains—the Kansas, Pawnee, Sioux, Cheyenne, Blackfeet, Crow, Arapaho—were always nomadic. Their subsistence depended on the buffalo, and they constantly moved quarters in pursuit of the herds. But in their ways of life and customs, the two groups were very similar. The Indians of the forests—of the *Last of the Mohicans* style—lived in wigwams; those of the Wild West— Buffalo Bill style—in tepees. Inside these dwellings, the earth was usually leveled down and a central hearth was used for cooking. Benches set along the walls served as beds or seats. When a tribe moved, the various objects which it took with it were hoisted on sloping planks shaped like hand barrows and drawn by horses or dogs, under the supervision of the women and children. The men rode around the column as it advanced.

What is surprising is that the Indians were in fact dressed as they are shown in the movies. Moccasins, leggings, long tunics, glass beads, bright, sometimes ankle-length feathers are not a product of legend. Fashions varied according to regions, but the main lines changed very little. Great attention, in particular, was always given to their hair. The men used bear grease to make their hair more shiny, and lampblack to make it blacker. Most of them cut their hair short on either side of the head, leaving a sort of coxcomb which descended threateningly from the forehead to the nape of the neck.

Not for nothing were the Indians called redskins, for they did in fact daub their faces with glowing red paint. Their women were no less fond of making up their faces. They set off their complexions by liberal applications of the brightest possible crimson on the forehead, temples, and cheeks. The more "elegant" women put black round their eyes and perfumed themselves with aromatic herbs. Some wore their hair long, proudly letting it fall—when they could —to their hips; others put their hair up in a heavy chignon on the nape, in imitation of a beaver's tail, firmly held in place by strips of cloth. For the women as for the men, it was a strict rule of conduct to keep the hair greasy. Their clothing, in some southwestern tribes, amounted to no more than a rectangular piece of cloth folded around the waist as a skirt; elsewhere, they also wore jackets.

The women's role was by no means negligible. In some tribes they joined in the community powwows. Although their husbands were polygamous, they did not gather their spouses under a single roof, and each squaw was the head of her own family. Theirs was the sole responsibility for rearing the children. Naturally, cooking and the upkeep of the huts, as well as garment weaving and pottery work, fell within their province. In sedentary periods, they cultivated the soil; thanks to them, corn, beans, pumpkins, and a number of fruits varied the regular fare. The men had only contempt for these agricultural labors. They recognized only a single occupation—hunting—and only a single adequate food—meat.

It was no small job to ensure the subsistence of the community. It is estimated that an Indian ate four pounds of meat per day, and the average size of a tribe was about 100 persons. In the East, that meant killing an average of four bucks daily. In the Great Plains, the buffalo singularly facilitated the problem: by slaughtering two or three per month, the same number of mouths could be fed.

Hunting gave the Indians a sense of discipline. They were by instinct individualists, and their principles of organization always remained loose. Each group had a leader, but there was nothing arbitrary about his authority. He relied on the council of elders, and in matters of major importance the whole tribe would discuss the problem in endless powwows. There would be interminable talk, singing and, above all, prayers.

Religion was in fact the most powerful bond in the community. The Indians were sincerely devout. They felt themselves constantly surrounded by mysterious forces. Each had his own guardian, his totem, whom he particularly respected. But their gods were nevertheless accessible to all. Never visible, always present, they manifested themselves in the forces of nature, particularly thunder and lightning. "Thunderbird," the god who was supposed to have assumed the form of a bird and to originate storms, was the most venerated of all. The Indians presented offerings to each of these divinities in the form of sacrifices of food, clothing, and adornments.

The rites took place according to strict rules, in which the Indians delighted, being much addicted to formalism. First came the dances, with or without masks, each step and each gesture heavy with meaning. There followed the ceremony of the pipe, which was symbolic in the highest degree. The celebrant slowly made the round of the assembly, with an elegance of carriage and a dignity of bearing that not even the most savage detractors of the Indians could deny. Moving counterclockwise, he halted at each cardinal point of the compass. When he arrived before the pipe, he did not immediately grasp it. He advanced slowly, retreated, and repeated the movement twice more. Only the fourth time did he dare to touch it. When he took it in his hands, he held it with great caution, bent forward over it in prayer, then walked over to the fire to light it. Then he solemnly offered the smoke at the four points of the horizon, to earth and sky.

This subtle symbolism was very alien to the crude realism of the white man, who looked upon the Indian rites

as a childish waste of time. Nevertheless, the "palefaces"
were obliged to adapt themselves to local customs if they
wished to maintain good neighborly relations with the "redskins." These nervous pragmatists thus learned the virtues
of patience.

When a tribe was prepared to negotiate with the whites,
it sent over a few young braves who had to be given a little
tobacco to distribute among the principal heads of family.
Then the whole group would arrive and would pitch its
tents around the white encampment—usually a fort. None
of this, of course, was done in haste. Finally the hour for
action struck. The Indians formed a single line, in strict
hierarchical order, and moved silently toward the camp
gate. The camp commander came out to meet them, the
extent of his advance depending on the degree of courtesy
he wished to show his visitors. The Indians offered him
presents in the form of horses, furs, and skins. A particularly
generous negotiator would take off his tunic and clothe his
host in it; then he would remove his fur cap and place it
on his host's head. Sometimes the Indians seemed to want
to outdo one another in gestures of goodwill: tunics and
caps would accumulate on the body and head of the "great
white chief," who must at all costs remain impassive. Finally
everyone would get down to "business." In exchange for
their presents, the donors received money, firearms, and
especially whisky. If they were not satisfied, they would
demand the return of their horses. But they left skins and
furs behind, thereby indicating their order of values.

When things went well, the two sides would decide to
fraternize. Sometimes there were even budding romances.
Some of them were serious enough for some "palefaces" to
decide to stay among the "redskins." But most whites were
satisfied to attend the dances organized in their honor; such
dances had no religious significance. The pioneers gazed
with astonishment—never imagining that white men would

some day do the same—at the silent, grave, impassive Indians tapping the ground with their feet, raising and lowering their shoulders to the beat of the tom-tom, systematically jerking their bodies so that every muscle seemed to move in unison. They found the "begging dances," or dances of reconciliation, particularly funny: they have been compared to those surprise parties which are always more fun for the organizers than for guest of honor. Former enemies would suddenly descend upon the territory of a tribe with whom they had just made peace. They would each grasp one of their former enemies, clasp him affectionately, and cut a few capers. It was customary for the recipients of these tokens of affection not only to accept them with good humor, but also to return the compliment with a present which must not be too trivial. Many tribes preferred enemy raids to these overfriendly "begging dances."

These peace games were the exception. Encounters between whites and Indians more frequently took place to the accompaniment of the whistling of bullets and arrows. At first, the Indians gave the palefaces a friendly welcome. Unfortunately, however, all the early colonizers of America were not missionaries. Many took advantage of the Indians' weakness to exploit, rob, or kill them. In their greed for land and furs, they sold the Indians alcohol and firearms. Drink awakened in those primitive beings a thirst for battle which they were driven to assuage at any price; the firearms gave them the means to do so. Good neighborly relations gradually gave place to fierce conflict. The Indians treated their enemies as aggressors and robbers; how can we say they were wrong, since the country had belonged to them for so many centuries? The colonists regarded themselves as the heralds of the future and were not prepared to tolerate the obstacles of the past—but could it have been otherwise at that stage in their development? No country has come into being by virtuous means alone, and there is always an element of cruelty in the victory of the more powerful. The case of the New World is particularly shocking, however, because of the enormous disproportion between the forces of the two sides. The extermination of the Indians is a sorry chapter in the often glorious pages of United States history.

So long as there was available territory, the problem of the coexistence of the two races remained relatively simple; it was hoped that it could be resolved by displacement. Andrew Jackson brutally carried out the policy recommended by Jefferson; from 1829 to 1837, ninety-four treaties were signed with Indian tribes and thousands of individuals were transferred—willingly or not—west of the Mississippi. Even so, there was no lack of violence. In 1832, when an Indian chief, Black Hawk, dared to cross the river in search of food, the Illinois militia (Abraham Lincoln was captain of it) indiscriminately massacred his tribe—men, women, and children. Six years later, the Cherokees, who had for centuries been settled in Georgia, learned that possession is not always nine tenths of the law. Gold was discovered in their territory. They were given $5 million and ordered to move out. The Supreme Court, under the influence of John Marshall, ruled the decision illegal, but the ruling was in vain. Vain, too, was Emerson's protest that such contempt for all faith and all virtue, such denial of justice, such refusal even to listen to the cries for pity were without precedent in human history, in time of peace, and in a country's dealings with its own allies and dependents. In 1842 the Seminole of Florida also found out that the federal government did not share the moralist's view on the Indian problem. For some years they resisted the American troops but finally gave up after their chief, Osceola, had been treacherously taken prisoner during what had ostensibly been armistice negotiations.

At the end of Jackson's second term, one of those transitory solutions had been arranged which politicans like to call permanent. Of some 350,000 Indians living between the Atlantic and the Pacific, there remained, so it is estimated, no more than 12,000 within the states themselves. The others were henceforward to live in the great plains, where the climate, many felt, was too extreme for white men. A line of demarcation, marked by military outposts and supervised by cavalry patrols, was supposed to separate redskins and palefaces, from Lake Superior to the Red River, passing through Wisconsin, Iowa, and the western frontiers of Missouri and Arkansas. Nothing remained of this administrative fiction after the great migrations of 1843 and the following years. In 1834 Congress had solemnly forbidden anyone to penetrate into Indian territory beyond the Missouri without special permission. Such formalities did not worry the pioneers at all.

Now natives and conquerors were really face to face, and the area in dispute shrank steadily. Their implacable hostility focused on three points—land, horses, buffalo. To gain possession of the land was an obsession with the pioneers; we shall refer later to the legal problems to which this occupation gave rise. The Indians stood in the way of this fierce ambition, so it seemed expedient to get rid of them. But the Indians did not always sell their lives cheaply. Scalping was not an invention of James Fenimore Cooper. It was carried out very scientifically. The operator would grab his victim, cut a circular groove around his skull, raise the skin on one side, grip it between his teeth, tear it off, and then joyfully brandish his trophy aloft. When he returned home he would give it to his wife, who would dry it over a kind of hoop and then fix it on a pole around which the hero would subsequently dance his victory dance. Many redskins liked to flay their enemies alive, and then leave them to die slowly. In 1866 the bodies of sixty-seven soldiers were found; the men had been ambushed, stripped of their clothing, scalped, gashed, and mutilated to the

point of being virtually unrecognizable. Reprisals were useless, since they were taken against men who feared neither
death nor suffering.

The Indians launched incessant and often effective
guerrilla bands against the white men. The guerrillas would
gallop up, encircle the column or camp, slide down into an
almost horizontal position on their mounts, and shoot their
arrows from under the horse's neck or over its back, which
served as cover. After they learned to use firearms, their
assaults became even more savage. They often attacked by
night. Their principal object was to steal the whites' horses
—an art in which they were past masters. This was yet
another cause for conflict between the Indians and the conquerors of the prairies. As we know, before Cortez' expedition, horses had been unknown west of the Atlantic. After
the sixteenth century, herds of wild mustang progressively
emigrated from Mexico toward the Great Plains of North
America. The Indians were quick to tame them and even
quicker to realize what valuable aid these animals would
give them in their perpetual struggle with the buffalo.

It is estimated that about a century ago there were
50 million buffalo between the Missouri and the Rockies.
The only value of the figure lies in its contrast with the
present, when the buffalo has virtually been wiped out.
More impressive than statistics are the accounts of travelers,
all of whom insist on the gigantic proportions of these
monster-like beasts: the bulls up to 11 feet long and 6 feet
high and weighing up to 2,000 pounds. All describe the
hundreds upon hundreds of buffalo which they saw, moving
in serried ranks and forming a veritable wall as far as the
eye could see. Woe to any man who found himself in the
path of a stampeding herd! A stampede was no less feared
than a hurricane. A compact animal mass would bear down
irresistibly, terrifyingly, in a direction dictated only by panic,
propelled by the instinct to escape some sensed danger.

These animals provided the Indians with everything they needed: meat for immediate consumption or to be dried for the winter in the form of pemmican; skins which they used for clothing and with which they covered their tents; tendons for their cords, threads, and bows; bones for their arrowheads and tools; pelts for their commerce with the fur traders; and even fuel.

The buffalo were naturally cautious. When grazing, they protected themselves by a row of sentinels which gave the alarm by furious bellows and wild tossings of heads and tails. At night they formed real encampments, with the cows and calves in the center and the seasoned bulls forming a ring around them, ready to repel any assault by the wolves which always pursued them. The problem for the Indians was to approach the animal within arrowshot. Then one had to aim accurately at the only point in the body where a wound would be fatal—behind the shoulder, at the inter-section between the mane and the rest of the body. If the shot reached its mark, the blood spurted up in torrents, the animal executed a few convulsive leaps, then fell to its knees, head to the ground, and died.

The white men became great experts at this game. They waged a ruthless war against the buffalo, and the number of animals slowly diminished. The Indians were the main victims of these massacres, which certainly hastened their defeat.

Even more effective as agents of Indian demoralization were syphilis, tuberculosis, firearms, corruption and, especially, whisky. The Secretary of State for War wrote as much to the governors of Missouri, Arkansas, and Iowa in 1847. He would be wasting their time, he wrote, if he reminded them of the extent of the ravages which that instrument of evil had inflicted on the red race of the continent, for they knew it as well as he did. Beyond any shadow of doubt, he added, alcohol more than any other thing was responsible for the rapid decline of that race, both morally and numerically. As an American historian puts it, what happened was that Indian civilization disintegrated, and that the Indians took little else from the whites than their vices.

Demoralized, crushed under the weight of the conquering mass, the Indians vainly recalled the solemn promises which had been made to them barely twenty years earlier. The building of the railroads and the land speculation which accompanied it rendered their claims even more intolerable. Gradually they were herded into reservations, which had some striking similarities with concentration camps. There they lived under the supervision of a federal official, the Indian agent, who was supposed to pay them an annual grant and, at least at first, to ensure them adequate food supplies. The instructions that came from Washington revealed an extraordinary lack of understanding of these unfortunates. They urged them to give up living in tents and to build cabins, to cultivate the soil (in their eyes, women's work), to dress like everyone else (sic), to cut their hair. It is hardly surprising that this forced adaptation to the American way of life did not take place without clashes.

*Chapter XIII*

# THE PRAIRIE
# CONQUERED

Now the conquerors were in possession of the territory. What would they do next?

Some, the most individualistic, became trappers. These men would be gone for months at a time, alone in the Rockies in quest of furs, leading a rude and primitive life. Certain curious traditions were associated with the occupation: hair must be worn nearly shoulder-length, but beard and whiskers were taboo, and a trapper worthy of the name must always be freshly shaven. Their dress was almost uniform: buckskin vest and pants with long fringes for draining off the rain and facilitating quick drying, and Indian-type moccasins. The trapper carried a long, heavy, single-barreled rifle, a cartridge pouch, a powder flash, and a hunting knife, as well as a hook for catching squirrels. He traveled with two or three horses, which carried the rest of his equipment. He fed almost exclusively on what he hunted. When the trapper was lucky enough to kill a buffalo or a bear, he cut it up according to strict rules: the skin was stripped off and spread on the ground, fur side up; it served as a recipient for the meat, which was cut up into long strips, plunged into pickling brine, and hung up in the sun. After four or five days, it became hard, black, and dried out. It was known as "carna seca" or "jerky," and served as reserve provender. When trappers wearied of this type of food, they granted themselves a week's relaxation at some outpost of civilization in the upper valleys of the Platte or the Missouri. Orgies and primitive debauches fully satisfied their not very complex natures.

Trappers had become scarcer by the middle of the century. The newcomers increasingly preferred the role of settlers. The process of installation was always much the same. Some daring individual began by "occupying" the land. He arrived alone or with his family. His capital consisted of a horse, a cow, a wagon, some tools. His first job was to clear the ground. Poor trees! Any method would serve to chop them down or destroy them. Once the land was more or less cleared, the new arrivals built a temporary shelter. They were particularly concerned to sow corn and to lay out vegetable gardens, from which they hoped to harvest potatoes, cabbages, beans, cucumbers.

Then a second wave of pioneers would turn up, usually with more funds. The needed investment was estimated at $1,000 to $1,500. They bought land, built log cabins, opened up dirt roads, built bridges. Speculators and entrepreneurs followed later. Plots of land changed hands, their price rose. Here and there villages emerged.

The great difficulty was to define property rights. Did the land belong automatically to the first occupant? The problem was always a controversial one. As early as 1785 a federal ordinance established the principle that the territories west of the Alleghenies and north of the Ohio would constitute public domain pending the creation of other states; land there might be sold at a minimum price of $1 per acre, in lots of 640 acres. In 1796 the price was raised to $2, but for the benefit of pioneers of smaller means it was provided that the lots might be variable in size. Twenty-four years later, after the panic of 1819, the rules of sale were again modified: $1.25 and a minimum of 80 acres.

When Jackson took office, the question had become a burning one. The West favored a policy of cheap land to encourage settlement. The North and South opposed it, fearing the impact on the Atlantic seaboard of too heavy an emigration. The debate rose to the constitutional level: once more some effort must be made to define states' rights as against the rights of the federal government. It led, on January 26, 1830, to the famous speech of Daniel Webster, who asserted, with burning eloquence, the inalienable pre-eminence of the Union. More practically, two new principles were adopted that year: the price of $1.25 would be progressively reduced if the land remained without a purchaser for a certain time; in addition, *de facto* occupants of land which was ordered sold would have the right to preempt it at a minimum price.

Mass migrations rendered the problem even more complex. The established settlers eyed the host of intruders with hostility; as for the latter, they had not endured all the hardships of the trek to be denied their place in the sun. Disputes proliferated; speculation, too. George Henry Evans and Horace Greely put forward the idea of a "homestead," or inalienable family property, which would be granted free to every settler; Congress refused to adopt it in 1846, although five years earlier it had voted a measure which was very similar. (The Log Cabin Bill of 1841 had in fact authorized every citizen who owned at least 320 acres of land to appropriate 160 acres of public land and subsequently to pay the minimum price of $1.25 for it.) The development came to its logical conclusion during the Civil War. In 1862, it was finally decided that every occupant of over five years' standing should be entitled to own and work an 160-acre homestead on condition of paying a nominal price.

Can any description of the West omit the cowboys? Actually, these perennial heroes of the Western films were few in number before the Civil War. It was the Mexicans who taught the Americans, after the war of 1846, the art of lassoing and branding cattle. The practice began to spread between 1850 and 1860. At that time, a few cowboys (known as cowpunchers) were to be found in the West, and particularly in Texas, garbed in what was destined to be their legendary attire. Each item of their clothing was functional. The ten-gallon hat served a variety of purposes: it was an umbrella in rainy weather, a protection against the sun, a hood when it was cold, a pillow at night, a drinking vessel. The kerchief served as a protection against dust and the burning heat of the sun. The high boots were made with narrow heels so that the foot would not get caught in the stirrup in case of a fall, and to help the cowboy grip the ground in case he lassoed an animal on foot. The pockets of the riding breeches were very deep so that their contents would not spill if the rider was thrown. Finally, there was the saddle, every detail of which was designed with the utmost care: it was heavy and wide to the point of covering almost half the horse's back, with a raised pommel surmounted by a roughly perpendicular knob which enabled the rider to tighten the lasso, and it had wooden stirrups, encased in leather, to protect the rider's boots from thorny bushes and cactuses.

The cowboys lived in primitive "ranchos" consisting of cabins with bunk beds, a barn, and a shed, all this surrounded by barriers. When they rounded up the cattle and brought them home from their pastures, two or three chuck wagons followed them with cooking stove and provisions. Their three mortal enemies were the rustlers, who stole horses and cattle, the settlers, who limited their freedom of movement, and sheep, which ruined good pastures with their deplorable feeding habits.

The properties in Southern California were far more aristocratic. They were vast ranches which had usually been in the same family for several generations and were often staffed by hundreds of servants who lived on the premises, rather as in a medieval feudal estate. All trades were plied there. In each establishment a "majordomo," accompanied by a "corporal" and ten or twenty assistants, or "vaqueros," periodically inventoried the grazing herds and horses. The rodeo originated here—a spectacle whose popularity in America today may be compared with that of the bullfight in Spain.

Cowboys, settlers, trappers were not particularly disposed to submit to authority. Authority was useful, they felt, only in a local and strictly limited context. Somewhat in the manner of the Germanic tribes, they made personal loyalty the basis for all authority and all obedience. In any case, during the actual migrations, questions of government did not arise. Each column, as we have said, had its own leader, and he would settle any problems that arose, in a spirit of purest pragmatism.

This individualistic and empirical approach proved inadequate when so many of the pioneers turned from a nomadic to a sedentary existence. Most of them, it is true, lived on isolated farms and had little contact with the outside world. Nevertheless, a number of villages gradually grew up, and even some small towns. A minimum of law and law enforcement became indispensable. Had no provision been made for such situations, the West might have collapsed in helpless anarchy. Fortunately for the United States, the young Republic had from the outset foreseen the consequence of its inevitable expansion. The Northwest

Ordinance of 1787 had included clear provisions for the administration of the lands beyond the Alleghenies, toward which a migratory movement was bound to develop sooner or later. At first, they were to be administered by governors appointed by the President. But this intervention of the federal government would be only temporary. As soon as a region included 5,000 free men of voting age, it would be authorized to elect an assembly and to send a representative to Congress, but without voting rights. When the territory attained a population of 60,000 it would be entitled to adopt a constitution, form a state, and request its admission to the Union on a footing of complete equality. That was how, between 1787 and the Civil War, Vermont, Kentucky, Tennessee, Ohio, Louisiana, Indiana, Illinois, Alabama, Mississippi, Maine, Missouri, Arkansas, Michigan, Florida, Texas, Wisconsin, California, Minnesota, Oregon, Iowa, and Kansas added twenty-one stars to the United States flag.

The West soon had its folklore, its braggarts and its heroes, its chroniclers and its poets. It developed an egalitarian spirit through the force of circumstance. Common perils and ambitions created an identity of sentiments and interests among the pioneers. In those endless plains, alone with nature, they felt a bond of kinship and a sense of dependency on one another. So long as the land stretched on seemingly without limits, they found more grounds for cooperation than for rivalry. Gradually, of course, the jealousies and rivalries inherent in all human groups reappeared. But for a time, at least, a real solidarity prevailed. Each column left directions along the way for the columns that followed. At halting stages, information about camp sites or difficult routes would be exchanged, as well as views on methods of dealing with the Indians. The women contributed powerfully to the creation of this common mentality. Some showed real heroism; all had energy and patience.

Often they would have to remain for days on end, isolated in their wretched dwellings, waiting for their husbands to return from a hunting or a fishing expedition. They therefore did all they could to develop habits of neighborliness. The success of the revivals, for example, must be largely attributed to the women folk.

Everything served as an occasion for getting together. Some gatherings were motivated by a very strong sense of cooperation: thus it was traditional to help one's neighbors —often living at a great distance—when they built their cabins or barns, or when they were sick and unable to cultivate their fields. At other times, work was merely a pretext. The settlers would all husk corn together, and the person who found a red kernel might claim a kiss from his neighbor. They arranged to peel potatoes together, to collect maple syrup together, and all this was occasion for endless chatter. These gatherings often concluded with juvenile games; "Blind Man's Buff" and "Pop Goes the Weasel" were the most popular. The men's chief passion was foot racing, wrestling, weight- and dumbbell-lifting contests, cockfighting. The women were equally passionately addicted to square dancing.

All these gatherings, furthermore, gave the women a chance to show off their culinary talents. They did not claim to be chefs for connoisseurs, but they would have felt themselves disgraced if they had been unable to prepare the standard feast which concluded the social events of the West: barbecued beef or pork, buffalo tongue, roast opossum, boiled corn meal, corn fritters fried in bear oil—all this washed down with much-needed whisky. The alcohol loosened tongues. There were raucous bursts of laughter and crude jokes embellished with many superlatives, in a dialect of incredible richness, but which would not have been approved by the gentry of New England.

Above all, it was the chosen hour for the tall-story

teller. Needless to say, hunting expeditions furnished him
with the essential material for his talents. "Two thousand
squirrels killed in one day, not by buckshot, but by the
vibrations created in the air by the shot as it skimmed past
the animals without touching them. . . ." "Sixty bears,
twenty-five bucks, one hundred wild turkeys—all the result
of a single day's hunt." The greater the exaggerations, the
better these naïve audiences were pleased. They never wearied of listening to the standard jokes: about the man, for
instance, who was so tall that he needed a razor to shave
himself; the clipper that sailed so fast, it left its shadow
three and a half miles behind it; the runner who got the
best of bears by making them run until completely winded;
the boat that was so flat it needed only a good dew to sail
the prairie. Before any combat, a challenge must be delivered in the Homeric manner. To hear some of these heroes,
they were prepared to tear the other man's eyes out, twist
his thumbs, break his hand, tear his nose and eyelids to
shreds with their teeth. Mark Twain tells how he heard two
men engaged in such an interminable verbal duel on a
Missouri boat, in the course of which they appeared on the
point of bludgeoning one another to death. When it became
clear, he continues, that neither intended to go beyond
words, the very smallest man on board calmly walked up to
them and without a word gave each of them a solid punch.

As in all epics, reality was embellished by legend. Imaginary exploits were added to genuine ones—although there
was no lack of genuine ones—to the fascination and delight
of the listeners. Daniel Boone in the eighteenth century,
Uncle Dick Wootton, Davy Crocket, Kit Carson, in the
nineteenth, became symbols of the "prairie spirit," com-
pounded of courage and ferocity, of devotion and cynicism,
of disinterestedness and harshness, of gravity and humor.
Davy Crocket was the hero of what was wittily called "coon-

skin democracy." The man of the great open spaces was contrasted with city politicians, and the Whigs used his name in the 1840 "log cabin campaign" to get Harrison elected. Nothing was lacking in his legend—he even died in defense of the Alamo against the Mexicans in 1830. His autobiography is a frontier classic. Kit Carson's—according to his publisher—reveals him as "a veritable Bayard of the nineteenth century." Poor Bayard—his knight's life sounds very tame compared with that of the adventurer of the prairies. Yet to anyone without pioneering blood in his veins, Kit Carson's extraordinary adventures (lying wounded in the open, his blood freezing as it leaves his body; attacked by an Indian, whom he scalps and kills; and so on) are unbearably monotonous. James Fenimore Cooper is preferable.

*The Last of the Mohicans* appeared in 1826, and was followed by an abundant literature, sometimes realistic, sometimes romantic, dedicated to the glory of the pioneers. In his *Georgia Scenes*, published in 1835 and 1840, Augustus B. Longstreet, who was later to be president of the universities of Mississippi and South Carolina, humorously described the primitive ways of frontier life. William T. Porter's *The Spirit of the Times* and Thomas Chandler Haliburton's *The Traits of American Humor* and *The Americans at Home* (published under the pseudonym Sam Slick) were also great successes in the libraries of the day. In a more sentimental vein, Rufus B. Sage's *Romantic Glimpse of the West*, Timothy Flint's *Daniel Boone*, James Hall's historical studies, and especially Emerson Bennett's *Prairie Flower* which sold 100,000 copies in 1849) were enthusiastically received by the reading public. With the appearance of the dime novel, the prairie was made familiar to the population as a whole. It was left to Mark Twain, Bret Harte, and "Uncle Josh Billings" (Henry Wheeler Shaw)—especially after the Civil War—to highlight the humorous aspects of the great adventure.

# Chapter XIV
# THE GOLD RUSH

James Wilson Marshall was a pioneer like the rest. Born in 1810 in New Jersey, he decided, when he was about thirty, to try his luck in the West as so many of his contemporaries had done. He went farther than most of them and settled in California in 1845. There he met John Augustus Sutter, a Mexican citizen whose birthplace was even farther away than the Atlantic seaboard. He had left his native Grand Duchy of Baden in 1834, attracted, like many other Germans, by the mysterious New World. He had not remained long in the East. He had gone first to Santa Fe, then Oregon. He had finally landed in California in 1839 and had founded a colony there, on the site of what is now Sacramento. He and Marshall formed a partnership in the operation of a sawmill. Little did they know what awaited them. If they had only known! On January 24, 1848, some strange pebbles were observed at the bottom of a mill course which brought water to their mill. They had an unusual sheen. The two partners held their breath: could it be gold? The idea was not absurd, for small quantities of the metal had in fact been found in California. The nuggets were submitted to experts, who were unanimous in identifying them as gold.

The magnitude of the discovery speedily became apparent. The wondrous metal seemed to turn up everywhere. Here the story takes a sad twist; or perhaps it teaches a lesson. Marshall and Sutter were abandoned by their workers, who set off to seek their individual El Dorados; their cattle were stolen from them; their property was invaded and occupied by squatters. Marshall ended his life in poverty and madness. Sutter went bankrupt; in the last years of his life the state of California granted him a pension of $250 to save him from destitution.

News of the gold did not reach the East until the end of the summer, and was received with skepticism. Nevertheless, the evidence accumulated and, strangely enough, was consistent. In September the New York *Journal of Commerce* published a letter providing details calculated to convince even the most incredulous.

Official confirmation arrived three months later. Two detailed reports left California in August. The first, from the governor to the Department of War, was accompanied by a box of gold dust and nuggets. The second was brought to Mexico by an officer of the federal troops. These two documents left no doubt about the veracity of the previous reports. So far Washington had maintained a prudent reserve—the attestation of miracles demands reflection—but now hesitation was no longer possible. President James Polk officially proclaimed the news to Congress on December 5, almost apologizing for so unexpected a message. The reports received on the rich gold deposits, he explained, had been so extraordinary that it would be hard to give them the slightest credence had they not been corroborated by *bona fide* reports from responsible officials.

His words spread like wildfire through the Union. The skeptics, a few months earlier, had talked of Aladdin and his magic lamp; now they bought "goldometers" at $3 apiece, purported to be capable of uncovering gold wherever deposits existed. The most enthusiastic set out right away. Winter made the continent impassable. There were two possible maritime routes: (1) via Central America, crossing Mexico, Nicaragua or, preferably, the isthmus of Panama, and (2) around Cape Horn. The latter was safer, but excessively long: it sometimes took as long as a year from New York to San Francisco. The other route was much shorter—at most, seven weeks; on the other hand, the Panama route entailed grave risks. Yellow fever and cholera were very prevalent, and there was often a wait of one or two months for transportation on the Pacific coast. Both routes had their partisans. In any case, there was usually no choice at all. Within a few weeks of the President's message, there was not a place available in a boat on the Atlantic coast. Soon the aspiring conquerors of Californian gold had to resign themselves to being herded on deck like slaves. Although a year later, at the end of 1849, the travel fever had begun to abate, Bayard Taylor, who was going to California for the *New York Tribune*, reported that his boat was packed with such mobs of people that it was practically impossible to take the slightest exercise, and as for trying to sleep, that, every night, was an adventure!

With the return of fair weather, the land routes attracted most of the prospectors. The movement took on the proportions of an avalanche. It is estimated that in two years some 100,000 persons set out on the adventure. The risks and dangers of the trek meant little to this "golden army," this horde of people united only by their passion for gold. Every class was represented: peasants, industrial workers, office clerks; rich, poor, young, old—even members of the clergy, who abandoned their churches at the call of

Mammon. Fierce rivalry predominated: this time there was no question of sharing the seemingly limitless spaces of the prairie; gold deposits, it was well known, were not inexhaustible. Woe to the man who allowed himself to be outdistanced! Repugnant incidents occurred, of a kind unknown among the earlier pioneers. One traveler, for example, would spoil food which he was unable to take along with him rather than leave it for someone else. Another—a small-size Attila—would burn the grass behind him as he went; he was caught and put to death. Others used less brutal methods. They would be assisted by white women, "diabolically seductive under their rough clothing" with the result that their rivals sometimes forgot even the lure of gold. They would be led to some deserted place, where they were well and truly robbed.

Nevertheless, such incidents were rare, and most of the prospectors arrived at their destination safe and sound, for the routes were now sufficiently well known. The journey would normally take some sixteen or seventeen weeks, either along the Oregon Trail, which the traveler would leave in the upper reaches of the Snake to follow the California Trail to the southwest, or along the Santa Fe Trail, which had the disadvantage of leading to Southern California. In both cases it was necessary to go through deserts, of which even less was known in those days than about the Sahara. For scores of miles, there was no hope of finding water. The traveler would walk on endlessly through empty, burning spaces where the only living things were herds of antelope and deer, jaguars, coyotes, and foxes, and above all innumerable scorpions, snakes, and lizards. And overhead he might see a few quail, or some screechowls, and an occasional eagle. Another trail—a more direct one—crossed Colorado and Utah. Its disadvantage was that it passed through Mormon territory. Having been forbidden by their leader to take part in the Gold Rush, Brigham Young's followers

did not feel like smoothing the way for their more emancipated brethren. They charged travelers very stiff prices for
food and directions and levied tolls at fords. One trading
practice was particularly profitable: they would exchange
one animal in good condition for three which were travel-
weary; then they would put those animals out to graze and,
once they were in shape again, repeat the deal in the same
proportion of three to one.

The prospectors tolerated these practices without too
much bitterness. At the Great Salt Lake, the proximity of
the "Promised Land" blotted out injustices and misfortunes.
When things were going too badly, they would console
themselves by singing their favorite song:

> Oh! the Good Time has come at last
> We need no more complain, Sir,
> The rich can live in luxury,
> And the poor can do the same, Sir,
> For the Good Time has come at last.
> And as we all are told, Sir,
> We shall be rich at once now,
> With California gold, Sir.

Often, too, they would adapt the "O Susanna" of their
predecessors to their own circumstances;

> Oh! California,
> That's the land for me;
> I'm off for Sacramento,
> With my washbowl on my knee.

The song, actually, was hardly an exaggeration of their
feelings. Many believed, at first, that a little luck and a
"washbowl" would suffice to make their fortune. Their
equipment consisted merely of a shovel, a rough sieve to
eliminate the top layer of earth, and one or two wooden
bowls for washing the sand. Some contented themselves with
scraping stream beds with a knife.

Improved methods soon became necessary. The gold sometimes lay under rocks. Lying flat on his back, the prospector would slide painfully into an opening little larger than his body and hack at the rock above him, bringing down upon himself a rain of stone and—he hoped—nuggets. Nevertheless, those who worked in the open envied such miners, for in summer, in the gorges, where most of the deposits lay, the temperature often exceeded 100°F.

Native Indians excelled at separating gold from earth. They would simply pick up the sand in a vessel, lift the vessel up, and slowly empty it into a blanket spread out at their feet. After the operation had been repeated a few times, the miraculous dust would have been at least partially cleaned. Then, placing the bowl in one hand, they would rotate it so fast that the heavier grains of sand and small pebbles it might still contain would be tossed up into the air; these they would catch, carefully heap them together, and later extract the nuggets.

There was hardly a country that was not represented in California. Alongside Americans from all parts of the continent there were Mexicans, Chinese (Chinese pagans, they were called by the rest; they kept to themselves, eating their rice in silence and cutting each other's hair as a form of entertainment), South Americans, Europeans of every nationality. (One of the most extraordinary adventures was that of eighteen Basques who came on horseback all the way from Argentina; it took them a year and a half to reach California.)

The French came in relatively large numbers—of the total 25,000, about two-fifths, it is estimated, came from France. The news from California had aroused intense interest in Paris, coming as it did after the financial crisis of the early days of the Second Republic. Many associations, some ideological, others more concerned with gain, were formed to exploit the resources of this new cornucopia. To judge by statements recorded in the official *Journal des Débats*, the gold fields extended over an area at least 800 miles long and 100 miles wide—certainly matter enough to whet appetites and excite imaginations. A Daumier sketch shows two shareholders heatedly arguing over the respective merits of the "Society of California Twenty-Franc Pieces" and the "Society of the Golden Carrot." The flow of departures from France was highest in 1849 and the beginning of 1850. It slowed down after a monster lottery (6,200,000 tickets at 1 franc each) was organized to enable Frenchmen to rely on luck as well as on adventure to acquire some of the precious metal. The proceeds of the operation enabled the public authorities to send to California some more or less desirable elements, whose imperfect knowledge of English immediately earned them the nickname of "Keskydees" (a phonetic rendering of the question *"qu'est-ce qu'il dit?"*—What is he saying?—which the Frenchmen must constantly have been asking).

The average gold digger was dressed in classic pioneer fashion: red or blue woolen shirt, coarse cloth trousers tucked into heavy boots, and low-crowned, wide-brimmed hat; he carried a pistol in his belt and a big hunting knife, known as a Bowie knife, in his right boot. Hair and beard were worn long. The correct gait was a casual slouch. Contrasting with this standard uniform were a few Panama hats, boldly worn by anticonformist Central Americans, and even top hats, symbolizing the scruples that must have been bothering "respectable" members of the middle class who suddenly found themselves catapulted—almost in spite of themselves—into the Californian adventure.

Living quarters were more than primitive. At first there was nothing but tents, but it quickly became apparent that even the best canvas gave little shelter in the rainy season. Gradually, therefore, wretched cabins were put up, with chimneys made somehow or other out of stones and dried mud; when the weather was too bad, the apertures were stopped up with rags and blankets. Later, whole groups of such dwellings made up those Gold Rush villages immortalized by Charlie Chaplin.

During the first phase of the Gold Rush, honesty and good fellowship seem to have prevailed in these villages, and law and order was maintained by elected committees which served both as police and magistrature. When fortunes began to be made—while at the same time the field of expectations narrowed—passions could no longer be held in check. Fights were frequent and often ended very badly. As for punishing the guilty—usually the strongest—that was rarely possible. Local folklore, reflecting this wave of violence, has preserved some real bogeyman tales on the subject. None can equal that of the terrifying "Keating," who spends his winters in the freezing mountains, feeding on the flesh of his erstwhile companions, whose bodies he carries with him. He is finally discovered, alone, like a vampire, surrounded by corpses, his face and hands streaming with blood, and a cauldron of human flesh bubbling over a wood fire at his side!

Local diversions were not always so spine-tingling. Their principal elements were drinking and gambling. Tossing off champagne was a success symbol which was generously employed. It was not unusual to find prospectors eating their frugal meal of barely cooked meat or fish, and washing it down with champagne at $10 a bottle. "Buckshot"—another legendary character, but of a more amiable type than Keating—was said to have spent on drink the whole of the $30,000 or $40,000 which he had earned prospecting. He belonged to the race of solitary drinkers, and never invited anyone. Perhaps he was taking his revenge; the story would not be complete if it did not go on to tell that in his previous life he had been a barman.

For many, there was something quite unreal in the sudden acquisition of all this money. They had got it by some kind of miracle, and they saw it disappear without undue surprise. Poker games were not the only road to ruin. The prospectors speculated on everything, and overnight the "new rich" could find themselves as poor as they had been before. The wiser ones divided their wealth in two. The part acquired before they discovered gold, and which was the product of years of labor, was sacred; they did not risk it in uncertain schemes and relied on it as a last resort in case of misfortune. And they curbed their ambitions knowing that, one day or another, ambition would lead them to disaster. It was a sign of good judgment not to stay in California too long. When the wives came along, they urged their husbands to move out of the "Promised Land." In any case, they did not have much fun there, and had few opportunities for spending money. Sandy Bowers was right: "There ain't no chance for a gentleman to spend his coin in this country, an' so me an' Mrs. Bowers is goin' to Yoorup!" Lucky Mr. Bowers, to have such a sensible wife at his side! Everyone was not similarly blessed, and the lack of women was very strongly felt.

Women were so rare that one would have thought they were a species in process of extinction. When the gold prospectors saw one, they could hardly believe their eyes. It is estimated that as late as 1850, there was not one woman for every ten men in California. And in any case, they were unlikely to venture near the mining operations. One, however—a good businesswoman—did venture to cross such an area in a covered wagon; 3,000 miners each paid $1 to raise the canvas of her wagon so that they could look at her. No effort was too much for these knights of courtly love if they could only—even for a moment—breathe a feminine atmosphere; one man traveled some thirty miles only to set eyes on the woman companion of one of his friends. The arrival of a man bold enough to bring his wife into the camp touched off unparalleled excitement. The next morning, pistol shots saluted the dawn. To those who were unaware of the great event it was explained: "A flesh-and-blood woman spent the night in this very tent!" The "sanctuary" was soon surrounded by a turbulent crowd; a man came out, looking rather worried. He was informed of the community's desires: "Friend, we still know that we were born of women, but it's so long since we saw one that we can't even remember what they look like. It seems you've managed to hook one. We'd like to do some prospecting. Would you agree to show her to us?" The husband, according to this eyewitness to the scene, was a man of good sense; he agreed to the request and showed them "the animal" (sic). We are not told what happened next.

In any case, platonic diversions were not to the taste of most of these seekers of violent sensations who had responded to the call of gold. Soon prostitutes from all parts of the world streamed to California. They constituted a formidable challenge to the local señoritas, splendid fandango dancers, in black silk stockings and white muslin dresses, who for a time had had a corner on that kind of market. Whenever a boat arrived, "experts" would send the captain a message in Morse code: "Are there any women aboard?" If the answer was affirmative, it was good to know in advance, since local prices were likely to be adversely affected. This type of business, however, despite continued imports, remained very profitable for several years. A French contemporary deplored American naïveté in this respect: "If only those poor fellows knew how these women lived in Paris, and how they could be picked up in the streets, they wouldn't be so crazy as to offer them $500 or $600 just to spend one night with them!"

San Francisco rapidly became a fashionable city. In 1848 it was no more than a village. The discovery of gold began by ruining its harbor; boats, abandoned by their crews, simply lay there rotting. But soon swarms of people began to arrive: emigrants reaching their final destination, local prospectors who had already made good. They had to be housed: cabins mushroomed; then houses. Wild speculation accompanied their construction. Land brokers were fond of telling the story of two of their clients whose father had died leaving $40,000 in debts, but also a well-situated piece of land. They had wisely done whatever they could to delay a settlement of the estate. Finally, after discouraging the creditors, they had found themselves with an income of $40,000 as a result of the prodigious rise in land values.

Food supplies, at first, were a serious problem; many products were simply not to be found and had to be imported at fantastic prices. Eggs, at one point, cost $10 a dozen, and a plate of the stock "ham 'n' eggs" cost $3.

The road system long remained primitive. In 1849 there was not even a semblance of a system. In winter the roads were mere rivers of mud; it was not uncommon to see unfortunate animals, or no less unfortunate human beings, sunk in a brownish liquid to the neck. These extreme conditions improved later, but up to above 1855 there were no paved roads at all. The young city was prey to incessant fires.

In those days, most shelters were in the form of tents, and at night the city lights shone through the tent cloth, turning the city into a dazzling display of lights. The substitution of wood for tent cloth did little to reduce the danger, but soon excellent volunteer fire services were formed; in San Francisco, as elsewhere, they responded with as much zeal as pleasure at the news that a fire had broken out.

Gradually, in response to the demand, the refinements of living began to be introduced. Shops were opened with window displays containing luxury articles previously unknown west of the Rockies. One such shop, which still exists, was founded by a Frenchman, Félix Verdier, in 1850, and specialized in merchandise from Paris. It became a sign of breeding to intersperse a few French words in the conversation. Fashionable ladies were always talking of *"haut ton"* (breeding), and rakes loved to seduce *"les petites dames"* (the little ladies) who arrived from France, taking them up to the *"cabinets particuliers"* (private rooms) on the first floor of fashionable restaurants. To a lady of *haut ton* who had been curious enough to accept such an invitation, but cautious enough not to lose her head, a Don Juan severely recalled the rules of the game: "You must know, Madame, that no woman has ever gone up the stairs of a French restaurant in order to say her prayers!" In short, people were learning the arts of civilization.

Yachting and riding contests soon began to take the place of bear fights and bull races. Women strutted about in crinolines and wore jewels which bore but faint resemblance to nuggets. The men vied with each other in elegance: checkered trousers, fancy waistcoat, long frock coat, wide-brimmed hat; and they had no objection at all to rings, watch chains, and charms, all as huge and ostentatious as possible. Duels became common. The arrival of Lola Montez gave gilded youth all the opportunities it desired to prove its mastery. The former mistress of Ludwig of Bavaria affected dazzling silk gowns, short black velvet coats, and enormous hats trimmed with lace which floated behind her. It was enough to turn one's head! The precursors of modern Café Society thronged to her receptions at Grass Valley. Respectable women frequented less mixed gatherings. All were present at the splendid affair organized in 1854 to celebrate the introduction of gaslight. A gallant master of ceremonies proposed an irresistible toast: "To the women of San Francisco, whose eyes alone are capable of eclipsing the gaslight!" After such wit, it could no longer be doubted that "breeding" had definitely come into its own.

California was not the only part of the West to experience the intoxication of precious metals. In 1859 there was a stampede to Colorado at the report—much exaggerated—that gold deposits had been discovered there. A year later the movement was to Montana. In both cases, disappointments were more plentiful than successes.

On the other hand, the Nevada silver mines, which began to be worked at about the same date, led to the making of immense fortunes. They were developed systematically; it was no longer a case of individual prospectors armed with a pick and a sieve. Powerful companies were formed which introduced mechanical processes unknown to their predecessors. (The machines were so expensive that people said that one had to own a gold mine in order to be able to work a silver mine!) The results were even more impressive. Riches sprang up from the soil at an even more rapid rate. Horace Greeley—author of the famous exhortation "Go west, young man"—proceeded to follow his own advice. The Hearsts owe their wealth to the silver of Nevada. For a time, Comstock Lodge was as famous as the Sacramento valley. Mark Twain has left a picturesque description of Virginia City, the headquarters of the silver rush: firemen, brass bands, barrel organs; hotels, theatres; gambling dens open to everyone; parades, political harangues; street fights; murders, investigations; uprisings; a whisky factory every few steps.

The games in vogue were "monte," faro, poker, and roulette. Women often acted as croupiers. Winners and losers met, according to their tastes, either in the "two-bit houses" or in a bar with a mahogany counter facing a long mirror, with dazzling chandeliers and walls decorated with flashy pictures in heavy gilt frames. There was conversation, singing, and especially dancing.

Again, we find some of those extraordinary characters of adventurers emerging with which California had swarmed in 1849. Two of them quickly became legendary—both, oddly enough, women. Lillie Hitchcock was a young lady "of good family" with a passion for the fire service. She never missed a fire. The rest of the time she drove her own four-horse carriage, played poker, fired her revolver, and wore wigs to match the color of her dresses; worst of all, she smoked! Despite so many eccentricities, it is asserted that she remained "a lady." Such an adjective was the last thing "Old Charlie" Parkhurst—or "One-Eyed Charlie"—would have cared about. He drove stagecoaches at breakneck speed, and his passengers at least had the consolation of knowing when the road was going to be dangerous: they would see him chewing tobacco plugs of such dimensions as to force their admiration. "Old Charlie" liked whisky too; on payday, his capacity for soaking up that liquid was quite phenomenal. People never quite knew what to expect with him. And he went on surprising them to the very end. After his death, "he" was discovered to have been a woman, and a woman who had known childbirth.

Very appropriately, "One-Eyed Charlie" had been an employee of Wells Fargo—legendary names in the saga of the West! Both were natives of states on the Atlantic seaboard; together, they foresaw the role that transportation would play in the progressive settlement of the territories beyond the Mississippi. They organized the American Express in 1850 and, two years later, the company which bore their name. Through a series of mergers worthy of a Rockefeller, they soon possessed a *de facto* monopoly. Their activities were many and various: they were carriers, hotel keepers, bankers, money changers, brokers, guides, and even musicians, having their own orchestra. They provided body guards for anyone who so desired; when Lola Montez ventured into the mines, she had a Wells Fargo man accompany her, in silk suit and top hat, with a double-barreled gun slung across his back. This was a good advertising stunt, but in many other cases the firearms were not mere stage props. When Wells Fargo men served as postal couriers, and especially when they weighed and transported the freshly mined gold, a couple of pistols were by no means superfluous equipment.

*Chapter XV*

# PLANTATIONS AND SLAVERY

Atmosphere, ways of life, problems—everything was different in the South, even stripped of the usual aura of legend.

Here, everything revolved around cotton. Toward the close of the eighteenth century, the discovery of mechanical processes permitted the rapid development of the cotton industry. Cotton growing became far more important than tobacco, rice, cane sugar, or indigo, hitherto the principal money earners of the region. From South Carolina and Georgia, where cotton growing had at first been concentrated, it gradually covered Alabama and Mississippi, occupying the valley of the great river as far as Memphis, and then continuing on its right bank, along the Red River, through Louisiana and even into a part of Texas. The sugar plantations around New Orleans, the tobacco plantations in Kentucky, the more varied crops in North Carolina, and some wheat in Virginia were about the only exceptions to the monopoly of cotton.

In 1820 the crop was 320,000 bales of 500 pounds each; in ten years it had quadrupled; in 1850 it was over 2 million

bales; on the eve of the Civil War it consisted of more than
4.5 million bales, and corresponded to three-fifths of the
value of American exports. This indicates the degree to
which the social structure and ways of life of the South
were influenced by "King Cotton." Its kingdom was separated from the North by the imaginary Mason-Dixon line,
extending from the southwest border of Pennsylvania to the
town of Newcastle, Delaware. Baltimore was within the
South; Philadelphia was outside it. It is estimated that at
the time of secession, 8 million whites and 4 million Negroes
lived in that immense territory, approximately as extensive
as Western Europe excluding Scandinavia and Italy.

Over three-fourths of the white population were not
dependent on slavery. They constituted a class of independent peasants who sometimes owned the soil but more
often cultivated it as tenant farmers or farm laborers. Some
2 million persons depended in different degrees for their
livelihood on the plantations themselves. A very small minority—some 350,000 persons—owned all the slaves, that is,
according to the 1860 census, some 3,838,765 persons. Small
estates were the rule: 250,000 planters had fewer than 10
slaves; 68,000 had only one; 1,500 had over 100; 250—the
local aristocracy, most often of recent origin (Jefferson
Davis' parents had lived in a log cabin)—had over 200, nine
had between 500 and 1,000, and only two had over 1,000.

The Negro population had increased fivefold since the
beginning of the century, and its population density was
particularly great in Virginia, South Carolina, the Georgia
coast, Alabama, the valleys of the Mississippi and the Red
River, and around the Texan ports. In these areas Negroes
made up 50 per cent or more of the population. The per-
centage declined progressively in the more northerly and
westerly regions. On the frontiers of King Cotton, it was
often under 10 per cent.

A handful of Negroes who had managed to buy their

freedom—about 200,000 of them—theoretically enjoyed the status of free men. In fact, they led a miserable existence. They were forced to wear a special badge, to register, to deposit a bond. They lived in special districts, were excluded from all public office, enjoyed no civil rights, and found a thousand obstacles placed in the way of their education. They earned their living as best they could as agricultural or unskilled laborers. Frequently, such men were kidnapped and returned to slavery.

New Orleans was an exception to this rule. There the "free colored" were treated far more humanely. Some achieved a sufficient degree of culture to be recognized as specialists in the French-language poetry which flourished in Louisiana in that period. Many were wealthy; born of a *liaison* between a white man and an "octoroon" (one of those beautiful ladies with barely a trace of Negro blood in their veins who served as mistresses to the dandies of the day), their fathers had often left them substantial fortunes.

Life in the South has been much romanticized. In fact, any generalized description would give a very distorted picture of it. There was very little in common between life on a large plantation and on one of the farms which made up the greater part of the agricultural holdings.

Let us take a look first at the vast estates—those which belonged to a mere handful of owners. These owners were certainly aristocrats, nor had they any doubts on that score; there was much, indeed, that was purely feudal about their position. They did not repudiate the liberty cherished by their ancestors, creators of the Declaration of Independence, but regarded it mainly as a justification for their privileges. They felt—not unreasonably—more civilized than most of their fellow citizens, and they prided themselves on the fact. Some could boast of a family tree over 200 years old, and they always liked to recall that Virginia had been the first of the thirteen colonies. They prized traditions, in which they found the justification for their own existence, and they tended to regard them as immutable. "Honor" was their code; it entailed living up to one's pledges, carrying out one's civil responsibilities (as conceived by the gentry of that place and time), and practicing a courtesy which lent their hospitality its incomparable charm. They were lavish in their external attentions to the ladies; not to have given a woman one's place in a stagecoach would have been regarded as an unpardonable breach of etiquette. For their "belles," or the "ladies of their heart," they eagerly fought duels, especially in Louisiana, under the influence of French customs. These nineteenth-century knights did not shrink from brutality, however. They considered it a sign of breeding to explode in violent rages and not always to confine such rages to mere words. Senator Charles Summer of Massachusetts learned this the hard way on May 22, 1856. Three days before, he had made a speech passionately denouncing slavery; in particular, he had attacked—very crudely and not very fairly—one of his fellow senators from South Carolina, Andrew Butler. The latter's nephew, Preston Brooks, violently assaulted Summer with his cane right on the Senate floor, striking him unconscious; Summer never recovered completely. The "exterminating angel" was given a triumphant welcome on his return to the South, and his admirers showered him with canes, on which they had taken care to have their names engraved.

The Southern gentlemen were, first and foremost, landowners. The church, the army, and the law were the only careers they felt able to embrace without indignity. Business for them was forbidden territory. Their crops were financed and sold by Yankees and Europeans; even the local stores were often run by foreigners. Agriculture—excluding, of course, any manual labor—was their normal means of existence. They did not all live on their plantations, although absenteeism among them has been much exaggerated; there were few absentee landlords save in the Deep South. Even when the owner was not at home, travelers experienced his liberality in the courteous and generous welcome which they received from his steward in his name. Most Southern gentlemen resided permanently on their estates. We have described their houses. They led the life of any country gentlemen: hunting, riding, supervising the property. Their responsibilities in the latter regard were heavy, even though they delegated some of them to a steward. The ladies of the house—those langorous creatures with magnolia complexions—were remarkable administrators. Very often it was they, rather than their husbands, who ran the plantation and saw to it that it was properly managed.

Different kinds of slaves lived on the plantations. This, for example, is a job breakdown of the sixty-seven slaves on a plantation on the James River in 1854. Thirteen were assigned to the house, thirty-six to the fields, and eighteen to maintenance. The first category included a butler and two parlor maids, a cook, four housemaids, a nursemaid, a washerwoman, a seamstress, a gardener, and a coachman. The second group included four plowmen, twenty-two hoe hands, two wagon drivers, four drovers, two stable hands, a cowman, and a pigman. Finally, in the third group of craftsmen, there were two carpenters, five masons, a miller, two smiths, two shoemakers, five spinning girls, and one weaving girl. In addition there were forty-five children and a number of old people.

The slaves constituting the domestic personnel often received picturesque names: Byron, Aida, Telemachus, Calypso. They were a part of the family, recited morning and evening prayers together with the family, and were fiercely devoted to their masters. The "mammies" would have given their lives for their masters' children. They had often nursed and reared them; for the young ladies of the family they often served as chaperones who would stand no nonsense, and once the young ladies were married, they initiated them into the secrets of maternity. Their word was law in the matter of babies. The other servants took part with similar interest in the events of the family's life: they rejoiced in the births and marriages; they grieved at the death of those they had served, perhaps for two or three generations; here they could perceive the hand of a mysterious fate governing all beings, and come to some perception of equality. Nevertheless, they did not regard themselves as the victims of injustice, and it would have been hard work to convince them that they were unhappy. Their owners treated them with a combination of kindness and severity—as they treated their house dogs.

There was considerable promiscuity between masters and slaves. The whites had no sense of shame in the presence of blacks: why worry with a creature who was not considered human? Mrs. Trollope could not get over it when she saw a young woman, who would not have let a young man so much as touch her hand, calmly lace her corset in front of a footman. She was no less astonished upon hearing from a Virginia gentleman that, since his marriage, a chambermaid had slept in the couple's bedroom every night. She asked why this was necessary. He explained: whatever would he do if he should happen to need a glass of water during the night and she was not there to give it to him?

Actually, Negresses bringing fresh water often came pretty close to their master's bed. This was the terror of mothers when their sons reached marriageable age. Soon they had to resign themselves to the inevitable. There were few plantations in which the masters had not had, or still had, one or more black concubines. The defenders of morality consoled themselves with the thought that in this way the virtue of white women was less imperiled. Statisticians attributed the large number of bachelors and of late marriages to the charms of these color contrasts. However that may be, the most sought-after women slaves were not necessarily the sturdiest. But their subsequent position of mistresses entitled them to only limited—and temporary—privileges. Their children were in no way set apart from those of the other Negroes. A look of astonishment, or perhaps of tenderness, from their father, quickly concealed, and that was all. When the children were grown, they often worked in the fields alongside the rest, and the overseer's whip made no distinction between one back and another.

The household Negroes, even if they had no white blood in their veins, were envied and resented by the others, who labored like beasts of burden. It was estimated that, on a first-class plantation, one man in excellent health was needed for every ten acres. Under very good conditions, a worker might produce up to 2,000 pounds of cotton; the usual average, however was 1,200 pounds. Even to achieve the lower figures, there should not be too much time wasted. Twelve- to fifteen-hour work days were common; at the height of the harvesting season, those figures were raised to sixteen or eighteen. Most of Saturday and Sunday, however, were days of rest. Hunting and fishing were permitted on those days, and occasional revivals—suitably supervised—provided edifying entertainment. The slaves wore a bare minimum of clothing: straw hat, cotton jacket, and pants in summer, and the same in winter, with the addition of shoes; women wore no more than a blouse and skirt; the children wore nothing but a shirt down to the knees. The slaves' quarters consisted of wooden huts, often whitewashed on the outside, and more or less plastered on the inside; thick wooden planks formed the roof. Often the inside of the house consisted of a single room, about 12 by 15 feet; sometimes two families shared it, with children and poultry running in and out at will; a crude hearth served mainly for cooking and heating water for washing clothes. The windows were closed by means of wooden panels. The furniture consisted almost exclusively of a bed and a few stools. The food consisted of an allowance of pork and corn. In some cases, however, slaves had the right to a patch of land where they cultivated vegetables and kept chickens; sometimes they even sold cotton to their master.

On the smaller properties, the Negro's life was more human but just as hard. There was no overseer eager to curry favor with the boss, and perhaps with an interest in the product of the crop. An average estate extended over some hundreds of acres and included from ten to forty Negroes. Their lives were not much harder than those of the whites. The planter's house was devoid of amenities. His food was fairly similar to that of the workers, whose staples were pork and oatmeal. There were no diversions. From time to time a visit to a town broke the monotony, but their life went on again in an atmosphere very different indeed from that of *Gone With the Wind*.

Even more primitive, if possible, were the very small properties which used only a few Negroes. By the force of circumstances, masters and slaves were in constant contact; relations between them were very close and differences of status became almost negligible. Often they took their meals together. Their quarters were so close that a kind of cohabitation ultimately developed.

Nevertheless, the owners of these wretched little plantations regarded themselves as aristocrats. They left the cultivation of the soil to two or three slaves whom they had managed to buy, often on credit. The "poor whites" could not do as much. They wielded the spade and the hoe themselves. In this category, with its pathetic—and over-simplified—appelation, situations varied considerably. The poor whites included small landowners and farmers whose con-

ditions were not much worse than those of many of the
planters. They worked their land with the help of slaves
whom they rented at about $10 and $30 a month. They
played a considerable part in the political life of the more
recent states of the Union, such as Alabama, Mississippi,
and Arkansas. They made no claim to refinement, and their
idea of oratorical joustings was somewhat crude; at the first
legislative assembly of Arkansas, the chairman, irritated by
an opponent, left his seat and stabbed the other man to
death. These spoilers for fights covered themselves with
glory in the armies of the Confederacy. But in the days
before they faced the Yankees, their two worst enemies were
the tutor and the schoolmaster, whose functions appeared to
them to infringe upon their freedom. And then there were
the hillbillies, less pugnacious and somewhat degenerate,
representing the scum of the region. They were hunters, fish-
ermen, cattle breeders, and subsisted as best they could in
the more or less deserted woods and abandoned fields, often
consumed by sickness and decimated by the moonshine
whisky in which they drowned their sorrows. They were
also known as "clay eaters," because they did in fact eat clay,
which gave them a yellowish complexion and accentuated
their sickly air. Nevertheless, they were "whites," and that
was enough to give them a sense of arrogant superiority in
relation to their racial "inferiors."

The Negroes despised them. But how did the Negroes
feel about other whites, and especially about their masters?

Passions have distorted the problem to a point where
it is almost impossible to answer the question. The conclusions of observers are consistently contradictory, so that
a single incident will give rise to directly opposing impres-
sions. Take, for example, as shrewd an observer as F. L.
Olmstead, whose descriptions of his Southern travels are a
classic. He tells of a "very pious lady" who made her slaves

work from 3.30 A.M. to 9 P.M. and on Sunday had them alter-
nately whipped and given religious instruction. Not far
from this plantation, he came to one with about a score of
Negro slaves who never, apparently, experienced corporal
punishment, who worked in very leisurely fashion under the
benevolent gaze of their master, and who ate the same food
as he did. On another occasion, he witnessed a scene which
sickened him. A Negro woman refused to admit a misde-
meanor of which she had been accused. The overseer struck
her with his whip. She still refused, whereupon he ordered
her to lift up her clothes to the shoulders and to lie flat on
the ground on her belly. She obeyed, and he proceeded to
beat her, while she writhed in the dust, moaning. The overseer's expression, Olmstead writes, was quite devoid of passion; it was simply severe and "business-like." A sickening
incident, but the only one of its kind mentioned in 500
pages. And the author's conclusion? That conditions were
deplorable in the South, but that it would be a mistake to
abolish slavery right away. The book was written in 1860.

There was certainly no lack of cruelty in the "peculiar
institution." Even if corporal punishment was not always
practiced, it was universally accepted. Jail was out of the
question: it would have slowed down production. The slaves
were wholly at their masters' mercy, and a Negro's testi-
mony was not admissible in court against a white. We recall
the advertisements which Dickens noted in the local papers,
which published lists of fugitive slaves: X branded with a hot
iron on his cheek; Y with several brand marks on his thighs
and hips; Z branded on his left gum. Or again: "A few days
before she ran away, I branded her with a red-hot iron on
her cheek and I tried to make an M"; "Molly, age 16, has
an R branded on her left cheek and inside her legs; a piece
of her ear has been cut off"; "Hewn has a ring and a chain
round his left leg"; "Fanny has an iron ring round her
neck"; "Dennis had a pistol shot in his left arm"; "Bandal

has an ear cut off"; "Mary has two teeth missing in her upper jaw" (breaking slaves' teeth was evidently an easy means of identification).

Should we generalize? Probably not. Such infamous practices were rare. Everything is not false in *Uncle Tom's Cabin*, but neither is everything true—far from it. Hounds did, in fact, patrol the borders of plantations, but they rarely had to display their ferocity. The candidates for freedom were infinitely fewer than those resigned to slavery. They were suspicious, moreover, of professions of disinterested good will. Some of their fellows, they knew, were periodically urged to try their luck by dishonest "liberators" who made a business of selling them back to their masters.

A systematic scheme organized by the abolitionists was needed before escapes could be made on any really extensive scale. In point of fact, the immense majority of Negroes were accustomed to their lot. Most of them were unreflecting, simple people; the harshness of their existence could not crush their spirit, and most accepted life as it was. They usually were on the very best of terms with their masters' children and loved to tell them stories in their rich and picturesque dialect. The "Uncle Remus" type was very common among them. Rebellions were few. They were always organized by freed Negroes or by whites, and they were often betrayed by the slaves themselves. If they managed to take shape, they were so brutally suppressed that for months on end there reigned an atmosphere of terror hardly conducive to further attempts. One fairly large-scale insurrection, led by Nat Turner in 1831, led to the massacre of some fifty Negroes. Yet even that insurrection involved only an infinitesimal minority. And during the Civil War, the Negroes gave abundant proof of their loyalty to their masters.

It would seem that passivity and obedience had become second nature with them, enabling them to endure the worst humiliations. They were bought and sold like animals, yet they retained their resigned equanimity. Accounts of these disgraceful practices abound and agree. For example: At a sale in the slave market, a Negro would be ordered to strip completely. A dozen white men would cluster about him and examine every part of his body, in particular his teeth. They would feel his arms, hands, and fingers and look down his throat. Or, again, the men were completely naked and were inspected from head to toe; women's hands, arms, legs, teeth, and breasts were examined, and if they said they had had children, their statement was checked by the condition of their breasts. When the bidding was about to begin, the slaves were ordered to walk up and down for a final assessment; often they were made to run, to give an idea of the suppleness of their muscles. The only ones to escape these indignities were domestic servants, who were presented in uniform: stewards in particular looked very fancy in striped pants, jacket, and top hat. Children were valued according to their weight and height, and babies were sold at so much per pound. Southern gentlemen, we should add, did not attend such sales; they sent their stewards, who were more capable of understanding and sharing the professional insensibility of the slave traders. One needed a strong enough dose of such insensibility after the hammer had struck. Nothing could have been more heart-rending than the expression on the faces of Negroes bought by a master whose cruelty they feared. Up to the last, they sought to establish some form of physical disability which would impede the sale. Wives were separated from husbands, children from their mothers, with total unconcern. Of all the aspects of slavery, this was perhaps the most cruel.

These sales continued right up to the Civil War. In fact, they had become increasingly active on the eve of the war. The supply had become inadequate, and prices rose in consequence. Average deals reached $800, and the best quality (eighteen to twenty-five years old, and in perfect health) would sell for as much as $1,800. Actual studs were established for the breeding of slaves, especially in Virginia. These young slaves were intended for the plantations in the Deep South, and they were led there, chained, in columns. Even so, the demand outstripped the supply. Around 1860, Southern logicians were prepared to demand the official revival of the slave trade—the only way, they maintained, of keeping their labor force up to strength.

Whether they were tortured as the abolitionists claimed, or spoiled, as the proponents of slavery claimed, the slaves were certainly not worse off in the middle of the nineteenth century than they had been fifty years earlier. We must look elsewhere than in the aggravation of their lot for the extraordinary wave of passion which swept the United States at that time.

It is estimated that in 1776, there were slightly more than 500,000 slaves in the thirteen colonies. Their emancipation north of the Mason-Dixon line, where only one-tenth resided, created no problem. Slavery there was speedily banned. The position of the South was far more serious. Even then, its economy depended on slave labor. If 400,000 Negroes were to be freed, would that not create a racial problem which, people liked to say, did not exist? Yet if they were not freed, would that not be a violation of the principles of the Declaration of Independence, in the adoption of which the delegates of the region had played so important a part? People sought the solution in looking to the future. No one, wrote Patrick Henry, would believe that he enjoyed being a slave owner. He was compelled to it by the difficulty of living without slaves; he would not and could not justify himself. His conduct, he knew, was wrong. He would pay his tribute to virtue, as best he could, by recognizing the excellence and logic of its precepts and by deploring his inability to conform to them. He was persuaded that the time would come when there would be an opportunity to heal this lamentable wound. For the time being, the Constitution confined itself to forbidding the slave trade for a period (twenty years), and remained silent on the problem of slavery as such. The only concession made to the partisans of abolition was to include only three-fifths of the Negro population in the census carried out for purposes of electoral representation. This was regarded as a means of reducing the influence of the Southern states in Congress.

The solution was a precarious one, even in the view of its authors. The expansion of the young Republic was bound, eventually, to upset it. In anticipation, the famous Northwest Ordinance of 1787 forbade slavery or involuntary servitude in the regions north of the Ohio. It did not, however, include the gigantic territory which Bonaparte sold to the United States in 1803 under the simplified name of Louisiana, and which comprised what is now Montana, North Dakota, part of Minnesota, Wyoming, South Dakota, Nebraska, Iowa, half of Colorado, most of Kansas, Missouri, Oklahoma, Arkansas, and Louisiana. A tacit compromise was gradually established. It extended an imaginary line from the Ohio valley beyond its confluence with the Mississippi, and decided that south of this line slavery would be tolerated. To maintain an equal balance, free states and slave states were admitted to the Union in alternation. In 1819 they had achieved equality in the Senate: there were twenty-two senators from each camp. In the House of Representatives, elected on the basis of population, the north was in a majority of 105 to 81. The candidacy of Missouri, situated almost entirely north of the fictitious frontier but populated by planters and slaves, triggered the great debate on slavery in 1820. Passions were already high. A compromise solution calmed them temporarily. Missouri—and its slaves—passed the admission test; but Maine—with its free men—was received simultaneously. And it was decided, further, that the thirty-sixth parallel should serve from now on as a barrier to the further expansion of slavery.

Relative calm prevailed for twenty years. The annexation of Texas, in 1845, the cession of Oregon by Great Britain in 1846, the victorious peace treaty with Mexico in 1848 (the territories ceded by Mexico correspond to present-day California, Nevada, Utah, Arizona, and a part of Colorado and New Mexico) revived the fires which had never ceased smoldering. After increasingly violent polemics, another compromise was attempted in 1850 to resolve an insoluble problem. It was proposed by Henry Clay, celebrated thirty years earlier for his restraining influence in the 1820 discussions. Webster, now aging, lent it the prestige of his authority in one of his last great speeches. The essence of his proposals was adopted in September by a Congress weary of eloquence. The specter of secession had constantly haunted the lawmakers. No one believed that it had been definitely exorcized; the optimists clung to the hope that its apparitions would, for a time, be less frequent. Vain delusions! Neither South nor North emerged from the debate satisfied. The slave states had had to resign themselves to accepting the suppression of the slave traffic in the District of Columbia, the admission of California as a free state, and the organization of New Mexico and Utah as territories that might later join the Union, on the slave or the free side at their choice. The free states, in return, had solemnly undertaken to refuse asylum to fugitive slaves and to return them to their masters. The principle was not a new one, but its legal application, this time, was ruthless. It was sufficient for the owner to assert under oath that the Negro belonged to him for the slave to be delivered over to him. A sickening procedure, Emerson wrote in his diary, to have been adopted, in the nineteenth century, by men capable of reading and writing! And he vowed, before God, not to comply with it.

Yet the sage of Concord was not among the extremists. He had even often blamed the fanatics who for several years had been demanding the immediate abolition of slavery with a passion equaled only by that of their opponents. His remarks, therefore, are all the more significant. In reality, behind the accommodations designed to save the Union, ideas were moving on either side, powerful, irresistible, ready to shatter irreparably the precarious edifice of the conciliators.

Patrick Henry's remarks, which we cited earlier, fairly accurately reflect the opinion prevailing in the South in his day. Slavery was a necessary evil, people felt, and it would gradually disappear. It was regarded as an ineluctable fact, and no attempt was made to give it a theoretical justification. This wholly pragmatic approach began to lose ground in the 1820's. Slavery, as we know, became increasingly vital to the economy of the region. At the same time, the West was offering its limitless expanses to planters: King Cotton and his servants succumbed to the lure of imperialism. The fulfilment of their dreams was dependent upon plentiful and cheap labor: what better source than the Negroes? And how reassuring it would be to give theoretical sanction to practical opportunism! Gradually a systematic theory developed, based both on facts and on principles. The Industrial Revolution, which had created slums and poverty, furnished it with arguments of considerable cogency. When the defenders of the status quo described the population of the big urban centers as "slaves without masters," they were exaggerating less than their adversaries claimed they were. In a comparison between factory workers and slaves on a plantation, the advantage did not necessarily lie with the former. Nearly all observers admitted that the Negroes worked less and that their lot was less cruel than that of many immigrants in the slums of the big cities of the East. However, these purely material considerations would not have sufficed to give slavery a lasting aura of respectability. The Puritan roots of the South were so deep that the slave owners could not help feeling the need for some moral demonstration of the righteousness of their cause.

It was provided them in various forms. They accused the North of practicing oppression. "Lord North," 1850 model, they claimed, was as arbitrary as George III's Minister had been. To oppose him was all the more justified since, like his predecessor, he had no understanding whatsoever of the situation. The Southern attitude was well expressed by Nathaniel Beverley Tucker, a scion of one of the oldest families of Virginia. The Yankees, he said, did not possess the qualities needed to understand the Negroes; their calculating egotism made it impossible for them to appreciate the devotion of those "simple souls"; what "our" slaves felt was as alien to them as the loyalty of the chivalrous gentlemen from whom "we" were descended had been to the Yankees' forefathers. The churches elaborated on the same theme, with the exception of the Catholics and Episcopalians (whose numbers, therefore, remained stationary). But the ministers of the Protestant sects found any number of arguments favorable to the existing social structure. The Hebrew prophets, St. Paul, each was used in turn. Sermon after sermon sought to prove that, physically and morally, the Negroes constituted an inferior race, intended by divine law to serve the chosen white race. In 1844, when the Northern Methodists had the poor taste to maintain that a bishop ought to emancipate the slaves he had inherited, a religious secession took place, anticipating by fifteen years the polit-

ical secession and resulting in the establishment of an auton-
omous Southern Methodist Church. Shortly after, the Baptists also split, with unanimous approval.

Politicians and writers did not let themselves be outdone by the clergy. Among the former, John Calhoun was
undoubtedly the one whose defense of slavery had the most
widespread repercussions. This planter, turned thinker
through circumstances, was an astonishing figure. His political philosophy followed that of Alexander Hamilton; in
other words, he had a clear understanding of the dangers
of disintegration which threatened the Union. He had
thought, at first, that a policy of military and economic
nationalism could limit them. The 1812 war with England
had found him in the forefront of the "war hawks." He had
voted in favor of the protective tariff of 1816, and actively
supported the construction of the great artery known as the
Cumberland Road, which, he hoped, would facilitate the
fusion of the Western states with those of the Atlantic seaboard. He soon revised his opinion when he realized that
tariff protection simply led to antagonism between North
and South. In 1828, when he conceived his famous doctrine
of nullification and secured its adoption by the assemblies
of South Carolina, his objective was the preservation of the
federal bond far more than its rupture. It was by safeguard-
ing the individual interests of the states that had signed the
Constitution that he hoped to ensure their fidelity to the
Union. According to him, the thirteen sovereign states of
1787 had not alienated their sovereignty in handing over to
a superior authority the power to exercise certain attributes
of sovereignty. They must therefore have competence to
judge whether the contract which had given birth to the
United States was being faithfully carried out. Their representatives, and not the Supreme Court, thus became qualified to judge of the constitutionality of laws. Should they
declare a decision of Congress unconstitutional, that deci-

sion would no longer be applicable in their state. The opponents of desegregation in the South today use the same arguments as did the proponents of slavery some one hundred years ago. There was only one exception to this principle: their opposition would have no legal basis if two-thirds of the states adopted a contrary position. The concession was wholly theoretical, given the balance of forces which existed between South and North.

The expansion of King Cotton, attended by his slaves, soon put this theory to the test of fact. As early as 1830, a celebrated case showed that nullification and secession were not incompatible. On the occasion of an official banquet, one speaker after another had expatiated on states' rights and supported their views by appealing to those of Thomas Jefferson. Jackson, who was President at the time, listened with growing impatience to these speeches, with their barely veiled threats. "Old Hickory" was not an advocate of centralization in the Hamilton manner, but he nevertheless recognized the ultimate sovereignty of the nation. When the toasts were proposed, he finally exploded. With a withering glance at Calhoun—his Vice-President—he lifted his glass "to the Federal Union!" and added, significantly, that the Union must be preserved. Calhoun hesitated, then rose in his turn: "To the Union!" he declared, but added an interpretation which in no way resembled the preceding one: "To the Union—with our liberty, our most precious possession!" Behind this abstraction, it was not difficult to recognize the facts. "Liberty," for the Southern states, meant, first and foremost, the right to preserve slavery.

It was Calhoun, again, King Cotton's legal expert, who provided these claims with a doctrinal foundation. In the middle of the last century there was hardly a gathering—even a society gathering—where this doctrine was not the principal topic of conversation. Its author, far from apologizing for the slave system as a passing evil, pictured the organization of the South as the ideal type of society. To hear him, in any human group the work of the masses was intended to ensure the survival of an elite. Whence the salary structure, in operation practically everywhere. That structure, according to Calhoun, was not really satisfactory, since it did not secure the happiness of the workers and contained within it the needs of revolutionary ferment whose effects were only too visible in Europe. It was quite otherwise south of the Mason-Dixon line. Here Providence had willed that a race physically and mentally inferior should have as its only *raison d'être* to minister to the well-being of masters who were manifestly superior. In return, these superior beings would provide for their servants and would thus free them from the fear of poverty which haunted the proletariat. Many, Calhoun went on, had formerly believed that slavery was a political and moral evil. Now it could be seen in its true light, as furnishing the surest and most stable foundation for free institutions. Indeed, he concluded, by relieving the whites of the sordid necessity of engaging in manual labor, it would permit them to accede progressively to that level of intellectual and moral eminence of which the founders of the Republic had dreamed.

Reference, of course, was made to the example of Greece. As though the South already felt the death sentence weighing upon it, it looked to earlier centuries to justify its ways of life. High society, as we have said earlier, was attracted to the traditions of medieval chivalry. However, the Middle Ages had been too feudal in character for its traditions to be able to captivate the population as a whole. Notwithstanding their claims to be different, the planters, like all Americans, had been influenced by the forces of egalitarianism. And then there were the "poor whites," who really bore very little resemblance to the Crusaders of the twelfth century. In a word, Greek cities were more able than medieval manors to provide models capable of pleasing everyone. There, slavery and civilization had not been incompatible; there, great thinkers had seen no contradiction between democracy and slavery. In anticipation of a new century of Pericles, a whole literature celebrated this theme. William J. Grayson idealized the lot of the slave in his poem, *The Hireling and the Slave;* George Fitzhugh compared the plantations to utopian communities in which profits were distributed according to the needs of each and all (his estimation of the needs of the slaves was not very high; in a pamphlet entitled *Cannibals All,* he barely conceded that the Negroes were human at all). Fitzhugh advocated the expansion of slavery into the limitless space of the West—if need be, with serfs imported from Europe. The Southern planters, he went on, would provide this society of great landowners with natural leaders, and thanks to them the United States would become the model of human societies.

Extraordinary incomprehension! But there was incomprehension, too, on the other side, where fanatics demanded extreme solutions of another type.

No one in the South, not even the moderates, advocated emancipation. Some, however, at least certain members of old Virginian families who were less extreme than the "fire eaters" of Charleston, were not averse to progressive emancipation, provided the freed slaves then left the country. For a time, a compromise solution along these lines had been hoped for. The American Colonization Society, financed primarily by planters, undertook to colonize Liberia by transporting Negroes there. The idea was a generous one, but not very practical. It could be judged by its results. In fifteen years, 1,400 Africans had been repatriated to their ancestral land. Clearly, the problem could not be resolved in this way.

On January 1, 1831, a young man twenty-six years of

age, a printer by profession, without financial resources but
with plenty of passion, published in Boston the first issue
of a journal significantly named *The Liberator*. In a few
weeks, he was to become one of the best known and most
hated men in America. William Lloyd Garrison did not
mince words: complete and immediate emancipation was
his sole watchword. He would fiercely champion this cause,
he wrote; on this subject, he had no intention of speaking
or writing with moderation; he would not budge an inch
in the matter; he would make people listen to him. On this
last point, at least, he was satisfied. His objurgations, his
invectives, his verbal excesses (he termed the sacrosanct institution of slavery a compact with satan), his calumnies
(according to him, every slave owner was a torturer) certainly did not pass unnoticed. His diatribes actually aroused
almost as much protest in the North as in the South. Labor,
and particularly the Irish, who were fearful above all things
of having to compete with colored workers, gave full vent
to their rage against the new prophet. One day he escaped
their fury only by taking refuge in a Boston prison.

Garrison was not the kind to be discouraged by such
a trifle. In 1833, he founded the American Anti-Slavery
Society, which only seven years later had a membership of
150,000 persons. The society was the focal point for patri-
cians of the type of Wendell Phillips, poets like John Whittier, evangelists like Theodore Weld, first-rate intellectuals
on the level of James Russell Lowell. The Quakers, it is
hardly necessary to say, communicated the flame of their
reformist enthusiasm to the movement. William Jay, son of
the former Chief Justice, and two influential businessmen,
Arthur and Benjamin Tappan, assisted by a Frenchman,
Francis le Moyne de Villiers, gave Garrison substantial
financial support out of their personal fortunes.

Some supporters were to be found even in the South.
Sarah and Angelina Grimke were not content to free their

slaves; they left their plantations to join the campaign of oratory whereby the anti-slavery movement hoped to arouse a still fairly somnolent public opinion. This propaganda was powerfully assisted through the lectures and published autobiography of a fugitive slave, Frederick Douglass, son of a white man and a Negro woman.

But for sheer sensation no one could equal "General Tubman," the "Moses of his people," alias Harriet Tubman, an expert in escapes. She is credited with having engineered hundreds of escapes. A Negress, she knew her people. She always carried a revolver, and pulled it out when necessary. "The dead can't talk," she would remind would-be fugitives if they showed signs of losing their nerve; "either you follow me or you die!" Before so clear an alternative, faltering spirits would revive. And what excitement, when the Northern frontier was reached! "Moses," then, would strike up "his" favorite hymn:

> Glory to God and Jesus too,
> One more soul is safe.
> O go and carry the news,
> One more soul got safe.

In the folklore of the "grapevine telegraph" and the "underground railroad," "General Tubman" holds a place of honor. The principal practical activity of the abolitionists was to hide fugitive slaves. South of the Mason-Dixon line, fugitives fended for themselves, hiding in the woods by day, guiding their steps by the pole star by night. Even the Northern fanatics would have considered it an infringement of state sovereignty to commit such a gross violation of state law as to aid and abet an escape on Southern territory. But once the frontier was crossed, the whole nature of the problem changed. Then it was a question of preventing the fugitives from falling into the hands of the federal authorities, who were bound, as we know, to return them to their masters. They were hidden in all kinds of ways: in hayricks, in barns, in the huge ovens of New England houses; they were disguised as women; their faces were concealed in Quaker bonnets; they were entrusted to the Express Company in crates labeled "Handle with Care"; one even achieved freedom in a coffin in which he had been substituted for a corpse.

The underground railroad never achieved very substantial successes. It is estimated that, around 1850, and even with the help of the anti-slavery movement, the proportion of fugitive Negroes never exceeded 3 per cent. An insignificant figure, but one which neither South nor North was prepared to recognize—in the South, because escapes served as a pretext for arousing the passions of the planters; in the North, because the abolitionists were not willing to acknowledge the mediocrity of their results.

Under the impetus of extremist passions on either side, the gulf between North and South steadily broadened. The "irrepressible conflict"—the expression was first used by William H. Seward on October 25, 1858—was clearly delineated on the horizon in the middle of the century. One million copies of *Uncle Tom's Cabin,* published in 1852, popularized the problem. More and more incidents took place. On June 2, 1954, Boston looked on powerless, in an agony of humiliation, as a fugitive slave was returned to the South by soldiers. His name—Anthony Burns—was soon to become famous throughout the United States. He was marched to the quay, in the midst of a crowd of 50,000 persons who abused and spat at his guards; the city police, twenty-four companies of state troopers, one federal company of artillery, four detachments of marine infantry, and a group of detectives in plain clothes were needed to keep order. The cost of the operation was estimated at $40,000. (Sympathizers subsequently bought Anthony Burns out of slavery. He became pastor of a Baptist church in St. Catherine in Canada, where he died in 1862.)

Some days earlier, under pressure from Southern representatives, Congress had revised the compromise decisions of 1820 and 1850 and adopted the principle of a "local option," which gave territories, whatever their geographical situation, the right either to adopt or to refuse slavery. The result, for a few months, was an anticipation of civil war in Kansas.

On March 6, 1857, the Supreme Court, in its turn, attempted to legalize slavery once and for all, by refusing the privileges of citizenship to any slave, wherever he might be. (This was the famous Dred Scott case. Scott, a slave belonging to a resident of Missouri, had been taken by his owner to Illinois, a free state, and Minnesota, a free territory, where he had lived for four years. After returning to the South, and being given the penalty of whipping, he had brought an action for damages against his master on the grounds that his stay in the North had earned him his freedom. The Court ruled that, as a Negro, he could not be a citizen and therefore had no right to initiate a legal action; in addition, he could not have been emancipated by the laws of Illinois or Minnesota, for this would have amounted to depriving his master of his rights of legal ownership.) The same year, Americans eagerly read *The Impending Crisis*, in which a "poor white," Hinton Rowan Helper, denounced the economic and social consequences of slavery and threatened the planters with a slave uprising. In the South, men were lynched for being found in possession of this book.

The hour had struck for violence. John Brown was one of the instruments of fate. He had already gained notoriety by massacring the opponents of his ideas in Kansas in 1856. Two years later, in the winter of 1858–59, he had led a column of a dozen fugitive slaves from Missouri to Canada via Kansas, Iowa, Illinois, and Michigan. He believed only in force (he was mentally unbalanced; thirteen members of his family, including his mother and grandmother, were insane). On October 16, 1859, he seized the arsenal at Harpers Ferry, West Virginia, and took hostages. Soon he was taken prisoner himself, and went to the scaffold on December 2, happy, as he wrote to his children, to die for God's eternal truth. The incident exasperated the South and strengthened the advocates of secession. Abraham Lincoln's success in 1860 touched off the final decisions. His opinions were known; he had stated them forcefully in his speech as candidate for the Illinois Senate in 1858. A house divided against itself, he had said, cannot stand. The United States Government could not subsist half slave, half free. He did not expect the Union to be dissolved; he did not expect the house to collapse; he did expect that it should cease to be divided. It would be either one or the other.

Either/or: the time for compromise had passed, and to save the Union Lincoln would not hesitate to employ force. He viewed the position in its true light, as a problem of unity, not of slavery. As he wrote to Horace Greeley on August 22, 1862, in this conflict his permanent objective was to save the Union, and not either to save or to destroy slavery.

The South had no illusions about the significance of his election to the Presidency. South Carolina was the first to secede from the Union. On February 8, 1861, Georgia, Alabama, Florida, Mississippi, Louisiana, and Texas formed, with South Carolina, a Confederated States of America. On April 14 the rebels seized Fort Sumter in Charleston. The first cannon shot had been fired; the die had been cast; soon the carefree days would be gone with the wind.

# PART THREE

# Intellectual and Moral Life

## Chapter XVI
# RELIGION

Religion played a fundamental role in everyday life, and the middle of the century was a particularly interesting period in that regard. Religious vitality was constantly in evidence, but it took on a variety of forms, often akin to incoherence and nearly always hostile to tradition. In addition, a new problem emerged; what were to be the consequence of the expansion of Catholicism?

Up to the time of the French Revolution, America and Europe had developed along more or less parallel lines with respect to religion. It might even be contended that the thirteen colonies lagged behind their mother country. Stern intolerance prevailed there. From Maryland to Georgia and in a part of New York, the Anglican Church alone was recognized; the Congregationalists enjoyed the same monopoly in Massachusetts, Connecticut, and New Hampshire; the exceptions were Rhode Island, Pennsylvania, New Jersey, and Delaware, which accepted the principle of separation of church and state.

The dissident sects were even more oppressive than the privileged churches. Adultrous women were no longer branded with a hot iron and sinners were no longer subjected to the penalty of the stocks, but the vituperations of Jonathan Edwards and the hysteria surrounding the "Great Awakening" had reminded any who might have been tempted to forget it that gentleness and Calvinism are hard to reconcile. (The "Great Awakening" was the name given to a series of meetings and sermons which took place in the middle of the eighteenth century, in which fanatical preachers sought to spread what they called the "new light.") In particular, the Puritan approach had impregnated the atmosphere. Puritanism justified wealth acquired through hard work, and it elevated individual effort to the rank of a kind of social service. As in our own day, it was less concerned with theology than with human relations; it had little understanding for the contemplative life and it reduced mysticism to a vague communion with the divine intended more to improve man on earth than to prepare him for happiness in the hereafter.

The Declaration of Independence did not free America of these tendencies. The founders of the Republic had no thought of challenging the basic principle on which the immigrants had built their societies. Where should they turn, save to the spirit of God and to his grace, the leader of the pilgrims had asked in the tragic winter which followed their landing on Cape Cod in 1620. The same year the colonists of Virginia, followed soon by those of Rhode Island and Connecticut, had placed their "social contract" under the protection of the divine power. And because of its superterrestrial references, the Declaration of Independence could speak of men's unalienable rights to life, liberty, and the pursuit of happiness. The Constitution itself, finally, was dated the seventeenth day of September, in the year of our Lord one thousand seven hundred and eighty-seven.

Nevertheless, the young Republic soon came to accept a concept which would previously have appeared subversive. The first ten amendments to the Constitution adopted in 1790, and collectively known as the Bill of Rights, prohibited any established church and solemnly guaranteed the freedom of all religious rites. One after the other, the states put it into effect. The last states to allow the churches to levy taxes for their support were New Hampshire before 1817, Connecticut at about the same date, and Massachusetts for another sixteen years. All this was new; yet in appearance only the legal status had been affected.

There is nothing more mysterious or more irresistible than the progress of an idea. Behind the illusion of immutability, the reality of change soon became apparent. Around the 1830's, it was clear that the seeds sown at the Revolution were bearing other fruits than those of the first harvest.

The cities of the East and South had as many churches as ever, well built, light, spacious. In the South they were square, made of marble and brick. In New England they were built of stone and wood, with slender towers. In the West they mushroomed under the feet of the pioneers; each year saw 1,000 new ones, according to estimates. The faithful continued to throng to them. In Boston, Congregationalists and Unitarians predominated; in Newport, Episcopalians; Providence was a Baptist area; in New York the ancient traditions of the Dutch Reformed Church had many adherents; in New Jersey, Episcopalians and Quakers were fairly evenly divided; the Quakers reigned supreme in Philadelphia; Baltimore, on the other hand, was a Catholic center; so was New Orleans. Generally speaking, the South and the West were the preserves of numberless Presbyterian, Methodist, and Baptist ministers.

There is nothing surprising about this diversity. Diversity was the essence of Protestantism from the first days of the Reformation. Nevertheless, it was more accentuated than elsewhere in the United States of the nineteenth century. It has been wittily observed that the country has such powers of absorption that it even naturalized Calvin. That, in fact, is what happened. The national optimism was not prepared to have its drives curbed by a doctrine of rigid determinism. In particular, by dint of glorifying individualism, people came to regard religion as a wholly individual affair; it seemed desirable that there should be as few intermediaries as possible between the believer and his God. But in that case, how was one to know whether between the deity and the human creature there existed that mysterious communion whereby the good might be distinguished from the evil? A thousand formulas were proposed—we might have said "recipes." Mrs. Trollope shrewdly voiced the belief that if a fire worshipper, or a Hindu Brahman, came to the United States, he would very soon find himself with a sizable following. Hundreds of sects were formed, each assured of possessing the Truth. Let us take a look at the swarm, some bordering on the ideal, others coming a little too close to reality.

The one thing we can say of Transcendentalism is that there was nothing mediocre about it. It was a generous movement, founded on a lofty conception of men, and was therefore designed for chosen souls, who alone would be capable of understanding it. Unitarianism had prepared the way for it. It had already attenuated the severity of the conclusions to which the Calvinists had been led by the extremes and the fanaticism of their logic. Nevertheless, this new interpretation of the Protestant ethos lacked vigor. Those who subscribed to it were for the most part worthy citizens and honorable paterfamilias; they were not of the breed of apostles or martyrs. Business was their lifeblood. What they looked for in religion was principally the assurance that making money was not incompatible with their salvation. In that respect, Calvinism had been very reassuring, since it had taken success as a signal of divine approval, but the anathemas with which it had surrounded itself had given it a forbidding and threatening aspect. Unitarianism was hardly gay, but it was infinitely less exacting. The afterlife concerned it only incidentally. Its followers had little interest in metaphysics. By practicing tolerance for others (unlike the Puritans), by carrying out their civic duties, by giving proof of philanthropy, by living in conformity with certain moral principles whose foundations they were disinclined to explore, they felt they had extracted from Christianity everything worth keeping. They felt secure in the esteem of men of the cloth, and derived satisfaction from the fact. One day, in Boston, so we are told, a minister interrupted the service to draw the attention of the faithful to the presence among them of a well-known businessman. Would they like to see one of the princes of trade, he asked them? His parishioners rose and pressed to see. "May God bless you, sir," continued the minister. "At your death, the angels will vie for the honor of carrying you to heaven on their wings!"

The businessman was probably less interested in such angelic enthusiasm than in the immediate admiration of his fellow men. The Unitarians did not live in a dream world. Transcendentalism, on the other hand, introduced its followers into a dream world by giving instinct and intuition precedence over reason. These mystics of optimism retained none of the Calvinist pessimism. In each individual they claimed to perceive so intense a penetration of the divine that the distinction between God and man appeared quite minor. They were persuaded that by correcting and purifying itself, the human spirit would become capable of transcending the frontiers of reason and of attaining spiritual perfection—which for them was the only genuine reality.

Because of the vagueness of this concept, it inevitably gave
rise to hundreds of different interpretations. In any other
country but nineteenth-century America, it could have led
a few extremists to a totally passive form of existence. True,
Hindu philosophies were much in fashion at the time, but
even in New England, that favorite refuge of eccentrics, it
would have been very hard to find any fakirs perched on
the tops of pillars. Some Transcendentalists were endowed
with a keen practical sense: witness the account book which
Thoreau kept meticulously up to date in his Walden Pond
retreat. Generally speaking, however, practical affairs were
not their specialty. Their literary conclaves were so refined
in character, so affected, even, that they were quickly isolated
from the rest of the country. Reformers abounded in their
ranks; we shall see how nebulous were their projects and
what obstacles they frequently encountered.

The itinerant preachers—Methodists, Baptists, Presbyterians—so typical of nineteenth-century America, and some
of whose characteristics are perpetuated today in Billy Graham, were of a wholly different breed. Their principal
means of action were house visits and the distribution of
religious literature. In 1859, preachers visited 3 million
families and distributed 8 million books and pamphlets
published by the American Tract Society. The Methodists
stood out from all the others for their inexhaustible zeal.
There was a saying in the West that when the weather was
exceptionally bad there was no one abroad save crows and
Methodist ministers. For nothing put them off. Take the
Reverend John L. Dyer—for sixty years he traveled through
the Middle West, on horseback in summer, on snowshoes
in winter. A dour zeal drove him on; he had never, so it was
said, been seen to laugh. Or take the Reverend William
H. Milburn—he himself described his missions in West Virginia, one of the most primitive regions in the United States.

Sometimes he found shelter with an inhabitant of the area, but under unbelievably rudimentary conditions; he would sometimes spend the night in a cabin 12 by 14 feet in area, inhabited by a family of fourteen persons, as well as pigs, dogs, and chickens. When the weather allowed, he slept in the open, but then his nights were disturbed by the howling of wolves in quest of prey. In twelve months, he traveled 4,000 miles and preached 400 times; at the end of his round, he noted that he had earned $12.10.

Or, again the Reverend Peter Cartwright. Cut out to be a boxing champion, he did not hesitate on occasion to use force. One day, so it was claimed, he "converted" the entire crew and passenger complement (including professional gamblers) of a Mississippi showboat—no mean achievement. People feared him, and he brooked no argument. It took no less a personage than Lincoln to disconcert him. In 1846 he stood for Congress in Illinois against the future President of the United States. In a public meeting he asked Lincoln where he would go if he did not repent and go to heaven. "To Congress, Brother Cartwright," Lincoln calmly replied.

Another such character—a Presbyterian this time, but no less fierce—was Charles G. Finney, president for fifteen years, until his death, of Oberlin College. He decided, during his tenure, to outlaw all external forms of merriment. One ravishingly beautiful female student, apparently, had not been conforming to his precepts. He met her; she smiled at him seductively; he remained stony-faced and said: "Good day, daughter of satan!" "Good day, Father," she replied.

Such an impudent reply would certainly not have been well received at a revival meeting. These were attended by immense crowds little disposed to dispute the statements of the preachers, and indeed gradually roused by the preachers to a pitch of hysteria at which they lost all self-control. There was always a good reason for putting on one of these big shows, and they became particularly frequent after the financial crash of 1857. According to a pessimistic preacher, however, they were not always altogether successful. "Brawlers, riffraff, and thieves have been converted," he lamented, "but my words have not made the slightest impression on the hardened sinners of Wall Street!" Fortunately for him and his fellow preachers, bankers did not normally constitute the majority of those who attended revivals.

Although some of these meetings took place in the cities, most occurred in the country. People would flock to revivals in a body, often in the hope of deriving some entertainment from them rather than with any determination to amend their lives. Friendships were formed. Amorous idylls began, and did not always stop half way. The number of illegitimate births increased with each campaign of religious "revival." A certain combination of sadism and ecstasy lent a special force to the enthusiasms of those occasions. This is how an eyewitness described the billing and cooing of a young couple: "Slowly, gracefully, they approached the center of the camp, singing, shouting, hugging each other, kissing. Finally, they reached the altar. There, they held each other tightly, their arms about each other's waists, and the man began to sing with all his might:

> I have my Jesus in my arms,
> Sweet as honey, thick as bacon!"

No one was surprised by these strange effusions. Actually, a successful revival required an atmosphere of hysteria. Conversion and liberation were synonymous, for the primitive beings who attended them. The soul of the sinner, they were told, is shackled; prayer alone is not enough to loose the bonds which bind it, and it must be accompanied by gesticulating and contortions as signs of repentence. The preacher would say that the more violent the convulsions, the closer God was. The goodwill of their flock often took somewhat excessive forms: people would deliberately break

an arm or a leg to show their zeal. Many barked. Like a
pack of hounds, they rushed at a tree, as they had seen dogs
doing to force down an opossum. They called it "forcing
the devil."

Meetings would start at dawn and go on late into the
night. One preacher after another would escort the assembly. Often, in the manner of the Barnum and Bailey Circus,
several would be speaking at once in various parts of the
camp.

The tension kept building up. Soon the faithful were
gripped by holy tremors. "The sound was like the roaring
of the Niagara. This sea of humanity seemed to be roused
as by a storm. . . . Some sang. . . . You could hear frantic
alleluias on every side; some prayed; others, in piteous tones,
implored the divine mercy; others yelled meaningless words."
The Methodist orators were particularly impressive: thundering, inveighing against their listeners. Dante's Inferno
seemed almost bearable compared with their descriptions,
one observer noted.

The Baptists had no intention of being outdone by
their rivals. If they made less noise, their stage setting was
no less impressive. At their behest, repentant sinners jumped
into the water, fully dressed, to receive baptism through
immersion. This practice ultimately persuaded simple souls
that paradise was an island and that you had only to swim
to it to reach it. The newly baptized were in a state of
ecstasy, and little concerned to respect human conventions;
they would change their clothes in full view of the assembled faithful; women were adjured to look the other way.

In this neurotic atmosphere, preoccupation with the
Last Judgment haunted the faithful. In 1843 a "prophet,"
H. William Miller, announced a precise date for it. He
attracted a considerable following, known as Millerites, and
organized yet another church, that of the Seventh Day Adventists. The new faithful prepared for the imminent end

of the world by halting their earthly pursuits, putting on white shrouds, and meeting on heights chosen by the Master. Alas, the Great Day went by and nothing happened! Miller was not in the least disconcerted: he simply put off his prediction for two years later. But again the Lord failed him. Many of his followers returned to their occupations; others remained undiscouraged, and their descendants are still waiting: there are some 250,000 Adventists in the United States today.

Shakers, Quakers, Christian Scientists, Mormons were the product of more complex inspirations.

Ann Lee, known as "Ann the Word" or "Our Mother Ann," founded the first of these groups—the Shakers—in the eighteenth century. Like so many reformers, she was a native of England, but America became the favorite testing ground for her ideas. Her disciples made a vow of perpetual virginity; they lived as brothers and sisters in excellently run communities and allowed only collective property. Their morals were unexceptionable, and they won respect for their honesty. They met from time to time for the curious ceremony which earned them their name. They would all wear grey shrouds and hoods. The service began with a short sermon and prayers, murmured slowly. Then they began to walk, dragging their feet. Soon the movement became faster; they began to sing and clap their hands in time, gradually they were gripped by convulsive movements; in the final phase, they achieved a corpse-like rigidity alternating with violent starts, as though they were moved by electric shocks.

The Quakers, more conservative in manner, never indulged in this kind of excess. By the middle of the nineteenth century, they could already boast a two-hundred-year history. William Penn's "holy experiment" had planted deep roots in American soil. The Quakers were always more concerned with results than with dreams, set social questions well ahead of metaphysical problems, and were eager for new ideas and reforms. They were in the forefront of the abolitionist movment.

The Christian Scientists, on the contrary, sought to establish a mystical and purely individualist bond between God and man, but they were as yet only a handful. Their influence grew only after the publication in 1875 of Mary Baker Eddy's book *Science and Health* and the establishment, four years later, of the Church of Christ Scientist.

The Mormons, on the other hand, were already getting themselves talked about in a big way. In 1820, in Palmyra, a little village in New York State, fifteen-year-old Joseph Smith had a vision. (He was descended of Puritan stock and, according to the ill-natured, somewhat too fond of money.) An angel, he claimed, appeared and announced to him that God had chosen him to restore the true church of Christ. Three years later, the celestial voices became more definite: they told him to go to a certain hill where, hidden beneath a stone, he would find a book inscribed in mysterious characters upon plates of gold. Nearby, he would find two stones, bearing the names Urim and Thammin, which would enable him, by the grace of the Most High, to decipher the hieroglyphics. Joseph Smith did not wait to be told twice. He rushed to the appointed spot; needless to say, the message he had received from the beyond turned out to be 100 per cent accurate. Nevertheless, a cruel disappointment awaited him. The angel was there too, and explained to him that in fact the fullness of time had not yet come: he must return four years later, day for day, and then he could take possession of the secret document which would reveal to him the divine will.

The forty-eight months which followed must have appeared long to the young prophet. At last 1827 arrived. This time there was no divine countermand. Joseph Smith did not feel he had the right to keep his discovery to himself.

He began to dictate the translation of the sacred text to a rich farmer, Martin Harris, who had been successively a Quaker, a Baptist, and a Presbyterian, and who was by no means disinclined to try a new religion. One hundred and sixteen pages thus saw the light of day. But Mrs. Harris, who was less enthusiastic than her credulous husband, proceeded to appropriate and destroy them. Prophets are not to be discouraged. Smith continued the work with his own wife—"his servant, Emma," as he condescendingly called her. (Emma finally wearied of his tyranny—and of his infidelity. He then brought out the big guns. In 1843, he had a "revelation" in which the Lord bade Emma be more docile. But Emma was quite unmoved and finally left her husband.)

In 1830 the Book of Mormon was published. Duly reindoctrinated, Harris was only too happy to mortgage his property to permit the printing of 3,000 copies. They were put on sale at $1 apiece, but the price soon had to be reduced to 25 cents, for lack of buyers. The mysterious work told the story of the ten tribes of Israel, who had finally, after endless wanderings, settled in America; the Indians were their descendants. The mission of the saints—that is, of the followers of God's messenger, Joseph Smith—was to free them from the paganism in which they had sunk and to recall them to the True Religion.

Which one? Here lay the difficulty. The new prophet was modest. He did not compare himself to Jesus Christ as did Ann Lee or Mary Baker Eddy. It was enough for him to be a "second Mohammed." But a Mohammed equal to the situation! After a new intervention from the beyond, in the person of St. John the Baptist himself, Joseph Smith decided to appoint twelve apostles and establish a church. No sooner said than done. A few months after the Book of Mormon was put into circulation, the Church of Jesus Christ of Latter Day Saints was duly established. All authority was vested in the prophet, who was both temporal and spiritual leader, and a carefully organized hierarchy was to carry out his orders. Only those of the faithful whose obedience was total would have some chance of salvation.

A first community was founded in Ohio, but they were rather far from the Indian descendants of Israel. In 1838, the prophet and his flock moved to Missouri, then to Illinois, where the little town of Commerce—on which they bestowed the more romantic name of Nauvoo—became their headquarters. It was a period of euphoria. Courted by the political parties in quest of new supporters, Joseph Smith managed to play the part of an undisputed dictator. He enjoyed great popularity. There was nothing of the Puritan reformer about him. Stylishly dressed, jovial, enjoying life in the open, he was said to "drink like a sailor and swear like a pirate."

Was it at a time when he was feeling in exceptional good humor that he had yet another revelation? However that may be, in 1843 his voices summoned him again and ordered him, this time, to think rather more systematically about the salvation of the weaker sex. They revealed to him the mysteries of the afterlife. If he could, would he not desire to join the group of privileged men who, after their death, were made divine (and thus preserved their bodies) because, on earth, they had practiced polygamy? A just recompense for their devotion. For by so doing they had ensured the salvation of their numerous wives who, without the "seal" of marriage, would have been incapable, on their own, of entering paradise. Such heavenly counsels did not fall on deaf ears. They came, in fact, at the most appropriate moment, for Joseph Smith and his intimates had already established their own little personal harems. Their joy was complete when they learned that, thanks to them, Isaiah's prophecies (Isaiah 4:1) had finally been fulfilled.

Alas, some schismatics, probably roused by their poorly

disciplined wives, dared rebel against the new instructions of the dictator-prophet. Incredibly enough, an opposition paper was published at Nauvoo itself. Repression was not long in coming. The polygamists, inspired by holy wrath, destroyed the printing press and put the unfortunate monogamists to flight. But this time the civil authorities felt impelled to intervene. Joseph Smith and his brother were jailed, and a few months later, in 1844, they were lynched.

Brigham Young picked up the torch. He was an even more astonishing figure than his predecessor. Like Smith, he came from the rugged, vigorous land of Vermont. In 1832, at thirty-one, he was converted to Mormonism. Three years later, he was admitted to the band of Twelve Apostles. He helped to organize the Nauvoo community, then went on a mission to England. He brought back with him thousands of converts who preferred anything to their wretched hovels. At Smith's death, the Mormons could boast of some forty communities; in particular, thanks to their industry and thrift, they had a well-stocked treasury. They were not inclined to leave the murder of their leader unavenged. Under the leadership of Brigham Young, who had succeeded the prophet and taken over five of Smith's twenty-seven wives, terror reigned for the space of two years in the Nauvoo region; a legion of "avenging angels" taught the "Gentiles" what it must cost them to oppose the divine dictates.

Nevertheless, the Mormons were but a handful and they soon had to bow before the law of numbers. In 1846 Brigham Young and 12,000 of them, in wagons, on horseback, many on foot pushing wheelbarrows, started off on their extraordinary migration to the West. Less than half of them persevered as far as the "promised land." They believed they had reached it in July 1847, and they burst out in loud hosannahs of thanksgiving when they reached the Great Salt Lake, lying below sea level, like the Dead Sea, and again, like the Dead Sea, traversed by a river which they compared with the Jordan. They decided to halt there and set to work.

Brigham Young ruled them with an iron hand, acting as administrator, judge, priest, and patriarch. Twenty-one wives (and forty-eight children) ensured his future divinization. One wife, Amelia Folson, was half his age and became his favorite in his old age, but in theory he refused to show the least preference. He demanded of his spouses to eschew needless make-up and coquetry. He even tried to impose a uniform on them: long pants rucked at the ankle, a coat going down to the knees, and a bowl-shaped felt hat. This time, the "sisters" dared show some opposition. A rare show of courage! Brigham Young and his flock did not like weepy women. And he had a splendid weapon to make them toe the line: the frightful threat of repudiation, heralding damnation. Few could withstand it. There was a fine sensation when one of Young's wives left him, in 1871, claiming that she had not had enough to eat or sufficient clothes to wear, and disclosed in a series of lectures the intimacies of Mormon married life. In Salt Lake City she was termed insane and was cited as a tragic example to insufficiently docile "sisters."

The Gold Rush posed another problem. Some of the members of the community had gone so far as to thrill at the fabulous tales coming from California. Brigham Young got up into the pulpit and started thundering even more than was his custom, telling them that if they, "the elders of Israel," wanted to go and work in the gold mines, let them go—and be damned! None dared go. They made up for it by striking hard bargains with the pioneers who passed through their territory.

The community continued to prosper—and its leader even more than the rest. When Brigham Young died, in 1877, he left a fortune of $1,626,510. Thanks to the Mormons, the desert was gradually transformed into a smiling and prosperous land. Up to the Civil War, they enjoyed *de facto* independence, and the exercise of federal control over Utah, established in 1850, was only nominal.

Given the spirit which animated these numerous sects, it is understandable that Catholicism should have had some difficulty in establishing itself in the United States.

Until about 1830, the question did not arise. Outside Louisiana, there were not even 100,000 Catholics in the United States. Before 1803, a single diocese, that of Baltimore, had sufficed for the whole country. Within twenty years, the situation had been transformed. In 1840 there were already 1 million Catholics, or 5½ per cent of the population. On the eve of the Civil War, one American in ten (3 million out of 31 million) owed spiritual allegiance to Rome.

We have referred to the practical problems arising out of the arrival of enormous numbers of Germans, and especially of Irish. Even more serious was the opposition they aroused in the religious sphere. The Protestant churches were deeply concerned over the intrusions of those newcomers. They felt themselves victims of some mysterious conspiracy. Prejudice against "Papism" had been slumbering. It awakened with an extraordinary virulence at the sight of these hundreds of thousands of immigrants firmly determined to remain loyal to the faith of their fathers. After the publication of the Protestant paper, *The Protestant*, a violent campaign was launched against Catholics. The question was tersely put: Was the Papacy that Babylon which St. John the Evangelist described in the Apocalypse? A disturbing question. There was no lack of volunteers to answer it.

In 1835 Lyman Beecher, father of the author of *Uncle Tom's Cabin*, published a book, *Plea for the West*, which revealed the degree and the tenacity of "anti-Roman" prejudice even among the educated. The author evoked the

specter of the "terrible confessional"; he assured his readers
that the aim of Catholicism was to divide the nation, dis-
rupt the Union, and overturn the country's free institutions.
Going one better, Samuel Morse, the inventor of wireless
telegraphy, described the Jesuits as puppets in the hands of
the Pope and summoned his fellow citizens to direct action:
let them place their sentries, and above all close their doors!
In 1836, the Protestant Reformation Society was founded:
its stated object was to coordinate the efforts already undertaken to convert Papists to Christianity. Innumerable lectures were organized, with really tantalizing themes, such as
the following: "The celibacy of priests and nuns: a history
of this modern innovation, and how it turns convents into
so many brothels."

The methods of "conversion" sometimes had a good
deal in common with those of a more primitive era of history. In 1831 the church of St. Mary was burned down in
New York; three years later, the Ursulines in Boston were
the victims of fanatics; their convent was set on fire, and in
the travesty of the trial which followed they were grossly
insulted. It must be acknowledged that simple souls had
some excuse for indulging in such excesses. Rumors and
calumnies were incessant. It was reported that the Catholics
were about to descend in a body on the fertile lands of the
West and seize them from their occupants; it was even suggested that the Holy Father had decided, for some obscure
reason, to leave Rome and settle in the Mississippi valley.
A slanderous literature enjoyed the success of sensationalism.
As examples of the accompanying illustrations, we might
cite that of a mother superior strangling her child, or of the
Inquisition with ghastly instruments of torture, or of a nun
"confessing"—her head on the priest's shoulder, and in the
background a huge bed, and so forth. In 1836 there appeared a book entitled *Awful Disclosures of the Hotel-Dieu
Nunnery.*

Under this promising title, a certain Maria Monk, who claimed to have managed with utmost difficulty to escape the clutches of the good sisters, produced "revelations" on convent life which the "respectable" hardly dared repeat. Their hesitation is understandable, since they read that a pit dug in the convent cellar was used to bury the babies of the nuns. (Maria Monk was convicted of fraud the same year, but more than a little remained of her calumnies.) Priests, it is true, did better still; according to another pamphlet, some of them had formed a secret society to "seize young virgins, kill them, and turn them into sausage meat"! The tension created by such stories occasionally reached such a pitch that a forceful bishop of New York, John Hughes, decided to establish a well-armed guard around every church. Needless to say, thousands of Irish immigrants, spoiling for a fight, offered their services. In Philadelphia, in 1844, two churches and a seminary were set on fire. In the ensuing riots, thirteen persons were killed and fifty wounded. *The Native American* drew the appropriate conclusions from the incident: the Pope's bloodstained hand had extended right to Philadelphia, to destroy it.

For some years, this kind of violence provoked a temporary reaction. In 1848 the federal government dared appoint an ambassador to the Vatican. It became fashionable among certain Protestants to send their daughters to Catholic institutions, where they were supposed to receive a more refined education than elsewhere. A new society, the American Protestant Association, sought to raise the level of the debate to questions of doctrine. Catholicism gained some distinguished converts, such as Isaac Thomas Hecker, the future founder of the Paulists, or Orestes Brownson, a former Transcendentalist. Brownson turned out to be a formidable polemicist. According to him, Rome was the true defender of freedom by reason of its systematic opposition to the state. Popular liberties, he dared assert, can be preserved only by a religion which is beyond popular control, which is above the people, which receives its inspiration from the beyond and which can command. His Protestant opponents, especially William Brownlow—"a man six feet tall, with a thundering voice, a man built to put fear into sinners"—could not get over such paradoxes.

The anti-Roman hysteria soon boiled up again. In 1849, the American and Foreign Christian Union was founded with the purpose of "converting Catholics to Christianity through light and through love." It would be a long struggle, to judge by the opinion of one delegate: Catholicism, he said, was and always had been a religion of fanaticism, persecution, and superstition. There was no crime, he went on, of which it had not been guilty, no sin against humanity which it had not committed, no blasphemy against God which it had not sanctioned. It was a power, he went on, streaming with the blood of the millions of murders it had committed, exhausted by a thousand years of debauchery, always ambitious, always bloodthirsty, always deceitful.

The Irish were not in the habit of leaving blows unanswered, and rather rashly they thought the time had come to take the offensive. In November 1850, a speech by the Archbishop of New York gave great offense. In an aggressive vein, the prelate declared that the Catholic Church's mission was in fact to convert the entire universe, including the Americans—city dwellers and country dwellers alike, army officers and naval officers, members of Congress, members of the Cabinet, the President, everyone. In these circumstances, a visit of the papal nuncio, Monsignor Gaetano Bedini, unwisely arranged for 1853, triggered off an explosion. Demonstrations took place all along his route, followed by pitched battles. A defrocked priest, Alessando Gavazzi, with hair to the shoulders and fiery eyes, wearing a monk's habit and with a dazzling gold cross on his breast, pursued the nuncio wherever he went, calling him the "bloody butcher of

Boulogne." When the papal envoy left, he had to embark secretly. The fanatics had no trouble rousing the populace. The Pope had sent a marble block for the construction of the famous Washington Monument; the crowd seized it and threw it into the Potomac. Streetcorner orators prolificated. One of them, modestly calling himself the Angel Gabriel, had his hours of triumph: every Sunday, he would ascend the steps of City Hall, blow loudly through his trumpet, and then proceed to thunder interminably against Pope, priests, and Catholics generally.

The conflict finally reached the political sphere. In 1850 a group of fanatics had founded the Secret Order of the Star-Spangled Banner to defend the Republic against "Roman" agitation. If asked about their activities, the members had undertaken to answer that they knew nothing about them—whence the name "know-nothings" which stuck to them. In 1854, the mysterious brotherhood achieved striking electoral successes. It all but gained control of New York state, and in Massachusetts it attracted a majority of the voters. The legislature which was elected under its influence spent most of its time making investigations of Catholic schools and convents which serious historians describe as buffooneries. The following year, however, the "know-nothings" began to lose much of their influence by adopting a stance in favor of slavery.

Around 1860, understandably, religious problems ceased for a time to occupy the center of the stage. What, indeed, were their eddies beside the tidal wave of the Civil War?

*Chapter XVII*

# EDUCATION

In 1650 the first settlers of Connecticut decided to adopt a statute, and immediately provided for the establishment of a school. The arguments advanced to justify their decisions have been cited over and over again: Since Satan, the enemy of the human race, finds his most powerful weapons in human ignorance; since it is essential that the wisdom of our fathers should not be buried with them; since the education of children, with the Lord's help, must be one of the principal concerns of government. . . . Thus, from the very foundation of the country, knowledge, progress, and virtue were linked together.

Nevertheless, the public authorities did not do very much for education before the second quarter of the nineteenth century. Up to that time, education was essentially the province of parents and the churches. Except in New England, there were few schools financed out of taxes. Parents sent their children to private establishments of varying excellence according to their means. The teaching in these schools was wholly founded on classical culture and religion.

For the "poor" there were schools run mainly by the

Quakers and dependent upon charity. Many hesitated to send their children to these schools, since that would constitute proof of their poverty. Sunday schools were more popular, but religious instruction was their only object. In point of fact, a large number of children received no instruction at all—some 50 per cent in New York in 1820, it is estimated.

The idea of free, state-run education began to spread at about that period. At first, it aroused fierce opposition. A member of the Indiana assembly could think of no choicer epitaph for himself than: "Here lies an enemy of free education." The directors of the private schools regarded the plans as an attack on their privileges; they accused their opponents of endangering the principle of free enterprise and succumbing to the seduction of foreign theories. To many, the idea of paying taxes to enable other people's children to escape ignorance seemed the rankest injustice. Moreover, to be forced by law to send one's children to school seemed a violation of the rights of parents. And for what purpose, anyway? "My boys don't need to know how to use anything but the Bible and their hands," was an old peasant's reply to an apostle of novelty. Another zealot of reaction observed that books cost too much and wasted too much time. These traditionalists spoke for thousands of their contemporaries. Even the churches were divided on the question. The Calvinists, faithful to their Puritan origin, supported the new principle. The more conservative Lutherans contended that to remove the schools from official control was the necessary counterpart of the separation of church and state.

These were rear-guard actions. The future clearly pointed in another direction. A variety of circumstances ensured the success of the state schools. Toward the left of the political spectrum, their expansion was identified with that of democracy. In the Jacksonian era, it became increasingly fashionable to talk of civil rights and responsibilities. Future citizens, it was asserted, should be taught the significance of those rights and responsibilities from their tenderest age— all citizens, and no longer just some, for the era of the common man was opening and that of the elite was closing. These arguments terrified the conservatives; they saw them as auguries of inevitable catastrophe.

Eventually, however, conservatives began to wonder whether education, after all, might not be used as a factor of social stability. The influx of immigrants from 1840 strengthened them in this hope. Hundreds of thousands of poor immigrants, as we know, landed on the Atlantic coast, ready for anything to justify the risks they had taken. "Respectable" social circles had nightmares about demagogues and revolutionaries exploiting this situation. Would not the discipline inculcated by the schoolmasters be a rampart against anarchy? Their fears became even livelier when the religion of the new arrivals became known—Papists, nothing but Papists, and still more Papists! These people would surely be harder than any others to "Americanize." It seemed, therefore, essential to get the children of the immigrants onto school benches as speedily as possible in order to rid them of the anachronistic and subversive principles with which they had been impregnated through the fanaticism of their priests and parents. The resources of the private schools were not, of course, adequate to the task. More and more people began to subscribe to the idea of public schools. With the advance of industrialization and urban development, the unions, which were quite active up to the 1837 crash, lent the movement their not insignificant support.

Nevertheless, the idea would not have spread as fast as it did but for the dedication of some strong personalities and the resources of a well-organized publicity campaign.

In this context, the name of Horace Mann is legendary in the United States. A native of New England, he began a brilliant career at the bar and in politics. But he was too much of an idealist to be satisfied with this kind of activity. At the age of forty, he decided to devote himself solely to problems of education. He was appointed secretary of the Massachusetts Education Board and became the life and soul of the reforms which were gradually to transform the educational system. Ardently idealistic, and at the same time pragmatic like so many of his contemporaries, he was interested in both theory and practice. Under his influence, Victor Cousin's report on education in Germany, and particularly in Prussia, came to be widely known in the United States. Mann took two ideas from it especially, and constantly urged their application: the need for a certain centralization of education by the state, and the usefulness of teacher-training schools. These were long-term plans. In the sphere of immediate achievements, Massachusetts owed him the modernization of a large number of school buildings, more uniformity in teaching methods, and especially—a perennial problem—the improvement of salaries. On the last point there was room enough for improvement: so far, an annual salary of $65 for women teachers was apparently the rule.

Another forerunner of modern American education was Henry Barnard (not to be confused with Frederick Barnard, who was president of Columbia from 1864 to 1889, and after whom the women's college, inaugurated six months after his death, was named). The earlier Barnard's action covered mainly Connecticut and Rhode Island. It earned him such hatred that a peasant once threatened to kill him if he dared set foot in his house. Maybe this incident discouraged him from continuing direct propaganda. He devoted himself, in later life, chiefly to the spreading of information. In 1855 he

began the publication of an encyclopedia which was ultimately to comprise thirty-one volumes of 800 pages each,
or a total—so it was said—of 12 million words. This king of
compilers did not shrink from any sacrifice. The undertaking cost him his fortune, and he died a poor man.

Barnard's "victories" were limited, perforce, to the small
group of professionals who used his learned publications.
Libraries were more effective; thanks to them, the public
was able to discover new ideas. It is estimated that in 1850
over 50,000 libraries (30,000 of them in Sunday schools, and
therefore very elementary, 18,000 in educational institutes,
and 3,000 in cities) were offering their readers nearly 13 million volumes. But reforms were mainly popularized through
lectures. Lectures, as we know, were enormously in demand
before the Civil War.

With the creation of lecture groups, a huge enterprise
of popularization got under way. There were apparently
some 3,000 of these associations, which functioned in villages as well as in the cities of the East. Speakers received
a fee of from $10 to $50. The greatest celebrities made tour
after tour under their auspices to promote the spread of education. In the West the Western Academy Institute played
somewhat the same role.

By mid-century, the reformers had virtually gained the
upper hand. Agreement was almost general on certain basic
principles. Most Americans approved the idea of free public
education at the primary and secondary levels. At least up
to a minimum age, they accepted compulsory education,
with the understanding that the parent's right of choice
would be respected; the rights of private education were
thus formally recognized. Nor was the advantage of giving
professors and teachers special training disputed. Ideas about
higher education remained more vague. No one considered

that it might not be restricted to a very small, fee-paying minority. A majority still believed that the role of the university should be confined to propagating general culture; nevertheless, the merits of specialized schools were coming to be increasingly recognized.

It is estimated that in 1850 there were 80,000 primary schools, in which 90,000 teachers taught 3.5 million pupils. In the rural districts, schools were open daily in winter so that the children could do their share of the work in the fields. Elsewhere, the scholastic year was nine months. School hours generally were from 9 A.M. to 12 noon, and from 1 to 4 P.M., five days a week.

The curriculum consisted essentially of the three R's, plus a smattering of grammar, history, and geography. (It was only after the Civil War, with its shattering of the national unity, that it was felt necessary to inculcate a sense of nationhood in children, and hence to teach them their country's history in greater detail.) Morals and civics held a place of importance. Girls attended the same classes as boys, but they were also taught sewing and knitting.

Until about 1840, the "Lancastrian" method—so called after its inventor, John Lancaster, an English Quaker who emigrated to the United States in 1818—was in effect in most of the states. This method was to assemble the children in huge halls with a capacity up to 1,000, then to divide them into groups of ten under the supervision of monitors selected from the oldest and the most intelligent students. These acted as tutors, teaching their fellow students what they had just learned. Thus emulation and discipline were the foundations of the system. Since it was intended for mass education, it was of course inappropriate to the village. Here there would sometimes be only a single teacher. Classes varied between 55 and 75. The children sat on benches, boys and girls separated by a central aisle. The boys' rows were

not always very orderly, and good biceps were often as useful to a teacher as a good brain, for he often had to grapple
with youngsters almost as big as he was. If he lost the battle,
no intellectual prowess could save his reputation. Such incidents were rare, however, for discipline was strict and corporal punishment was frequently used. The buildings were
in general very inadequate and poorly heated. The "little
red school house" has passed into American folklore. For
idolizers of the past, it has become the symbol of former
virtues in contrast with present-day vices.

The more progressive educational ideas of the Swiss
Johannes Pestalozzi gained ground in the 1830's, but they
had little influence before the Civil War, except perhaps in
the teaching of mathematics. In all other subjects, pedagogy
relied mainly on memory. The recitation of lessons learned
by rote took up the main part of the class. Primers were
therefore of utmost importance and some were prodigiously
successful. For example, some 122 million copies, apparently, were published of *First and Second Readings* by William H. McGuffey, a preacher and educator. For nearly fifty
years, all American school children used them. They were
filled with virtuous sentiments. No less didactic and almost
as popular were Noah Webster's *Reading Lessons*, published
in 1783, which were still in use a half-century later. Their
success—some 80 million copies must have been printed in
the century following their publication—enabled Webster
to spend twenty years working on his famous dictionary, the
first issue of which appeared in 1828. His *History of the
United States*, together with another history textbook by
Samuel Goodrich, were the basic works used for the teaching of the past. Both were elementary and purely descriptive, and permeated with conventional patriotism. Jebediah
Morse's *Elements of Geography* and Joseph Ray's *Arithmetic* completed the bookshelves of young Americans.

It gradually became customary to spend eight years in primary school. The vast majority of children went no farther. A chosen few, however, went on to secondary studies. Most of these schools, in the 1850's, were still private. They were known as "academies," and taught mainly Greek and Latin, the Bible, and Shakespeare. Some were more advanced—Philipps Exeter, for example—offering a choice of two programs, one entirely based on the classics and intended for future scholars, the other more practical and having no other aim than to prepare students for "the ordinary business of life." Some more daring establishments, finally, were already succumbing to the intoxication of "progressive" education. The most famous of these sanctuaries of progress was Temple School, which Bronson Alcott managed to open in Boston in 1834 in an atmosphere of mystical Transcendentalism. For a time he succeeded in gathering some forty pupils within its walls—children of parents with "advanced" ideas. Each was to develop as he pleased, at the pace appropriate to his nature. There were no punishments save those freely agreed to or imposed by the majority of the students. Everything went more or less satisfactorily until Alcott decided to institute discussions on the mystery of Christ's nativity and on sexual problems. Sex, according to him, was sacred, purely spiritual, transcendental, and sublime. Though well disposed, the parents could not believe their ears, and three-fourths of them withdrew their children. The 1837 crash completed the collapse of this noble experiment.

The high schools did not indulge in such indiscretions. The teaching there was along the same lines as in primary school, and under the same conditions, since it was free. But these institutions were absurdly few in number: 321 in 1860, more than one-half in the three states of Massachusetts (78), Ohio (48), and New York (41). An insignificant number beside the 6,085 academies and their 12,260 teachers and 263,000 students.

The number of colleges and universities at about that date has been estimated at 246, only about thirty of them situated west of the Mississippi. The vast majority were private, confessional establishments. Many were located in the heart of the country. These small rural colleges exerted a profound influence on the development of the national character. Among the best known are Amherst, Dartmouth, and Union. The student body rarely exceeded 200 or 300; the teaching staff, about a dozen. The atmosphere was a family one, in which everyone knew everybody else. Discipline, however, was not excluded; still less, religion. The day began at 6 A.M. with a religious service in chapel; Saturday was devoted to religious instruction and Sunday was spent in the sinister atmosphere of the Puritan sabbath; occasional revivals would stir up lukewarm students. The program included Greek and Latin, some philosophy, a little French or German and, of course, literature, duly expurgated. Chemistry and physics were much in vogue, accompanied by a few—cautious—elements of biology and botany. Life was simple and monotonous. Sports, especially baseball and rowing, did not make their appearance until 1850; previously they had been virtually unknown. The main forms of recreation were bullying newcomers and periodically getting really drunk—one way of getting rid of one's complexes. This was the period of the emergence of college fraternities, those semi-secret, semi-snobbish student associations which are often designated by Greek letters: Kappa Alpha, Sigma Phi, and so on.

Other establishments, which prided themselves on more closely resembling European universities, were situated in or near cities: Harvard near Boston, Yale in New Haven, Brown

in Providence, Princeton in Princeton, Pennsylvania in Philadelphia, William and Mary in Williamsburg, to mention
only a few. The influence of German methods predominated, especially at Harvard. Strongly idealistic and aristocratic traditions were cultivated. The principal objective
was still the training of an elite, and only condescending
reference was made to the education of the masses.

Seventeen state universities were in operation by 1860,
each built on land granted free by the particular state assembly. Most of them made no claim to intellectualism. The
University of Virginia, proud of its seniority (it was founded
in 1819) and of its founder (Thomas Jefferson), tended to
draw its inspiration from the principles of Athenian democracy. Elsewhere there was more interest in the advent of the
"common man." This new type of student, it was felt, should
receive a new type of education. Some educators—obstructed,
incidentally, by the trustees—advocated less rigid programs
of instruction, with a minimum of compulsory classes. In
particular, there were in these universities many enthusiastic
supporters of technical education. Nevertheless, such education was only very slowly put into effect. Before the Civil
War, virtually the only engineering school was the Rens-
selaer Polytechnic Institute, founded in Troy in 1824. Medical schools were more numerous and better attended, and
especially law schools, in which the national mania for procedure was already being given full scope.

Bluestockings were almost universally despised. The
ideal of womanhood, as we have said, was the romantic type.
There was incompatibility, it was felt, between intellectual
effort and physical development. Everything in women's
education must aim at preparation for marriage, and it was
generally accepted that knowing too much was not the best
way to find a suitor. A few secondary schools, however, were
opening their doors to the daughters of parents presump-

tuous enough to take the risk. In the 1850's an academy founded in Troy, New York, by Emma Willard, one of the leaders of the feminist movement, could already boast a thirty-year existence. More recent, but no less famous, was the Mount Holyoke Female Seminary, opened in 1837 by Mary Lyon. They worked hard there, to judge by a student's letter. On Thanksgiving morning, she wrote, they had been allowed to sleep as late as they liked, provided they were ready for breakfast at 8 A.M. She had risen at 5—an hour later than usual—and worked for two and a half hours before breakfast. The establishment was later transformed into a college, but its example was followed by no more than some sixty institutions. Prior to the Civil War, not more than a few thousand women were receiving academic training. Moreover, young men and women never—or virtually never—attended the same establishments. Oberlin College, Ohio, created a fine sensation in 1803 by opening its doors to students of both sexes; it was followed twenty years later by Antioch, in the same state, and then by Iowa State University in 1856.

In the South, such promiscuity was not so much as to be thought of. The little instruction which girls received they received at home. It would have appeared contrary to both human and divine law to let them go to school. Boys, on the other hand, received a fairly good education. The very rich provided tutors for their sons; others sent their sons to the best private schools and colleges in the South, or even in the North. They did not seek to make scholars of them, but "honest men," nurtured on the common culture, and conscious of their civic duties. Representatives of the South predominate in the roster of pre–Civil War statesmen. There was, of course, nothing democratic about these practices. They benefited only a selected few; the mass of the people in the realm of King Cotton was even more ignorant than elsewhere. As for the slaves, they were barely literate. In some regions they were not even permitted to learn to read and write.

It is estimated that of a population of 23 million in 1850, 1 million were illiterate. Nevertheless, the education crusade had begun to bear its fruits. The Civil War slowed down the advance but did not halt it, for even at that time the search for knowledge was a constant objective in America.

*Chapter XVIII*

# LETTERS, ARTS, AND SCIENCES

Who would think of reading an American book, an English critic asked in 1820. Who, indeed, and how, if we are to believe Emerson, who asserted that not a book, not a speech, not a conversation, not a thought had seen the light of day in the thirty years that followed 1790. Was this no more than an outburst of irony on the part of a man of letters naturally contemptuous of the material conquests of the young Republic? Possibly. Nevertheless, the period following independence was in fact characterized by extreme intellectual poverty.

The same could not be said of the middle of the nineteenth century. Twelve years earlier, Emerson's intellectual declaration of independence had sounded like a clarion call: Americans, he said, had listened too long to the sophisticated muses of Europe; the era of their dependence and long apprenticeship was coming to an end; the time had come for Americans to use their feet for walking, their hands for working, and their brains for thinking. Edgar Allan Poe died in 1849, *The Scarlet Letter* was published in

1850, *Moby Dick* in 1851, *Uncle Tom's Cabin* in 1852. Two years later came *Walden,* followed a few months later by *Hiawatha.* And 1855 was indeed a fertile year; it also saw the publication of *Leaves of Grass.* In the space of twenty years, Emerson, Poe, Hawthorne, Melville, Thoreau, Longfellow, Whitman had written the works which have made them immortal.

This literary harvest had been preceded by an intellectual revival centering in New York.

For a score of years, the Knickerbocker Group (so called after *Knickerbocker's History of New York,* published by Washington Irving in 1809) dominated the literary scene. It could boast of being the first manifestation of a truly national literature. Washington Irving made a universal reputation for himself in the group, in the first place through his imaginative works, written with humor and charm, and secondly through his historical works, in particular his *Life of Washington,* which made a contribution of major importance to the study of the first years of the Union. Better known still, abroad as well as in his own country, was James Fenimore Cooper, who soon came to rival Sir Walter Scott. From his books, a great many Europeans were persuaded, once and for all, that all Americans wore feathers, Indian style, wielded the hatchet like redskins, and smoked the peace pipe at every opportunity. His missionary zeal and his taste for polemics did not simplify life for him. He sought to explain America to Europe and Europe to America— a perilous venture which earned him equal unpopularity on either side of the Atlantic. William Cullen Bryant, the third best known member of the Knickerbocker Group, was untroubled by any such ambitions. A typical Puritan and a no less firm liberal, he expressed respectable and generously accepted ideas in prose or verse with no great fervor but with deep conviction.

None of these works could be said to have been the product of genuine inspiration. It was left to New England, so austere and passionate, to generate the flame which would finally give life to American literature. Here, all three creative elements of any civilization were present: tradition, leisure, and a taste for the things of the spirit. The seed which had been ripening for two centuries bore its fruit in striking fashion around 1840. A number of groups emerged, all enamored of the intellectual life. Some, of the Back Bay type, were less concerned with reforming society than with civilizing young America. These tendencies were perfectly embodied in Longfellow, James Russell Lowell, and Oliver Wendell Holmes, the first by his poetry of a serene simplicity, the second by his brilliant satire, the third by his essays and his sparklingly witty lectures. The historians, too, were more eager to describe the past than to fashion the future. Bancroft, Prescott, Parkman, and Ticknor wrote works at this period which were soon to become classics.

The preoccupations of the Concord group were of a very different kind. In that romantic little village so typical of the Boston area, in an atmosphere resonant still with the echoes of the War of Independence, a few idealists had gathered around Emerson, determined to change the face of the earth. They claimed to found their ideas on philosophical principles—a claim of well-nigh revolutionary audacity. De Tocqueville, at about the same time, noted that in no civilized country was there less concern with philosophy than in the United States. The Transcendentalists, therefore, were bound to remain in the minority. This role was not to their taste. Apostles of democracy that they were, they were wholly disinclined to shut themselves up in an ivory tower. Emerson's words are significant in that connection: to walk without the people, he wrote, was to walk in darkness. They regarded the distinction between "intellectuals" and "the masses" as a purely transitory one, which would vanish with the diffusion of "light." Nevertheless, they were forced, willy-nilly, into the role of an elite, the complexity of their doctrine being such as to make them hard to follow.

Emerson's talent, and the reason for his success, was to render universally accessible a philosophy whose essence was so hazy. For there were two Emersons. There was the philosopher, the mystic, who adjured the pioneers plodding westwards to hitch their wagon to a star, or who wrote, of himself, that when his feet were touching the soil, when his head was bathed in the air joyously circulating about it, when he felt himself lifted toward infinite spaces, his self—his hateful self—dissolved. He was no longer anything, he continued, but he saw everything, and through him there circulated the currents of the universe. He was a part, a particle, of the divine. Or again: we see the world only fragmentarily; sun, moon, animals, trees—all these are only parts of a whole which is the soul. And in the same vein, he wrote that all are born believing: man bears faith within him as an apple tree produces apples. But such raptures did not prevent him from coming back to earth. His lectures abounded in sayings which Benjamin Franklin would not have disavowed: the sole principle, the vital principle of a true republic is goodwill; never to change one's mind is the mark of a petty spirit; God offers every brain a chance between truth and rest. Platitudes, we may say, but platitudes through which he succeeded in communicating to his audience his faith in human perfectibility, his unshakable optimism, his search for happiness which he was incapable of dissociating from his search for the ideal. He was the most eloquent standard-bearer of this thrilling period of gestation in his country's life. One of his biographers wrote of him, recently, that the world had never seen anyone like him before, and may never again see his like. Future generations may confirm that tribute.

More original, probably, but less profound, Thoreau

exerted influence only on a handful of logicians, prepared like himself to follow the consequences of their individualism to their extreme conclusion. America in 1850 was not lacking in idealists eager to absorb Emerson's precepts. Nevertheless, to refuse to pay taxes and to pay them in the form of a prison term required such a special form of logic that although a good many admired Thoreau, no one followed his example.

In Hawthorne, there are eddies still of the Transcendentalist current, but how attenuated, how transformed! He was no mystic and he was not afraid, like his Concord friends, to lift the veils and reveal man in his often unattractive nudity. He did not shrink from the conclusions to which his somber imagination led him. He restored the rights of pessimism which Emerson had so stubbornly sought to banish. But it is the form of his works, even more than his ideas or his style, that assure him a place of honor. He proved himself a master of the short story form which was to play so great a part in American literature.

More illustrious in this sphere, and in any case better known outside the United States, Edgar Allan Poe resembled none of his literary confrères. By the originality of his personality, by his instability, and especially by his turbulent life, he stood apart from his times. He suffered hunger, cold, poverty; he sought escape in suicide—and failed; he consoled himself in the bottle—and succeeded only too well. Lowell said of him that he was "three-fifths . . . genius and two-fifths pure fudge." If posterity has revised this judgment, it has been in the direction of modifying the expressions of contempt it contained.

The contrast is striking between the two poets Poe and Whittier. We refer to them together because they have nevertheless the trait in common of never having belonged to a coterie. For Poe, poetry was the rhythmic creation of beauty, and its object was pleasure, not truth. For Whittier, on the other hand, it was an investment in the service of an ideal. Whittier was the perfect specimen of a Quaker, with all the generosity and extremism that characterizes the Quaker mentality. He never ceased to protest against what he called injustice, intolerance, inhumanity. He championed every reform, especially the abolition of slavery, and for thousands of his contemporaries he was the bard of the crusade which they had proudly espoused.

Walt Whitman's name need not have been included in the present study, since he was virtually unknown before the Civil War. The publication of *Leaves of Grass* in 1855 went unnoticed. With the exception of Emerson, who recognized Whitman's inspiration, the pundits paid no attention to the work. Three enthusiastic reviews appeared, it is true, but unfortunately they had been penned by the author himself. Many would have signed them twenty years later.

Melville, the pessimist, and perhaps the greatest worker of the period, did not have the good fortune to enjoy real popularity at any point in his lifetime. He was actually too far removed from his time. He found certainty neither in religion, in science, nor in progress. He even went so far as to dispute the very "mission" of America: the man who hated the oppressors, he wrote, might well become an oppressor himself—that was often the case with nations as with men. After *Moby Dick*, which enjoyed only relative success, despite the symbolism of the theme, so obviously inspired by the national philosophy, Melville lived for forty more years in almost complete obscurity, and his salary as a customs clerk brought him more money than did his literary work.

As in present-day America, there was considerable prejudice against intellectuals in general. They were regarded as incapable of making money and therefore incapable of contributing to the development of the country, dangerous because too open to foreign influence, tending to take an "aristocratic" view of life. It was the virtual consensus that literature should be left to the women—under certain cautious provisos, of course.

What did the women read? Some works enjoyed considerable popularity. Up to 1 million copies of *Uncle Tom's Cabin* were printed. Over 300,000 of Longfellow's works appeared. Without reaching such figures, *The Scarlet Letter*, Prescott's *The Conquest of Mexico*, Thoreau's *Walden*, and Emerson's *Essays* may be regarded as having made the best-seller list some one hundred years ago. A book in vogue could be expected to sell between 10,000 and 20,000 copies. Until about 1840, the price averaged $2 to $3. Some 200 books appeared each year. At about this period popular editions appeared at 50 or even 25 cents. In spite of the poor quality of the paper and the printing, they were extraordinarily successful. Female readers, in particular, thrilled over Mrs. Southworth's melodramatic novels, where "villains" alternated harmoniously with "heroes." In the South, William Gilmore Simm's works were in constant demand— a demand that was well satisfied, since he produced sixty-five books.

There were no copyright laws to protect foreign books. Works by popular authors were immediately published in what were rightly called pirated editions, for they entailed no payment at all of author's royalties.

French authors, of course, were read with considerable hesitation. Balzac, Dumas, and Victor Hugo had their admirers, but as a critic severely recalled, they were "characterized by an unprecedented degree of extravagance and immorality." As for Eugene Sue's work, it was rubbish, according to the *New York Herald*. English authors were more successful. Although Byron and Shelley shocked "respectable" people, Walter Scott, Thackeray, Tennyson, and Bulwer Lytton were in all the libraries. Dickens too, even more so, perhaps, after his adverse comments on the country. As Fanny Kemble wrote to one of her friends, a book cannot enjoy success in the United States if it does not criticize the Americans. British travelers must have shared this opinion, to judge by the comments of "Boz," Mrs. Trollope, Harriet Martineau, Fanny Kemble herself, and a number of others.

All these books, whether good or bad, circulated only in "polite society"; they virtually did not penetrate the countryside. In an average farmhouse you would find the Bible, *Pilgrim's Progress,* Walker's dictionary, a surveyor's guide, and a few novels by Jane Porter, James Fenimore Cooper, or Walter Scott. To this list might sometimes be added George Fox's and John Woolman's *Journals* and, after 1850, Webster's dictionary and Pike's arithmetic primer. *Godey's Ladies Book,* and *Frank Leslie's* and *Peterson's* magazines were intended for housewives. The entire family, however, delighted in almanacs. We have already mentioned *The Farmer's Almanac;* accompanying it, usually, was Benjamin Franklin's *Poor Richard's Almanac,* filled with wise precepts, Landredth's *Rural Register* for agriculture, Dr. Jayne's *Medical Almanac and Guide to Health,* Hostetter's *Illustrated Almanac* and Ayer's *Almanac* for kitchen recipes and housekeeping hints, as well as "funny" stories to while away winter evenings.

On the subject of art, there is not much to say. Even more than in regard to literature, there was a clear cleavage between artistic circles and the rest of the country.

Architects, as we pointed out earlier, confined themselves, between 1820 and 1850, to imitating the principles of antiquity, some with more talent, others with less. The result was a neoclassical style, of which the University of Virginia in Charlottesville is the happiest example. When Gothic came into style in the middle of the century, its imitation was equally lacking in originality. There was little promise, in that period, of the magnificent concepts of modern American town planning.

Painting made laudable efforts, but was handicapped in any numbers of ways. In the first place, it was virtually impossible to get artistic training at home. A voyage to Europe—a very costly enterprise—was a must for those daring spirits whom the demon of art held in his sway. Düsseldorf, as much as Rome, Paris, or London, attracted great numbers of students, since this was a period of Germanophilism. But on their return, they had to find purchasers—a difficult undertaking. Art patrons were few. Those who were willing to give an artist some encouragement usually confined themselves to ordering their own portraits, or those of their wives, in an atmosphere hardly conducive to inspiration. Some artists nevertheless gained fame by this means: one of the best known, Thomas Sully, is credited with producing 2,600 portraits. George C. Bingham, William S. Mount, and even Morse, until his genius showed him another road, also painted considerable numbers of portraits. But the daguerrotype, which became immensely popular after 1840, was a formidable rival in this respect. Historical scenes were a surer field, with certain subjects mandatory. Portraits of the Founding Fathers, the signing of the Declaration of Independence, the Battle of Bunker Hill, and George Washington crossing the Delaware adorned the walls of countless houses. The portrayal of such scenes at least gave painters an excuse for dissimulating behind an already intense spirit of nationalism their own aspirations toward a beauty of which the immense majority of their fellow Americans were instinctively suspicious. Moveover, by glorifying the past, they avoided charges of immorality—no small consideration in a society with very rigid standards of morality.

Under the influence of Romanticism, landscapes came into fashion. The dreamy and grandiose horizons of the Hudson Valley inspired the disciples of the Hudson River

School—a pale anticipation of the Barbizon School—to produce a large number of canvases which were competent but
devoid of emotion. But here again, modern techniques com-
peted with the artist's brush. In the first place, the colored
Currier and Ives lithographs rapidly became a standard
component of interior decoration. Secondly, and especially,
huge mobile panoramas drew enormous crowds; landscape
painters cut a poor figure in comparison. Two such panoramas were particularly popular: one representing the battle of New Orleans in 1812; the other, extending over half
a mile, unfolded before the spectators a series of views of the
Mississippi valley from the river head to its mouth.

For a short time, a statue drew public attention to sculp-
ture—an art that was even more despised than painting. But
woe to him who might give scandal! In 1843, Hiram Powers,
an artist much in vogue, dared exhibit a "Greek Slave"
which aroused a storm. For she was completely unclothed.
The question was raised—horrors!—whether the sculptor had
used a live model. The Cincinnati clergy instituted an in-
quiry; after carefully examining the *corpus delicti*, they gave
it, so to speak, their *imprimatur*. Encouraged by his success,
the sculptor subsequently produced an Eve before the Fall,
adorned with not so much as a fig leaf. But these were exceptional exploits. His more prudent competitors followed
the example of the painters and chose their subjects pref-
erably from history. Horatio Greenough made busts of La
Fayette, Alexander Hamilton, John Quincy Adams. In particular, he fashioned a gigantic George Washington, half
naked and nobly draped in a toga. There was a considerable
problem in finding a home for it; it was eventually accepted
by the Smithsonian Institute.

In so poor an artistic environment, music stood out for
its vitality. It received a considerable impetus from the arrival of German immigrants. Young ladies of good family
began to play scales on the Chickering pianos manufactured

in Boston. It was considered in good taste to attend concerts. The New York Philharmonic Orchestra was founded in 1842. At its first performance, on December 7, it gave the Fifth Symphony, the Oberon Overture, and *Fidelio*. Tours were soon organized by European artists. The Norwegian violinist Ole Bull, a pupil of Paganini, plunged his listeners into ecstasy. We referred earlier to the welcome extended to Jenny Lind, the "Swedish Nightingale," when she toured the Union between 1850 and 1852 under Barnum's aegis.

A few composers sought to emancipate themselves from foreign influences. Lowell Mason, in particular, gained fame through his hymns, among them *Nearer, My God, to Thee*, which the passengers of the *Titanic* are said to have sung as it went down. Another musician sought to imitate Walt Whitman, claiming that in harmony he had found means of expressing his country's soul. He must have been somewhat difficult to understand, for at a performance in the White House, President Tyler interrupted him with the request that he play some good old Virginia air instead. Regional music was, indeed, the most popular of all; people never wearied of its nationalistic and sentimental themes. *America, Old Folks at Home, Home, Sweet Home*, brought tears to many eyes.

Science was far from acquiring the unparalleled prestige which it was subsequently to enjoy. Its development was still obstructed by the churches, which feared that science might dispossess them of their traditional privileges. The publication of *The Origin of Species* in 1859 went more or less unnoticed. The din of civil conflict was such as to deny Darwin's ideas any resonance, and it was not until after the war that they began to arouse passionate controversy. The theory of evolution, however, did have its ardent champions —at their head, Asa Gray, who was dubbed the Christopher Columbus of American botany—but circumstances constrained them to walk warily on so explosive a terrain. True, as far back as 1835, the great scholar Benjamin Silliman—founder of the first American scientific periodical, *The American Journal of Science and Arts*—had hinted, in a series of lectures on geology, that the Bible should not, perhaps be too literally interpreted. At about the same date, the discovery of dinosaur bones in Connecticut had raised other questions concerning the antiquity of the planet.

Orthodox theories had their distinguished defenders too, chief among them Louis Agassiz, a well-known Swissborn naturalist who spent the last twenty-five years of his life, from 1846 to 1873, at Harvard. He claimed that the species had remained immutable since their creation. Nevertheless, respect for tradition did not prevent him from having a very inquiring mind. He was a great adversary of theoretical science and constantly urged his followers to employ methods of direct experimentation. Practicing what he preached, he would carry snakes in his pockets.

Another naturalist, John J. Audubon, a native of France, operated in the more poetical sphere of ornithology, and his *Birds of America* has become a classic.

Botany and geology were probably the two branches of science which developed most rapidly in that period, although physics, too, made considerable strides. We know the part played by Morse. Joseph Henry was no less ingenious. He was an emulator of Faraday and, like him, an expert in electromagnetic research. He initiated those meteorological bulletins which Americans have learned to read with implicit faith, despite the fact that these learned predictions are repeatedly upset by the whim of a tropical hurricane. Joseph Henry's reputation rests at least as much on his position as the first director of the celebrated Smithsonian Institution as on his discoveries. In 1829 an English chemist, James Smithson, left 100,000 pounds to the United States for the founding of an establishment in Washington dedicated to the increase and diffusion of knowledge among men. The terms of reference were vague. Traditionalists, and Calhoun in particular, looked askance at the project. It needed the intervention of John Quincy Adams for the bequest to be finally accepted. Even then, Congress considered using the funds principally for a sort of museum of curiosities, Barnum style, in Washington. It is largely to the impetus and drive of Joseph Henry that the Smithsonian Institution owes its present position as a scientific center of worldwide renown.

*Chapter XIX*

# NEWSPAPERS
# AND PERIODICALS

In the America of the early nineteenth century, news was transmitted mainly by word of mouth. Posting houses and general stores served as information centers. The introduction of a steam-operated printing press by Daniel Treadwell in 1822, the industrial manufacture of this new type of machine thanks to Isaac Adams and Robert Hoe, the invention of rotary printing presses by the latter's nephew, Richard Hoe, in 1847—all these together formed the springboard for the expansion of the press. Thirty-seven news organs were circulating in 1776; it would really be more accurate to call them leaflets or fliers, since the format was small and they did not contain more than four pages. We may recall, in this connection, the part played by the *Federalist* ten years later, in the ratification of the Constitution. By 1810 there were 359 such pamphlets in circulation, 861 in 1828, and 1,403 in 1840.

All these papers were local in character and served mainly as the means of expression and influence of their owners. Typical in this respect was the *Springfield News*, founded in 1824 as a weekly by Samuel Bowles. It was later to become celebrated through its vigorous anti-slavery campaign. But the circulation of such organs was, in the nature of the case, limited; moreover, their price was still very high —6 cents—and hence accessible only to a minority.

The *New York Sun*, launched by Benjamin H. Day in 1833, was the first one-cent paper. It soon began to specialize in sensation. Accidents, duels, gambling, immorality—duly reprobated, of course, in virtuous editorials—provided it with matter calculated to appeal to a wider public; within a few years, its circulation had leapt from 4,000 to 19,000. In 1835, it achieved an unprecedented triumph through a hoax which has remained famous in the history of American journalism. One of its reporters at $12 a week, Richard A. Locke, published a series of articles purportedly reproducing a report by Sir John Herschel, son of Sir William Herschel, who had discovered Uranus in 1781. In this document, the English astronomer described life on the moon as he claimed to have perceived it through a new telescope at the Cape of Good Hope. The public was thrilled with descriptions of the winged creatures resembling humans and the smoke-producing beavers which supposedly populated our satellite. Locke's triumph knew no bounds when he confessed his trick, after having allowed several scholars to engage in a serious discussion of the subject.

Almost immediately after the *Sun*, the *Philadelphia Public Ledger*, then the *Baltimore Sun* extended to other cities than New York the privilege of having a press with a wide circulation. The first of these papers won fame by adopting a series of maxims exceedingly typical of the American approach, such as: "Don't say you know when you have only heard tell"; or "You have to write simply if you want to make a hit with illiterate readers"; or finally, this one, in which we seem to hear, in anticipation, an echo of John Dewey and relativism: "Before you decide, try to understand both sides of the question, and remember that there are always at least two sides to every question."

James Gordon Bennett cared little enough for this principle when he established the *New York Herald* in 1835. This Barnum of journalism was an astonishing personage. It has been said that his success was due to "crimes of passion, Wall Street panics, and Gordon Bennett himself." He exerted a strong influence. He expected God himself to collaborate with him; nothing, he wrote, and no one, could prevent his paper from succeeding save the Almighty—and the Almighty was entirely on his side. There was nothing he did not use for copy. When he was about to get married, he informed his readers of the fact, explaining that the weather was so fine, everything was going so well, the prospects of a moral and political reform were so good, that he could no longer resist the divine instinct inherent in every honest nature. He was therefore, he continued, going to marry one of the most marvelous women in respect of intelligence, heart, soul, propriety, looks, and manners that he had ever met in the course of his interesting pilgrimage through life. He must give the world an example of blissful married life. In a few days, in accordance with the sacred rites of Holy Church (he was a Catholic), he would become the husband of one of the most remarkable, accomplished, and beautiful young ladies of the day.

The arrival in New York of the first steamer to cross the Atlantic, the *Sirius*, was another pretext for talking about himself: he had decided, he wrote, to go to London in a few days' time, first in order to see the coronation of Queen Victoria on June 21, 1837, and also to set up agencies in Europe in order to be ahead of all other papers on the American continent.

To have sole rights on a piece of news, or at least to be the first to publish it, was in fact an obsession with this master journalist. He would sometimes send fast boats on their way to America and bring back newspapers and news before they did. He had an admirable knowledge of the unsophisticated readers who delighted in the *Herald*. He knew they were more interested in the gossip column than in political news. Who cared about the elections of any particular candidate, whether it be the President or a police commissioner? He was first to publish the stock exchange prices, first to report on religious functions, first to tear down the veils traditionally surrounding society gatherings. From a circulation of 17,000 in 1840, the paper had achieved a circulation of 100,000 just before the Civil War, when Gordon Bennett came out violently on the side of the slave owners. The *Herald's* influence nevertheless remained limited, despite its headlines and its exaggerations.

The *New York Tribune* enjoyed far greater authority. The first issue appeared in 1841, following a merger with the weekly *New Yorker*. The new journal differed in every way from the *Herald*. First of all, with respect to the mentality of the founder: whereas Gordon Bennett was concerned only with sensation, Horace Greeley claimed to be interested only in ideas. The former was an activist; the latter did not scorn to moralize: a lazy man, he wrote, is always the pitiful victim of a bad education. Or again: it was his invincible determination to become wiser today than he had been the day before. From the outset, there was an aura of intellectualism about the *Tribune*, often *avant-garde* and a trifle snobbish. Karl Marx was one of its correspondents for a time. Albert Brisbane, an apostle of Fourierism, was one of its contributors. Charles A. Dana, who became editor-in-chief in 1847, had for five years taken part in the Brook Farm experiment, to which we shall refer later. The new journal reflected these somewhat contradictory influences. Generally speaking, it took a liberal line. It played a decisive part in the anti-slavery campaign. In less than twenty years, its circulation rose tenfold: 26,000 in 1847, 112,000 in 1854, and 287,750 on the eve of the Civil War.

The *New York Times*, founded in 1851 by Henry Jarvis Raymond, appeared insignificant beside these two giants. It adopted from the start a position of objective responsibility and morality which characterizes it still. Passionate commitment to political goals, on the contrary, characterized the *Brooklyn Eagle*, in which Walt Whitman sang of America's "Manifest Destiny," or the Boston *Liberator*, in which William Lloyd Garrison wrote on behalf of the most extreme abolitionists. And at the same time, fiery editorials by William C. Bryant, who was at once a poet and a polemicist, brought renown to the *New York Evening Post*, in existence since 1801. In the West, finally, the papers with the largest circulations were undoubtedly the Louisville *Journal* and the Chicago *Tribune*.

A French-language press operated in several parts of the country. In Louisiana, *L'Abeille* and a very large number of other papers consistently refused to use English; in New York, the French population was large enough for the celebrated *Courrier des Etats-Unis* to have appeared as far back as 1825. It existed peacefully until 1851, taking both an anti-abolitionist line for America and a Republican line for France. The *coup d'état* of December 2 brought it a rival, *Le Phare*, which was actively Bonapartist. For a time, the two papers were locked in fierce combat. The hostilities ended with a merger which enabled the *Courrier* to retain its name while adopting the views of its rival. The standard of freedom was then taken up by *Le Républicain*, and subsequently by *Le Progrès*, but for barely a year.

In the West, the *Journal de l'Illinois* was published in 1857 by the remnants of the Cabet expedition. In San Francisco, the French soon felt the need to read the news in their native tongue. The *Echo du Pacifique* appeared in 1852. It was destined to enjoy a remarkable longevity, since it still exists under the name *Le Courrier Français des Etats-Unis.*

Periodicals led a precarious existence. Almost their only source of revenue was subscriptions. Advertisements were confined to a few pages, and it would have appeared undignified to them to include any ads but those for publishers and stationers. Increased postage rates, in particular, more or less precluded a wide circulation. Even by paying their contributors very little, periodicals found it hard to balance their budgets. Most of them folded up during the Civil War.

About 1850, the *North American Review*, which could already boast a thirty-five-year existence, was unquestionably in the forefront of the literary reviews. It had been founded in 1815 to neutralize the influence of the French Revolution and to rid the young Republic of the British literary hegemony; it was the vehicle of conservative and nationalistic ideas, presented with distinction and without histrionics. A number of other periodicals emerged in its wage, seeking in rather obscurer tones to diffuse the Transcendentalist ideal. Their readers were few, their existence short. The *Dial*, first under the enthusiastic direction of Margaret Fuller, then under the more reticent direction of Emerson, lasted only four years. The *Harbinger*, organ of the Fourierists, and the *Massachusetts Quarterly Review*, in which, in 1847, the Rev. Theodore Parker took over from the *Dial* as the standard-bearer of Transcendentalism, fared no better. *The Christian Examiner* at Harvard, the *New Englander* at Yale, and the *Princeton Review* were in a less precarious position because they enjoyed the support of their respective universities; they cautiously sought to reconcile the claims of orthodox Protestantism and the reformist spirit. Catholics tended to read *Brownson's Quarterly Review*, although the ideas of its founder, Orestes A. Brownson, newly won over from Unitarianism, were not always accepted without reservations. The South delighted in the *Southern Literary Messenger*, at one time edited by Edgar Allan Poe, which exalted local traditions, bathing them in an atmosphere of poetry.

The general public was little interested in these overly subtle publications. Nevertheless, in New York, the *Knickerbocker* managed for nearly thirty years, from 1833 to 1859, to preserve its popularity while at the same time maintaining high literary standards; Washington Irving, Longfellow, Oliver Wendell Holmes, and William Cullen Bryant were among its many contributors. The *Democratic Review* was its active competitor and made a point of discovering unknown talent: Walt Whitman did his apprenticeship there. *Graham's* held sway in Philadelphia, but by mid-century, after achieving unprecedented acclaim under Poe's direction, it had begun its decline.

At about the same period there appeared two magazines which were destined to fame. *Harper's*, launched in 1850, had a circulation of 50,000 by the end of six months, and 130,000 three years later. The boldness of its policy accounted for its success. It used a large number of illustrations and quite shamelessly pirated English literature. The *Atlantic Monthly*, the first issue of which appeared in November 1857, did not lower itself to such commercial methods. From the start, it aimed at establishing itself as a purely literary journal. Oliver Wendell Holmes published his *Autocrat of the Breakfast Table* in it, in serial form, followed by other works. Emerson, Whittier, and Lowell wrote in it regularly.

Among the female reading public, only the bluestockings regaled themselves with these highbrow reviews, all more or less stamped with Europeanism. The favorite fare of the vast majority of women was *Godey's Ladies Book*, the predecessor of the *Ladies' Home Journal*. Here everything combined to attract the female reader: gorgeously presented fashion prints alternated with recipes and household hints;

novels and verses, always sentimental, but always "decent," satisfied the secret aspirations of the heart without imperiling the dictates of reason. Thanks to its considerable circulation—150,000—it could command excellent contributions. Poe, Longfellow, and Holmes wrote in it, to the delight of the ladies. Its influence was considerable; it was thanks to' a campaign led by its directress, Mrs. Sarah H. Hale, that Thanksgiving was finally recognized as a national holiday in 1863.

Annuals and "gift books" were more popular even than magazines, and far more prosperous. People would give them as presents to their friends, less with the idea that they would be read than as a token of affection. There were many different kinds: some in big format, with luxurious bindings, with gilt-edged pages, sometimes encrusted with mother-of-pearl, in the fashion of the day; they cost up to $12. Others, intended for all purses, made no claim to a sophisticated presentation—such as the small volumes, poorly printed on poor quality paper, which Sunday school teachers would hand to their pupils in a burst of Christian benevolence. In both cases, the content was always literary: the difference was in the quality of the works. The cheap "gift books" contained more or less genuine selections from published works; their aristocratic rivals prided themselves on containing only original works. Illustrations, of course, held a place of honor. Whatever the public for which they were intended, they represented mainly romantic landscapes, chaste lovelorn maidens, and distracted—but always tactful —suitors.

This fad had come from Germany. It exactly suited the sentimental America of the time and spread very rapidly. In the 1850's some sixty books of this type were published annually. Major writers consented to contribute a few lines, which were generously remunerated. Some annuals enjoyed extraordinary success; for example, *The Token*, in which Hawthorne published many of his stories, or *The Rose of Sharon, a Religious Souvenir*, whose title is indicative of its spirit, and which for eighteen years, from 1840 to 1858, continued to spread the good word.

# PART FOUR

# Civil Life

## Chapter XX
# POLITICS

At sight of the "new men" invading Washington on March 4, 1829, for Andrew Jackson's inauguration, elderly American ladies, it is said, were reminded of the days just preceding the outbreak of the French Revolution. Their fears were very exaggerated, for there was nothing revolutionary about "Old Hickory's" admirers. Nevertheless, the "new men" certainly lacked decorum, and they were as little concerned about their dress as the *sans-culottes*. The occasion itself was marked by good humor rather than by ceremony. With a few faithful followers, and without any military escort, the President walked to the Capitol through the mud of Pennsylvania Avenue. Standing at the head of the great stairway, he swore to uphold the Constitution and read his message to Congress. Then he mounted his horse to ride to the White House. He did not lack style, sitting erect and slender, with his hawk-like profile and his shock of white hair, but his supporters did him no credit. They followed him, some on foot, some riding in carriages, dressed in the weirdest variety of costumes and obviously determined to take advantage of the occasion. They were not awed by the White House. They scattered through the building, tracking the carpets with their muddy boots and breaking glasses. The refreshment tables had to be moved to the lawn outside to entice the guests to evacuate the reception rooms.

Jackson's election has been referred to as the "1828 Revolution." In more ways than one, the expression is apt. For a different America came to power on that day.

Since the Declaration of Independence, the United States had been governed by an aristocratic minority. Some of its members, following the traditions of Hamilton, sought to strengthen federal ties. Others, inspired by Jefferson, were more concerned to uphold regionalism than to promote centralization. These differences, however, were minor beside the principles they held in common. They all believed in progress, eighteenth-century style: liberty and equality for them were goddesses whom they worshiped with unaffected sincerity. They preferred ordered development to sudden change, and abhorred demogogy. They feared the adoption of universal suffrage, and suffered little embarrassment at the paradox of having a limited electorate in most of the states of the Union.

Gradually, as always, the movement of ideas swept aside the obstacles set up in its way. "Nose-counting democracy" became conscious of its own power. It demanded the ballot and more and more frequently obtained it. By 1828 the movement had acquired irresistible force. In thirty years the number of eligible voters tripled. The "gentlemen" of the old school were succeeded by the modern "masses," bringing with them ideas and ambitions which would profoundly transform political life in the years leading up to the Civil War.

The "aristocrats" quickly found out what affronts they were liable to suffer. Old Hickory put them to a hard test when he sought to have "decent" ladies receive the wife of the Secretary of Defense, a certain Mrs. Eaton, whose past had admittedly been unconventional. The "old guard" put up a common front. Under the exalted leadership of the Vice-President's wife, Mrs. Calhoun, the wives of official Washington made the unfortunate Mrs. Eaton aware of their disapproval in no uncertain terms. They declined her invitations, turned their backs on her, and refused to speak to her. The President's own niece preferred to leave the White House rather than obey her uncle's injunctions. Jackson was not a man to acknowledge defeat easily. Before a Cabinet meeting, called expressly to discuss the "affair," he personally guaranteed Mrs. Eaton's virtue and declared her as chaste "as a virgin." This certificate of good morals did not still the passions that had been aroused. The "skirt war" flared up more fiercely than ever, and the seductive sinner continued to be snubbed wherever she dared show herself. The President had to give up the struggle, but he was extremely bitter about it; the incident precipitated his break with Calhoun, whom he never forgave for this opposition.

The triumph of the self-styled guardians of tradition was a hollow one. They shook their heads despairingly when they saw the manners that now prevailed in the White House. It was a far cry from the stylish living of George Washington's day! "Old Hickory" liked to loll in shirt-sleeves in a chair of state and preferred the company of journalists—who cared little for fine manners and were masters of the art of spitting, as he was himself—to that of high society. (Jackson, incidentally, was subsequently accused of extravagance for ordering twenty spittoons at $12.50 apiece. But under the circumstances, the expenditure may have been justified.)

This hail-fellow-well-met attitude was maintained by a number of his successors. Zachary Taylor was apparently ignorant of the use of a comb. In winter he would stroll about in thick woolen socks pulled over his boots and saw nothing wrong in his wife's joining him in smoking a corncob pipe, at least when they were among themselves. The White House was open to anyone who wanted to come in; there were no more guards, there was no checking of visitors. This free and easy atmosphere led to certain not unexpected consequences: an Englishman who came to visit the President wished to leave his umbrella in the lobby; he was advised to hold on to it if he wanted to see it again. No ceremony, no precautions surrounded the President's travels. The "reactionaries" were surprised at this. A journalist reminded them that outmoded customs should not be preserved. Only the most abject of slaves, he cried in indignation, only a man fit to be no more than a subject of the Grand Turk, could imagine the President of the United States traveling in any other way. They have all done so, always, and all, thank God, will go on doing so. . . . The role of prophet is a thankless one.

After the first shock, the Whigs—or conservatives—came to realize that simple manners and Spartan ways might be as profitable to them as to their opponents. Harrison's election in 1840 was a triumph of demagogy. The main thing was to prevent "the good general" from expressing his views —a not unsurmountable difficulty. However, Nicholas Biddle, one of his most powerful supporters, intended to leave nothing to chance, and instructed the campaign organizers accordingly. No committee, he insisted, no convention, no city, no rally must ever get a single word out of him about what he thought or what he intended to do if he was elected President. This policy of silence might not have sufficed to ensure his victory, so he was also portrayed as a hero. "Old Tippecanoe"—so called in memory of the battle of Tippecanoe in the War of 1812 against the English—had had a respectable career in the army, but not one to win him undying fame; his campaign managers, however, presented him as a second Napoleon. This was a first step toward glory, Plutarch style. To set the final seal on his popularity,

all that was needed now was to attribute to him the tastes
of a Cincinnatus. The log cabin, as we know, held a place
of honor in American life. To have been born in a log cabin
was a distinction which one did not customarily allow other,
less fortunate mortals to forget. "Old Tippecanoe," alas, belonged to the F.F.V.—First Families of Virginia—and had
not seen the light of day in a woodcutter's hut. Worse still,
he lived in a comfortable, sixteen-room house and owned
nearly 2,500 acres of land in Ohio. No matter! Even in 1840,
no miracles were beyond propaganda's powers. Harrison was
presented as a poor farmer, and the simplicity of his style
of life was contrasted with the sumptuous living of the out-
going President, Van Buren. The log cabin and hard cider
on the one hand; a palace and champagne on the other.
The descriptions of the White House roused the electors to
a high point of indignation—understandably. For in one
such description, for example, attention was called to the
sumptuous drawing rooms, the dazzling reception rooms,
sparkling with lights, the bronze French-style lamps, the
gigantic, gilded mirrors, the sofas, settees, easy chairs, divans,
and footstools, the comfortable French armchairs, the mahogany beds, also French style, the gilded trays, the gaudy
artificial flowers, the ice-cream-colored vases, the gilded gob-
lets, the silver soup tureens, the spoons, the knives, the forks.
Forks, indeed! That was really too much. Crowds at campaign rallies would sing in chorus:

> Let Van from his coolers of silver drink wine,
> And lounge on his cushioned settee,
> Our man on his buckeye bench can recline,
> Content with hard cider is he,
> The iron-armed soldier, the true-hearted soldier,
> The gallant old soldier of Tippecanoe!

Not all Presidential election campaigns were as colorful
as that of 1840, but all of them learned from it. Parades, ban-

ners, emblems, banquets, rallies, songs, invectives, threats, promises, solemn undertakings—all were henceforth to be a part of American electoral joustings and to lend them that character of semi-consciousness, semi-buffoonery which sets them apart from all others.

Before the conquest of power by the masses—or more poetically, by "the Divine Average," to quote Walt Whitman—political life had remained the monopoly of a handful of the privileged. "King Caucus" reigned. A few months before the Presidential election, the members of the Senate and of the House of Representatives would meet and nominate their party's candidate. The electors were consulted only to the extent of accepting or rejecting him. In 1824, for the first time, "the sovereign people"—that is, the minority which represented it—rebelled against this procedure, to the rallying cry of "Down with King Caucus!" And for a few years, nominating powers passed from Congress to the state assemblies.

A new development took place in 1831, when, for the first time, the Democrats organized a national convention. In 1840 the Whigs followed their example. From that time on, the electoral "machines" began to operate with the efficiency for which they are renowned. Thousands upon thousands of professionals, strictly organized and graded, undertook at the city, state, and federal levels to remind electors of their duties—and their interests.

The spoils system, largely used by "Old Hickory," dates from this period. It consisted, as we know, in a massive weeding out of personnel and the replacement of the supporters of the defeated party by those of the victorious one. The switch was well worthwhile, for the working hours were far from excessive: from 9 A.M. to 3 P.M., at least in Washington. Two arguments were advanced in justification of this administrative earthquake. In the first place, one man was as good as another, so why should some have the monopoly of the public service? Secondly, the civil servants' job was not difficult, which was a good thing, since otherwise they might take over the government. It was implied, in a word, that anybody could do anything.

The implication did not pass unnoticed. Job-seeking became a profession. Poor Presidents! They paid dearly for their office. "Old Hickory" declared that he had had 500 applications for a single post. Van Buren—"the little magician"—upon arriving in Washington late at night after an exhausting journey, was surrounded by a horde of job seekers who pursued him right into his hotel room. "Old Tippecanoe" claimed that on the day of his inauguration, prospective functionaries would not allow him even to satisfy his most urgent needs. Their memory haunted him on his death bed, and with his dying breath, so it is said, he implored them to leave him alone: would their requests never cease?

The job seekers were, indeed, tireless, in their efforts, and extraordinary skill was needed to put them off with fine promises. The most tenacious of them periodically returned to the charge; the shy or the most wily got their wives to plead their cause.

Once established, the fortunate incumbents had no intention of letting themselves be dislodged. The surest way, they felt, was to control the party levers themselves. Postmasters, customs inspectors, district attorneys became both government officers and professional politicians. Each politician had his own team, whose members claimed jobs in turn within the party organization, in accordance with the universally recognized principle of rotation. Thus, in 1857 the Pierce clan was supplanted by the Buchanan clan, although both were Democrats.

These incessant changes did not facilitate administrative continuity. That, however, may not have mattered much in a country in uninterrupted transition, where the political system as such was unchallenged. What was more serious was the inevitable corruption engendered by the spoils system. Forged documents and fraudulent contracts appear to have been frequent occurrences. In 1838 the customers controller of the port of New York fled to Europe after purloining over $1,200,000. Twenty years later, the Postmaster General took refuge in Mexico, leaving behind a deficit of $160,000.

Three main lobbies covered the deliberations of the Congress: the tariff lobby, the land grant lobby, and the shipping lobby. Their activities, however, cut a poor figure beside those of their modern successors, and their methods were discreet enough to prevent scandal—at least as a rule.

What was far more obvious was the indecorousness of parliamentary customs. Foreign visitors—most of them, in fact, English—could not get over it. Mrs. Trollope, for example, visited the House of Representatives. The chamber, she wrote, was filled with men sitting in the most indecorous manner; most were wearing their hats, and nearly all were spitting in a way which decency would not allow her to describe. Another English visitor observed that the heat and airlessness in the chamber were such that women fainted. Some representatives slept, others whiled away the time whittling sticks, others again were lying back in their seats with their feet on the table staring at the ceiling, others were throwing spit balls, all were constantly banging their desks to call the ushers. As for the speaker, he droned on monotonously without anyone paying the slightest attention to what he was saying.

The Senate prided itself on greater dignity. Fashionable ladies often sat in the galleries, and their presence imposed some restraint on the deliberations. Then, too, there were the shades of ancient Rome, reflected in an often majestic eloquence which would have been highly compatible with the wearing of a toga. The hall rang constantly with those sonorous words: "star-spangled banner," "the sovereign people," "democracy," "progress." The senators spoke from their seats, nearly always without notes. Their colleagues' patience was infinite: some speeches lasted the whole day through. Straight faces were a must; in this regard, Calhoun was unrivaled. Henry Clay's description of him is unforgettable. He writes of the champion of the South rising to speak, erect as a rod, with careworn face, lined brow, haggard, gazing fixedly before him, giving the impression of dissecting the ultimate abstraction that could be conceived in a metaphysician's brain, and murmuring in a low voice that the country was in a state of crisis. Only Daniel Webster could surpass Calhoun in Olympian dignity. When he was to speak, the hall would be filled. He would look at his audience with eyes shining like live coals under bristling eyebrows, then start speaking, slowly, very quietly. Gradually the cadence picked up, the tone swelled, and sonorous period harmoniously succeeded sonorous period in a voice now deep, now melodious. He even made platitudes sound original.

Webster's eloquence was more picturesque than Calhoun's; above all, he dared to introduce an occasioned joke or anecdote at the opportune moment to relax his audience. His speech of January 26, 1830, in which he grandiloquently exalted the necessity of the Union, has remained a classic, and every American schoolchild has learned the peroration: "Liberty and union, now and always, one and indivisible. . . ."

Before the slavery issue opened its unbridgeable gulf, agreement between the political parties was relatively easy to achieve. Verbal violence, often expressed in highly colored language, sufficed to assuage passions. Thus the electoral platform of the Workingmen's Party, which suddenly and fleetingly came to prominence around 1830, had a few very simple ideas about property. Great riches, according to the party, should be seized from their owners, as a sword or pistol are seized from a robber. This program was not to everyone's taste. The upholders of order replied by asserting that those who advocated such ideas were lost to society, to earth, to heaven, that they were atheists, and that they should be ruthlessly hunted down like wild beasts thirsting for blood. The anti-Masonic party, some years later, was no more tender concerning lodge members. It referred to them as monsters who would stop at nothing, who crunch the bones of God-fearing men, whose hands reek of blood. Such imprecations, as we know, were not one-sided; we have referred already to the incredible abuse, in deed as well as word, of which Catholics were the target. Behind all this violence, however, there was a powerful bond uniting the whole country: to the immense majority the Constitution was as sacred as the Bible. And so long as the federal government's role was limited, no excessive strain was put on the Union.

There was no controversy about the principles of democracy. In 1829, when the *North American Review* wrote that the experiment of 1789 had already succeeded beyond the most optimistic expectations, it was voicing a unanimous opinion. Countless statements of this kind could be cited. Van Buren, for example, asserted in 1838 that it was incumbent upon the American Union to maintain the qualities of a government based on the constant exercise of the people's will. Experience, he continued, had shown that that system was as profitable in practice as it was just in theory: the intelligence, the wisdom, and the patriotism of the people had gone hand in hand with the development of official responsibility. Polk, nine years later, forcefully recalled that, three-quarters of a century after the birth of the free American Republic, the question whether men were capable of self-government did not arise. And when Lincoln declared at Gettysburg that government of the people, by the people, and for the people would not perish from the earth, he was expressing a conviction which the violence of the Civil War itself could not shake.

Thus the government must be a "popular" one. But what kind? And what exactly did the term mean? Here we already find differences of interpretation. Following the Hamiltonian line of thought, John Marshall, then his disciple John Story, patiently constructed a jurisprudence of authoritarian character. Rather like the jurists of the French monarchy, the Supreme Court justices sought by arguments based on law and fact to develop the powers of the central government. But their object was rather to preserve the Union than to justify administrative intervention in the country's life. It would be singularly mistaken to regard them as ancestors of a planned economy. Only a handful of reformers were sympathetic to the Socialist doctrines which were beginning to gain support in Europe. For Americans in 1850, the best government remained that which governed least, or rather, that which most strictly respected states' rights.

De Toqueville observed that for a European nothing was more striking in America than the absence of what in Europe was called government or administration. Except in its capacity as a great landowner, the central power in fact possessed very little means of action. On the eve of the Civil War, the budget stood at $74 million and the debt at $65 million. The federal government administered the postal service and of course the mint, but its actual administration was confined to those two areas plus a few arsenals. The list is just as short in the regulatory field. The executive branch exercised control over immigration; it imposed certain obligations on the merchant marine, some for security reasons, others for the protection of the local manpower; it granted subsidies to ship builders and arms manufacturers; it encouraged cod fishing; it granted funds to Morse for the laying of the first telegraph cable—and that was about all.

The customs tariff was virtually the sole appreciable form of government intervention in the economic life of the country. The question was a burning one, and we know what part it was to play in the explosion of 1861. But in the thirty years which preceded the Civil War, customs tariffs were consistently lowered despite the temporary increases resulting from the economic crises of 1837 and 1857. Protectionist theories received considerable publicity through the publication, between 1837 and 1857, of Henry C. Carey's *Principles of Political Economy* and *Principles of Political Science*. Nevertheless, in the middle of the century, free-trade theories still had many defenders.

We should not conclude from this picture that private enterprise subsisted on its own in the United States of a century or so ago. The passivity of the federal government was compensated by the activity of the states, which financed and controlled banks, transport companies, railroads, and shipping lines. State subsidies greatly facilitated the construction of roads, canals, and bridges. Not everyone profited from these undertakings, but very few complained of them. At first glance, the contradiction is surprising. Why accept administrative intervention by the states and reject it at the federal level? The explanation, perhaps, lies in the vitality of the regionalist principle, as it was then understood. We know how reluctant the thirteen colonies were before 1776 to accept the federalist position. Even after the adoption of the Constitution, the political unit to which Americans felt they belonged remained the state. The state, to them, was not an authority to be feared for its abuses of power, but rather an instrument, created by them, dependent upon them, and intended to serve them. Consequently they

did not have the instinctive fear of it which they felt about
the federal government, more distant and more anonymous.
The states to them were *their* government, whereas the
Washington administration was *the* government. That distinction explains why they welcomed action taken by the
former and feared that taken by the latter.

*Chapter XXI*

# THE SPIRIT
# OF REFORM

A typically American malady—"reformania"—reached its paroxysm in the mid-nineteenth century. They were an incredibly picturesque lot—the men and women who had caught the contagion, eager to improve the world. Some were akin to prophets; others verged on holiness; a small number were fanatics of the Torquemada variety; most, however, were Gandhis before their time, believing only in gentleness and passivity. All were more or less in the clouds, incorrigibly contemptuous of reality, caring little whether they were regarded as madmen, because they were so sure of possessing the truth. In short, they were sometimes irritating, often likable. To their fellow citizens, they were known as the "lunatic fringe."

Why this unrest? Change and progress have always been synonymous in the American vocabulary. The word "reform" is thus assured, whatever the circumstances, of a favorable reception. But its repercussions, a century ago, were particularly wide. The country had been subjected to shocks which rendered the atmosphere more receptive than

264

ever. In the first place, there were the great religious quar-
rels of which we have spoken. With the loosening of the
foundations of traditional Protestantism, Rousseau took the
place of Calvin. No limits were conceived to human perfectibility, man being "naturally" good. The improvement of
his lot depended on man and on man alone. It was up to
man to destroy the constraints and prejudices which delayed
his progress toward the new Eden. "Jacksonism" had been
a crude and probably unconscious expression of the same
tendencies. By glorifying the "common man," "Old Hickory" and his supporters had in fact, albeit unwittingly, put
Rousseauism into practice. Together with the Unitarians,
but in a less lofty sphere, they were in their own way knights
in the crusade which exercised such power over the minds
of so many Americans of that period.

A variety of foreign influences accentuated this development. Greek independence had been as popular an issue
in the United States as in England or in France. The words
"independence" and "freedom," recovered—in connection
with Greece—the magic which 1776 had imparted to them.
The affinities between the romantic spirit and the revolutionary spirit were obvious. And after 1815, the winds of
emancipation blew ceaselessly from Europe. Love of the people, pity for the weak, defense of the oppressed, criticism of
the vices of society, dreams of justice—all these themes had
no trouble gaining popularity in the United States. Utopia
had its apostles in the New World—sometimes, almost, its
martyrs. Their trials brought them a haughty satisfaction:
how splendid is a just man abandoned by everyone! They
had read Victor Hugo, and even more Saint-Simon, Fourier,
and Pierre Leroux. The European upheavals of 1848 rever-
berated powerfully in America. The socialism which had
inspired them was admirably suited to the natural optimism
and generosity of the "reformers." Its hazy doctrines, easily
adaptable to the vaguely metaphysical idealism with which

they had already been impregnated by German thought, positively went to their heads.

What was to be reformed? Everything! And so plans began to appear, from the most banal to the most unexpected, from the most exhaustive to the most limited. Emerson wrote to Carlyle, in October 1840, that he and those around him had all rather lost their heads with all these endless projects of social reform, and that he had become slightly crazed himself. It must indeed have been hard to keep cool in the heady atmosphere which surrounded the new ideas. The great high priest of Transcendentalism has left us a vivid description of a meeting of the "Friends of Universal Reform" in Boston in 1840. The assembly, Emerson wrote, was perhaps rather disorganized, but in any case very colorful: crazed men and women, bearded men, Muggletonians, agrarians, Adventists, Quakers, abolitionists, Calvinists, Unitarians, philosophers spoke in turn, tirelessly thundering, praying, preaching, protesting.

Public health—which, as we know, left much to be desired—was the subject of many of the reformist plans. Homeopaths, hydropaths, vegeterians each claimed to improve it in their own manner. For one healer, the secret of longevity lay in abstention from all fermented foods. Another, Sylvester Graham, gained fame by recommending the use of unsifted flour in the preparation of a new kind of bread which still bears his name. Another claimed that if everyone would work in the fields, all maladies would disappear. Another, concerned that nothing should jeopardize the course of nature, founded a society for the protection of earthworms and mosquitoes. But the flesh was not all; the spirit too had its specialists. Phrenology was the first fad to come into fashion following a lecture tour by Dr. Spurzheim, an associate of Gall. Then came mesmerism, introduced by a certain Mr. Pogen, a French Creole. And the "psychometrists" claimed to foretell the future by holding a relic in their hands.

Despite the extraordinary attraction which things "miraculous" held for a naturally credulous and, usually, uneducated public, these theories had few durable effects. One replaced the other according to the whim of fashion and, once out of fashion, their names were all but forgotten.

The great movements of ideas were quite another thing. Some were to effect a real upheaval in American life. Significantly—and this differentiates them from their counterpart in Europe—they were not political in character. No one advocated divine-right monarchy, or plebeian dictatorship, or the reign of the proletariat. The American Peace Society did, indeed, campaign for a league of nations and perpetual peace, but the subject had so little relevance to current preoccupations that it aroused little enthusiasm. Social problems, almost exclusively, held the attention of reformers: prohibition, feminism, labor questions, and especially slavery.

We have referred elsewhere to the repercussions of these movements on American life. Here we shall confine ourselves to sketches of a few exceptional figures less eager, perhaps, to improve the world than to improve themselves.

Should we start with Emerson? His name has appeared so often in these pages that we may perhaps leave him in the background now, invisible but present. Thoreau, in any case, cannot be ignored. He was the most reasonable of the reformers, for he had no ambition to make disciples; he was satisfied to push his personal ideas to their logical conclusion. Wearying of the "precious" atmosphere of Transcendentalism, he went off alone and with his own hands built himself a cabin in the country in which he lived for two years in solitude. He was required to pay taxes; his individualism would not allow him to do so. He went to prison, where, he said, he lost whatever respect he had had for the state and merely pitied it. Every aspect of modern life grated on his anarchical instincts, even—Americans of yesterday and of today may not recognize him as their brother—work! His Walden experiment convinced him of the absurdity of regular effort. He had subsisted, he wrote, solely through the work of his own hands, and he had found that by using them during six weeks of the year, he could provide himself with all he needed. Throughout the winter, and during much of the summer, he had been completely free and able to devote himself to study as he chose.

This somewhat self-centered taste for independence distinguishes Thoreau from almost all his fellow reformers. For the most orthodox, propaganda was an integral part of their action, and they measured their success chiefly by the extent of their recruitment. "The more of us lunatics there are, the happier we are" (not the merrier, for they did not laugh) might be quite aptly applied to these professionals of collective emotion.

Take Bronson Alcott, for example, the other sage of Concord. He began his career as a peddler; soon he became a peripatetic philosopher, then a schoolmaster. He discovered and was enthralled by the ideas of Pestalozzi, and decided to apply them in a teaching establishment—the Temple School—which he managed to open in Boston. His taste for novelty led him to one indiscretion after another. Already dangerously close to heresy, he ventured—as we saw earlier—on taboo territory. Storms, foreclosure, bankruptcy—what matter? In every reformer there slumbered a nostalgia for the "noble savage." Disappointed with society, he turned instinctively to the arms of nature, in which he found a refuge. Together with a few valorous companions, he founded a "vegetarian community" near Harvard. His daughter Louise, who was as humorous, it seems, as her father was serious, and who saved the always precarious family fortunes by the publication of her *Little Women*—a best seller—in 1868, has left an intriguing description of this venture. The daily schedule lacked variety: dawn rising, bath, "music," followed by a frugal meal of bread and fruit . . . and so on until bedtime. The meals, indeed, differed little in content: for lunch, bread, vegetables, and water; for dinner, bread, fruit, and water. The members of the group were conscious of the importance of their mission, but carried it out with subtle variations. One intended to prove that you could subsist perfectly well without sugar, milk, butter, cheese, or meat. Another of the elect seemed to think that concern with reform consisted primarily in wearing a white cotton suit and untanned leather shoes, and growing a snow white beard. A third, clothed in garments he had made himself, was chiefly concerned to use as few words as possible. A fourth claimed to secure his salvation by never eating cooked food, and living in a "state of nature." He had not yet reached that stage and confined himself to the contemplative munching of dried beans.

Such crass pastimes would not have satisfied the Oneida group of New York State. Its founder, John Humphrey Noyes, at first considered becoming a pastor, but this endeavor soon appeared superfluous to him, for at twenty-five years of age he already felt himself to be in a state of perfect purity. Such a blessing must surely not be kept from others. He gathered about him a number of persons of good will, eager to restore in nineteenth-century America the simplicity of the primitive communities. The "perfectionists"—as they modestly called themselves—defined their program in a manifesto in which they rejected all state authority and decided to elect Jesus Christ President, as they put it, not only of the United States but of the whole world. Until such time as the rest of the human race adopted their views, they would turn to nature too and live in community. Polygamy and polyandry were, for a time, the guiding principles of their amorous relations. Gradually, however, the philosophers of the new creation lost ground and more commonplace preoccupations gained the upper hand, which helped their community avoid financial failure. In 1848, some thirty years after its foundation, Oneida possessed a capital of $600,000 and had become specialized in the manufacture of steel traps and silverware, only the name of which—Community Silverware—betrays its origins. Here, then, all was well that ended well.

The same could not be said of that most fascinating, perhaps, of the community experiments, the illustrious Brook Farm, carried on for six years in Massachusetts by a group of sincere and idealistic Transcendentalists who had adopted a motto adapted from that of the Benedictines: "Think and pray." The cornerstone was George Ripley, not surprisingly a former pastor and a deserter from Unitarianism. He gathered about him—some hesitatingly, others with great enthusiasm—the best-known names of the *avant-garde*. Nathaniel Hawthorne stayed briefly at Brook Farm, but did not return. Had he really, he wondered, performed a deserving action in spending five precious months concerning himself with the feeding of cows and horses? He doubted it. William Ellery Channing—"our bishop"—was the representative there of a "spiritual" Unitarianism. Theodore Parker was the advocate of free thinking carried to the hilt. Elizabeth Peabody liked to relax there from the cares of her Boston library, a meeting place dear to the "pure." Margaret Fuller, the muse of Transcendentalism, was sincerely sympathetic to the adventure undertaken by her friends, but never associated herself with it directly. Emerson, for his part, remained skeptical: it was the Age of Reason, he decreed, reduced to picnic proportions—yet with so much good will! Weeding was done to the recitation of Tennyson and Browning, and the community studied music and foreign languages (especially German). The culture of the mind no less than of the soil was an integral part of the program, but unfortunately financial competence was not included. Albert Brisbane attempted to introduce Fourierist principles; he only aggravated the position. Fire precipitated the final collapse of the experiment in 1847.

Some fifty collectives are believed to have sought to apply Fourier's ideas in the United States. All of them failed, and their average duration was two years. Only three managed to survive a little longer. The North American Phalanx, founded in New Jersey in 1843 by Brisbane, Greeley, and Channing, functioned for twelve years. The phalansteries, one established in Illinois, the other in Texas, by two groups of Frenchmen, lasted even longer.

It is hard to believe that so dull a book as Etienne Cabet's *Voyage en Icarie* could have been so successful some five generations ago: five editions were published in six years. After its publication in 1841, the Icarians grew in number. How could one resist the author's call? "Forward, for the emancipation of the workers, for the happiness of men and women, for the well-being of humanity, for the salvation of all!" But where should the program be put into effect? The government of Louis Philippe turned a deaf ear to the idea. But then there was the New World—the natural refuge of utopia. Sixty-nine families decided to settle there. The womenfolk were particularly enthusiastic. The "sisters" did not weary of singing the verse of the "Icarian Farewell Song" which was dedicated to them:

> Do you see, oh sisters, the new dawn
> Of the day when all irons will fall?
> Up, daughters of God! Let us go, filled with zeal
> To remake the universe.
> Woman is equal to man
> Under the divine law of love . . .
> We will follow you to Icary,
> Soldiers of Fraternity.

Illinois seemed to be the chosen territory: Nauvoo, Illinois, was selected as the headquarters of the community. Cabet joined his flock there in 1848. Despite his presence, discouragement and nostalgia descended upon the *émigrés*. Where was the earthly paradise which they had been promised? Their sole prospect was a hard, miserable, hopeless existence; what a contrast between dream and reality! Many, suffering from varying degrees of homesickness, fled to New Orleans. Cabet followed them there, took them in hand, brought them back, and reorganized them in 1850. But he made the mistake of leaving them to themselves while he took a short trip to Europe; when he returned, the tares were causing havoc among the apostles. He died of grief, so it is said, in 1856. Gradually nothing was left of the colony. Some of its members continued to live in Illinois, but practicing a form of existence dangerously similar to the previously abhorred capitalism.

At about the same date, another phalanstery, also of French origin, was also nearing its end. In 1852, Victor Considérant, one of Fourier's most active disciples, arrived in New York. His friend, Albert Brisbane, took him to visit the North American Phalanx. He decided against associating himself with it because he found the experiment too communistic and not sufficiently "phalansterian." After looking for a site for his own colony in the Mississippi valley, he decided upon Texas. A new state, immense territories, a scattered population—it seemed to combine all the ideal conditions. Soon the Franco-Texan Company was founded. It proposed to apply strictly the principles of Fourierist association. Each of its members was assigned the job that suited him: 810 dispositions which, according to the theory, predominate among humans were to serve as criteria for such designations. Thus everyone would be happy, since everyone would work only within the framework of his desires. Actually, they would have to work very little, for the collective organization would do wonders: two harvests a year and seven meals a day. It was to be the metamorphosis of work into pleasure. The rich would bring their capital to the phalansteries, others their work or simply their "talent." However, those with nothing but talent to offer would be less well remunerated than their associates: 3/12 of the profits as against 4/12 for those who put up funds and 5/12 for the workers. All would live in groups of 300 families in vast buildings with common dining halls and reading rooms.

Allured by such attractive prospects, 200 initial adepts—French, Swiss, Belgian—arrived in Houston in 1855, after a sixty-day voyage from Antwerp. It took them twenty-five days more to reach the "promised land," symbolically called La Réunion, a vast 2,000-acre tract near Dallas, which at the time was a small village with a population of not more than a few hundred. They set to work. Applied to Texas soil, the principle of specialization turned out to be less profitable than it appeared in Fourier's works. Numerous professions were represented: tailors, shoemakers, jewelers, watchmakers, weavers, masons, pastry cooks, doctors, nurses, hat makers, artists, dance masters, musicians. Unfortunately, there were only two farmers—not quite enough for the seven meals a day. A succession of icy winters and torrid summers progressively cooled the zeal of the heroic pioneers. In less than five years they dispersed, and Considérant himself returned to France. In 1865 the American courts ordered the association finally dissolved.

The idea of the welfare state was in those days virtually unknown. Only a few daring spirits, who were immediately dubbed revolutionaries, presumed to advocate the idea, but their exhortations rarely reached outside the circle of their friends. Philanthropy remained an almost exclusively private affair.

Judging by the *North American Review* of October

1847, the rich were already in the habit of leaving a part of their fortune to charitable institutions. If they happened not to conform to that tradition, we read, their memory was disgraced and their heirs found it very hard to restore their reputation. In the prevailing Puritan atmosphere, such generosity was probably less a product of altruism than a form of self-interest. For many it was a way of putting themselves right with the Almighty—a form of investment, with the returns paid in the next world. Not until the end of the century, and largely through the influence of John D. Rockefeller, did the practice of bequests and donations come to be motivated by a spirit of social solidarity.

The contribution made by official agencies, in any case, was a very meager supplement, confined almost exclusively to prisons and lunatic asylums. Some cities had shelters for the destitute, but these had few inmates, for pauperism was rare, and living on public charity was regarded as a disgrace which even the most wretched sought to avoid.

Until 1830 the prison system was extremely brutal. In village prisons the inmates were often chained to the wall; a blanket served them as a bed and they were allowed a minimum of clothing. At the least misbehavior, they were flogged or confined in cells without air or light. The state institutions seemed almost sumptuous in comparison, but absolute isolation for the prisoners was long the rule. Many cases of madness resulted from this practice. Dickens has left magnificent and terrible descriptions of the prisons he visited in 1842. Subsequently, the rules were mitigated. In the first place, the number of prisoners was reduced substantially, for imprisonment for debt was abandoned. At the same time, corporal punishment became rarer. Above all, it was realized that the purpose of imprisonment must be to reform the criminal as much as to punish him. Prisons came to be called "houses of reform" or of "correction." And the

practice spread of having the convicts work together instead
of keeping them in isolation.

The lot of the insane also improved. It had long been
tragic. There had been a tendency to regard their mental
derangement as a sort of deliberate perversity. To "cure"
them, barbarous methods were used: straitjackets, gags,
chains, ice showers. It took the extraordinary determination
of a woman to bring this situation to a stop. In an honors
list of reformers, Dorothy Dix would deserve a very special
place. One wonders where this school mistress-turned-apos-
tle, of insignificant appearance, and in poor health, drew the
strength and the conviction to make so many visits and
tours, and to give so many lectures. She is said to have covered 60,000 miles in eight years. Nothing discouraged her,
neither insults, nor indifference. Angular in profile, a typical
New Englander, like so many of her fellow reformers, she
would get up on the platform and speak slowly, without
raising her voice, but with such conviction, such compas-
sion, that no audience could remain unmoved. When someone asked her the reason for her success, she replied, gently,
that she had never met obstacles which the needs of her mission had not enabled her to surmount. Indiana, Illinois,
Louisiana, Tennessee, Mississippi, Missouri, Michigan, Wisconsin, and the District of Columbia responded in turn to
her appeal and humanized the conditions in their insane
asylums.

In Samuel Howe, too, the feeble-minded and the blind
had a protector of tireless zeal. From his youth, he had
shown his devotion to the cause of the oppressed by signing
up as a volunteer for the Greek war of independence.

*Conclusion*

# THE NATIONAL
# CHARACTER

Such, then, were the Americans approximately one hundred years ago. The differences between them were seemingly immense; a different "everyday life" could have been written about every region. Not a single traveler to the United States failed to observe the fact; at the same time, every one of them was struck by the contrast between the diversity of customs and the uniformity of ideas. The only exception was the South, and this it was that spelt its tragic destiny. Everywhere else, on the eve of the Civil War, the *homo americanus*—that mysterious human type which had so greatly intrigued the Frenchman, Crèvecoeur, eighty years earlier— had arrived at a stage in his development at which he already stood out clearly from any other.

Let us picture that vast continent, extending as far, from shore to shore, as does the land area between the Atlantic coast of France and the Urals; with every type of climate, every form of wealth, every hope; with empty spaces stretching apparently to infinity; with a thrilling sense of limitless opportunity in the air.

Let us picture its several million inhabitants, some priding themselves that their forebears had inaugurated the great adventure which they, in turn, were looking to promote, others among the wave upon wave of immigrants, eager to find in the New World what had been refused them in the Old. All enterprising, all confident.

On the one hand, inexhaustible possibilities; on the other, men who denied the impossible: this concurrence of circumstances, perhaps unique in history, modeled the national character.

A first consequence was the identification of life with movement. Every city was an anthill. The incessant bustle forcibly struck Michel Chevalier, for example, when he came to the United States in 1834: "If movement and a rapid succession of sensations and ideas constitute life," he wrote, "then people here are a hundred times more alive than anywhere else. Everything there is movement, change, activity. One experiment succeeds another, one undertaking succeeds another. Wealth and poverty follow upon each other and in turn take each other's place." At about the same date, Dickens observed astutely that whereas the English said "all right," when they wished to signify their approval, the Americans used the expression "Go Ahead." Ahead? But in what direction? Never mind—anywhere, since the choices before you are legion. To stay put seemed absurd, when so many others, by moving elsewhere, had found success and wealth.

Movement, moreover, meant search, meant endeavor. This was an irresistible enticement for purely pragmatic minds, indifferent to theories, drawn by experiment as by a magnet. Emerson expressed this state of mind better than any one else. He put everything in doubt, he said; he regarded himself as a tireless searcher, with no past behind him. Nothing was sure, he continued, save existence, change, energy. No love could defend itself against a stronger love by promises or contracts. No truth was so sublime that it might not appear trivial in the light of tomorrow. Thus, not to become rooted was to respond to the call of life; it also meant taking risks, gambling on the unknown when the odds might be against you—the instinctive approach of the speculator, as was the American of those days. Stability and security were altogether alien concepts. Americans would have been greatly astonished had anyone been able to fore-tell that for their descendants these concepts would one day become essential stages in their pursuit of happiness. For them, living meant not merely avoiding a negative immo-bility, but actively confronting chance—that capricious genie, generous one day, hostile the next, but always attractive, for it was nearly always assimilated to that other genie, hope.

Optimism was the very air they breathed, optimism to the limits of the possible. How earnest they had been, a con-temporary reminisced, how self-satisfied, how full of their own praises! The expression "God's country" is marvelously descriptive of the way in which the citizens of the young Republic thought of their country. It was axiomatic for them that their country was the best, the biggest, the most virtuous of all. And if there were skeptics daring enough to doubt it, was it not enough to point to the influx of immi-grants, which never abated.

This success, however, this prosperity which every Amer-ican sensed was just around the corner, had to be earned—by work. Here we have another salient feature of the na-tional character: the universal taste for work. Rich and poor alike threw themselves into their work with fervor. The problem of leisure arose only for a few women, who were not very successful, as we have seen, in resolving it. Everyone else would have felt it a disgrace not to be constrained to ceaseless effort. Pioneers and prospectors had certainly not sought their fortune at such cost in order to jeopardize their success by laziness or indifference. But even in the more sophisticated cities of the East, where a dawning civilization might have been accompanied by a certain aspiration toward thought or dreams, the supreme law remained *action*. Few examples exist of a period or a country where intellectual life was so completely dissociated from everyday concerns.

Work was both a cause and a goal. It would be impossible to understand the Americans without taking into account the religious influence which held sway among them at the beginning of their history. The Puritans who colonized New England were men of iron. No other wave of immigrants ever managed to exert as much influence as they had. And that influence is still to be felt today, even among those who are not their descendants. They brought with them their narrow and austere conception of life, which ruled out all compromise and all pleasure. Joyous work, the work of which Péguy sang, they would have regarded as sacreligious. Work, for them, was an offering which man presented to his Creator. But for this offering to please their merciless God, it must be the result of effort, perhaps of suffering. They regarded work as not only a necessity but also a duty; a means of subsisting in this world and especially of acceding to eternal life.

The concept was implacable in its logic for these one-track believers, but it gradually suffered erosion. By the middle of the nineteenth century, the American idea of work was no longer the same. It is true that Americans continued to assimilate the words "virtue" and "effort"; what was easy, they felt, might be immoral: if their brows were not covered with sweat, they were not sure of being entitled to the bread they were seeking to earn. Nevertheless, work and redemption were no longer as loosely associated in their philosophy of life. Apart from a handful of dreamers, the population as a whole devoted its labors to a very specific

object: success, that is, money-making, other achievements
being very little esteemed.

Had materialism, then, won the day? Here, we must not
stop at appearances, which give rise to so many misunder-
standings. What had happened was that an interpretation
of Calvinism, less uncompromising than earlier ones, had
come to the aid of wealth. To make one's fortune, it was
explained, is not contrary to the divine law; far from it, for
success is a sign of encouragement which the Creator in his
goodness gives to those he wishes to favor. In any case, the
accumulation of dollars did not appear as an end in itself.
Everyone realized that money could well be lost overnight.
Wealth, once acquired, shared in the general instability of
life. The main thing was to acquire it, since that was the
most effective means of joining the ranks both of the elect
and of respectable citizens.

This exaltation of success, rendered all the more attractive since it was justified by moral arguments, led to interpretations which were not altogether disinterested. Woe to
the weak! Woe to the humble! read the new Beatitudes.
Competition became fierce. Everyone should have his chance
—but surely no more. As one of the manuals of good manners of the time puts it, true republicanism means that men
should be equal in principle, but that they should be free
to become in fact as unequal as possible.

That principle was well observed in mid-nineteenth-
century America; nevertheless, the national character was
devoid of envy and hate, those destructive sentiments which
undermine societies as rust corrodes metal. For the rivalries,
keen though they were, and the often considerable differences in fortune were attenuated by influences which made
them less damaging. In a country in perpetual process of
development, and egalitarian in spirit, failure or poverty
did not have the same meaning as in a static and hierarch-

ical civilization. The doors of wealth always seemed ready to open to anyone who pushed hard enough. Moreover, an instinctive cordiality and a simplicity of manners further softened the contrast between conditions. There were no titles, no special courtesy formulas. "He's Mister and I'm Mister too," said a Hungarian immigrant who could barely speak English, referring to Lincoln. As a result of walking arm in arm and calling each other by their first names, Americans came to believe themselves alike.

Alike they were indeed, in more ways than one. Save for isolated individuals in the prairies, condemned to a solitude which they hoped would be no more than temporary, Americans were moved by their gregarious nature to look for anything that would give them proof of their community of tastes and thoughts. They felt really themselves only when they were in a group. "We are in the same boat," they would say, speaking of their common lot. The descendants of the passengers of the *Mayflower* did not, it is true, disdain to recall their preeminence, and there was plenty of snobbishness in local manners. Nevertheless, even the clans which sought to differentiate themselves from the rest felt linked with the mass by so powerful a sense of solidarity as to render their claims to singularity almost ridiculous. Outside the problem of slavery—that sore which, one hundred years later, is festering still—there was tacit agreement on a number of fetishes raised to the level of dogmas.

In political life, the two-party system was considered superior to any other. Socially, the self-made man was the hero of the day. He embodied the qualities which were more highly prized than all others: courage, imagination, ingenuity, and especially self-confidence—that "self-reliance" which Emerson exalted in his triumphant lectures. To "make oneself" was not simply a proof of manhood, it was also a tribute to "free enterprise," and better still to Democracy, that immaculate goddess, messenger of the future. The Constitution, inspired by the commandments of Democracy, was sacrosanct. When the South ruptured the Union, it did not justify itself by some vague and abstract right of rebellion, but by a legal interpretation of the respective powers of the federal government and the states. In so doing, it was faithful to the historical tradition which, in 1776, had led the insurgents to brand the British demands as unconstitutional and to appeal to the Crown against the decisions of Parliament.

The Constitution, then, was unanimously revered, and it was the duty of the Supreme Court to preserve it with its majesty against all error. The Court enjoyed a prestige which time had not yet eroded. Its jurisprudence oscillated between the Hamiltonian and Jeffersonian positions; the conflict between those tendencies had weighed heavily upon the young Republic from the outset. On a number of essential points, the Court had no difficulty in reflecting the instincts of the country. The country approved the Court's action in limiting the powers of the central government except—as in the secession crisis—when the Union itself was in jeopardy. Again, the country counted on the Court to preserve the principle of private property inviolate; this was another key principle on which agreement was unanimous, even in the South, where it was appealed to against the Emancipation Proclamation which dared to recall that livestock and slaves could not be treated identically.

We talk of the "awkward age." The expression is marvelously apt as applied to America before the Civil War. Unpolished, clumsy, exuberant; bubbling over with vitality, eager for novelty; enmeshed in contradictions; cruel and generous; prepared to follow ideas to their extreme consequences; impassioned to the point of refusing to draw back from a conflict which might have spelt its doom; contemptuous and at the same time envious of older civilizations;

thrusting forward toward the future as toward a promised land; realizing, without being able to define its contours, that a great destiny lay before it; speaking at one and the same time of a "Manifest Destiny" and of an "American dream"; shamelessly confusing materialism and idealism; in short, confused, extreme, mysterious and, above all, unlike any other country, as it had been from its birth and as it has never ceased to be.

# BIBLIOGRAPHY

The list below does not pretend to be complete and is offered only as a guide to readers who wish to explore certain areas in greater depth. To avoid needless detail, the author has omitted journals and periodicals, names of which are given in Chapter XVIII. Nor has he thought it necessary to cite individually, with certain exceptions, reports of travelers or novels of the period, both important sources of documentation. Readers will find titles of these works either in the present volume or in those of the authors listed here.

ADAMS, JAMES T., ed. *Album of American History* (pictorial), 5 vols., New York, 1944-1949

ADAMS, JAMES T. *The American,* New York, 1943

ALTROCCHI, JULIA G. *The Spectacular San Franciscans,* New York, 1949

AMORY, CLEVELAND. *The Proper Bostonians,* New York, 1947

BEARD, CHARLES A. and MARY R. *The Rise of American Civilization,* 4 vols., New York, 1927-1942

BEEBE, LUCIUS and CHARLES CLEGG. *The Pictorial Epic of the Continent,* New York, 1955

BEEBE, LUCIUS and CHARLES CLEGG. *U. S. West: The Saga of Wells Fargo,* New York, 1949

BEIRNE, FRANCIS F. *The Amiable Baltimoreans,* New York, 1951

BERGER, MAX. *The British Traveller in America, 1836-1860,* New York, 1943

BILLINGTON, RAY A. *The Protestant Crusade: 1800-1860,* New York, 1938

BILLINGTON, RAY A. *Westward Expansion: A History of the American Frontier,* New York, 1949

BOWERS, CLAUDE G. *The Party Battles of the Jackson Period,* New York, 1922

BROMWELL, WILLIAM J. *History of Immigration to the U. S. from 1819 to 1855,* New York, 1856

BROOKS, VAN WYCK. *The World of Washington Irving,* New York, 1944

BULEY, ROSCOE C. *The Old Northwest,* 2 vols., Indianapolis, 1950

BUTTERFIELD, ROGER P. *The American Past, a Pictorial History of the U. S., 1775-1945,* New York, 1947

CALHOUN, ARTHUR W. *A Social History of the American Family from Colonial Times to the Present,* 3 vols., Cleveland, 1917-1919

*The Cambridge History of American Literature,* edited by WILLIAM P. TRENT and others, New York, 1944

CHANNING, EDWARD. *A History of the United States,* 6 vols., New York, 1905-1925

CHINARD, GILBERT. *When the French Came to California,* California Historical Society, 1944

COLE, ARTHUR C. *The Irrepressible Conflict, 1850-1865, "History of American Life"* series, vol. VII, New York, 1934

COMMAGER, HENRY S. and ALLAN NEVINS. *The Heritage of America,* New York, 1939

CUBBERLEY, ELLWOOD P. *Public Education in the United States,* Boston, new ed., 1934

CURTI, MERLE. *The Growth of American Thought,* New York, 1943

DAVENPORT, MILLIA. *The Book of Costume,* vol. 2, New York, 1948

DAVIDSON, LEVITTE J. and PRUDENCE BOSTWICK, ed. *The Literature of the Rocky Mountains West, 1803-1903,* Caldwell, 1939

DAVIDSON, MARSHALL B. *Life in America,* vol. 2, Boston, 1951

DAY, DONALD, ed. *Uncle Sam's Uncle Josh,* Boston, 1953

DE VOTO, BERNARD A. *The Year of Decision, 1846,* Boston, 1943

DICKENS, CHARLES. *American Notes,* Boston, 1890

DOOD, WILLIAM E. *The Cotton Kingdom,* New York, 1919

DRIGGS, HOWARD R. *Westward America,* Philadelphia, 1941

DULLES, FOSTER R. *America Learns to Play: A History of Popular Recreation, 1607-1940*, New York, 1940

DUNBAR, SEYMOUR. *A History of Travel in America*, 4 vols., Indianapolis, new ed. 1937

EATON, CLEMENT. *A History of the Old South*, New York, 1949

ERNST, ROBERT. *Immigrant Life in New York City, 1825-1863*, New York, 1949

FISH, CARL R. *The Rise of the Common Man, 1830-1850*, "History of American Life" series, vol. 6, New York, 1927

GABRIEL, RALPH H. *The Course of American Democratic Thought*, New York, 1940

GABRIEL, RALPH H. and others. *The Pageant of America*, 15 vols., New Haven, 1925-1929

HACKER, LOUIIS M. *The Shaping of American Tradition*, 2 vols., New York, 1947

HACKER, LOUIS M. *The Triumph of American Capitalism*, New York, 1940

HANDLIN, OSCAR. *This Was America*, Cambridge, 1944

HANDLIN, OSCAR and others. *Harvard Guide to the Study of American History*, Cambridge, 1954

HANSEN, MARCUS L. *The Atlantic Migration (1607-1860)*, Cambridge, 1940

HANSEN, MARCUS L. *The Immigrant in American History*, Cambridge, 1940

HARD, CHARLES. *Washington Cavalcade*, New York, 1948

HARLOW, ALVIN F. *The Serene Cincinnatians*, New York, 1950

HART, ALBERT B., ed. *American History Told by Contemporaries*, 5 vols., New York, 1897-1929

HOFSTADTER, RICHARD. *The American Political Tradition and the Men Who Made It*, New York, 1948

HONE, PHILIP. *Diary*, edited by Allan Nevins, 2 vols., New York, 1927

HULBERT, ARCHER B. *Forty-Niners: A Chronicle of the California Trail*, Boston, 1931

KELLEY, CLYDE. *U. S. Postal Policy*, New York, 1931

LA FARGE, OLIVER. *A Pictorial History of the American Indian*, New York, 1956

LANGDON, WILLIAM C. *Everyday Things in American Life*, 2 vols. (1776-1876), New York, 1937-1941

MCMASTER, JOHN B. *A History of the People of the United States from the Revolution to the Civil War*, 8 vols., New York and London, 1883-1913

MCPHARLIN, PAUL. *Life and Fashion in America, 1650-1900*, New York, 1946

MINNIGERODE, MEADE. *The Fabulous Forties, 1840-1850*, New York and London, 1924

MORISON, SAMUEL ELIOT and HENRY S. COMMAGER. *The Growth of the American Republic*, 2 vols., New York and London, 1930

MOTT, FRANK L. *A History of American Magazines, 1741-1885*, 3 vols., New York and London, 1930-1938

MUMFORD, LEWIS. *The Golden Days, A Study in American Experience and Culture*, New York, 1926

NEVINS, ALLAN, ed. *America through British Eyes*, New York, 1948

NEVINS, ALLAN, ed. *Ordeal of the Union*, 2 vols., New York, 1947

NEVINS, ALLAN, ed. *Washington to Coolidge: A Documentary Record of Editorial Leadership and Criticism, 1785-1927*, New York, 1928

OLMSTED, FREDERICK L. *A Journey in the Black Country*, New York, 1860

PARRINGTON, VERNON L. *Main Currents in American Thought* (vol. II, 1830-1860, *The Romantic Revolution in America*), New York, 1930

RICHARDS, CAROLINE C. *Village Life in America*, 1852-1872, New York, 1913

RIEGEL, ROBERT E. *America Moves West*, New York, 1930

RIEGEL, ROBERT E. *Young America, 1830-1840*, Norman, 1949

ROGERS, JOHN W. *The Lusty Texans of Dallas*, New York, 1951

SCHLESINGER, ARTHUR M. *Learning How to Behave: A Historical Study of American Etiquette Books*, New York, 1947

SPILLER, ROBERT E. and others. *Literary History of the United States*, New York, 1948

TALLANT, ROBERT. *The Romantic New Orleanians*, New York, 1950

TAYLOR, BAYARD. *Eldorado, or Adventures in the Path of Empire*, New York, 1884

TAYLOR, GEORGE R. *The Transportation Revolution, 1815-1860*, New York, 1951

TINKER, EDWARD LAROCQUE. *Creole City*, New York, 1953

TOCQUEVILLE, ALEXIS DE. *De la Démocratie en Amérique*, Paris, 1835

TRAIN, ARTHUR JR. *The Story of Everyday Things*, New York-London, 1941

TROLLOPE, FRANCES. *Domestic Manners of the Americans*, London, 1832

TURNER, FREDERICK J. *The Frontier in American History*, New York, 1920

TWAIN, MARK. *Life on the Mississippi*, Boston, 1883

TYLER, ALICE F. *Freedom's Ferment: Phases of American Social History to 1860*, Minneapolis, 1944

WECTER, DIXON. *The Saga of American Society: A Record of Social Aspiration, 1607-1937*

WHITE, LEONARD D. *The Jacksonians*, New York, 1951

WISH, HARVEY. *Society and Thought in Early America*, New York, 1950-1952

WISSLER, CLARK. *Indians of the United States*, New York, 1940

WITTKE, CARL F. *We Who Built America*, New York, 1939

WOODWARD, WILLIAM E. *The Way Our People Lived*, New York, 1944

WRIGHT, RICHARDSON. *Hawkers and Walkers in Early America*, Philadelphia, 1927

# INDEX